Girl Talk

Girl Talk

What Science Can Tell Us
About Female Friendship

Jacqueline Mroz

SEAL PRESS

Seal Press
Hachette Book Group
1290 Avenue of the Americas, New York, NY 10104
www.sealpress.com

Printed in the United States of America

First Edition: November 2018

Published by Seal Press, an imprint of Perseus Books, LLC, a subsidiary of Hachette Book Group, Inc. The Seal Press name and logo is a trademark of the Hachette Book Group.

The Hachette Speakers Bureau provides a wide range of authors for speaking events. To find out more, go to www.hachettespeakersbureau.com or call (866) 376-6591.

The publisher is not responsible for websites (or their content) that are not owned by the publisher.

Print book interior design by Amy Quinn

Library of Congress Cataloging-in-Publication Data has been applied for.

ISBNs: 9781580057677 (paperback); 9781580057684 (ebook)

LSC-C

10 9 8 7 6 5 4 3 2 1

To Simon, Lucas, Will, and Owen
And to all my wonderful friends who inspired this book

Contents

Foreword

— *Claire Messud*

OUR CULTURE DEVOTES endless attention to romantic love, and almost as much to familial relationships—whether in fiction or nonfiction, in film, television or photography. But in our lives— in women's lives, particularly—friendships often prove as central to our identities as do lovers, parents, and children.

Jacqueline Mroz, in this timely, lucid and thoughtful book, turns an illuminating eye upon the affective ties that shape us from childhood onwards: what constitutes a friend? How has this changed over time, or between cultures? Why and how do friendships unravel? How does literature mirror—or fail to mirror—our actual experiences? What might we seek in our friends at life's different stages? These are all vital questions, too rarely addressed.

It seems that friends are like breathing: We can't live without them, but we don't spend too much time thinking about it. Mroz's well-researched and careful taxonomy of friendship will enable readers better to understand how and why these relationships matter so much.

In mid-life, I look back over the decades and acknowledge that my memories are organized as powerfully around my friends as my family relationships. My family moved around a good bit when I was young, with the result that my recollections of friends are tied to particular places, and to distinct periods. When I was in elementary school, we lived in Sydney, Australia: thanks to social media, my sister and her best friend from those long ago days remain close still. Although for many years I lost sight of my besties from early adolescence in Toronto, I recently heard from one and discovered that they still go on holiday together, forty years after we all met. I regularly have dinner with a trio of beloved high school friends, as all of us live in the Boston area. Another friend from that time is now friends with my dearest college mates, and he texts me photos whenever they're together. I met my future husband in the early weeks of my graduate study in the UK, and a close college friend came to visit the next day: she got to know him at the same time as I did, and the three of us set off for Edinburgh and the Scottish Highlands that fall, on a trip of such memorable hilarity that we still joke about it. All these years later, she is still practically family; our kids have grown up knowing and loving each other too.

Girl Talk feels to this reader particularly relevant because in recent years I've been preoccupied with female friendship, and have written two novels—*The Woman Upstairs* and *The Burning Girl*—in which I've sought to explore passionate but complicated relationships in different stages of life. As a reader, I've reveled in diverse contemporary narratives of friendship—from Elena Ferrante's work to Zadie Smith's *Swing Time* to Emma Cline's *The Girls*, to Magda Szabó's extraordinary *The Door*, about the deep but tortured bond between a writer and her housekeeper. As a human being, I've marveled at the evolution of my understanding of these strange, aleatory, voluntary connections: what draws us to a new friend? What makes us give up on one, if we do? How much does friendship resemble amorous love, and how does it differ? How does it accommodate rivalry and envy, attraction and repulsion?

Friendships between women are as multifarious as insects or plants, as familiar and unknowable as weather. Friends dutifully forged of circumstance, who become something more abiding; love-at-first-sight friends, for whom one's heart leaps in recognition (but of what, exactly?) from the first conversation; friends formed of shared intellectual interests or political concerns; friends slowly stolen from other friends, wittingly or unwittingly; fair weather friends; fast friends; feckless friends; mad friends; the innocents; the loyal guard; the lost ones...There are those friends you always rather dread seeing, but whose company you invariably enjoy more than you expected; and those you can't wait to spend time with, who somehow always disappoint. There are the ones you always thought really 'got' you, until you realize belatedly they didn't at all, and then you wonder who they thought you were, and troublingly, who you thought *they* were, too. There are the solid, quiet ones you carelessly overlook, until you come shamefacedly to see they're solid gold.

Each one has something to teach us; each is remarkable, not least because we give them our hearts. We choose them—deem them special—as they choose us. When you consider how agonizing this process proves in our romantic lives ("who will ever love me?"), it seems all the more miraculous that, in friendship, we make our choices with abandon, sincerely, eagerly, often unthinkingly, and usually without prospect of measurable gain. In an era in which we obsessively measure value and take a disturbingly utilitarian approach to so much in our lives, friendship remains an essential extra, a gift that, even in its challenges, brings us more than we can truly know.

In addition to exploring the cultural and social histories of friendship, Mroz cites its many known benefits—including better physical and psychic health. But one of this book's abiding pleasures rests in its moving use of anecdote, the deft inclusion of moving stories told by ordinary women of all ages about the girls and women they have loved, with whom they've struggled, and upon whom they've relied. Every woman who reads this book will find echoes of her own experiences. In *Girl Talk*, Mroz grants these vital human connections the focus and importance they merit, a serious attention for which her readers will be lastingly grateful.

Introduction

A friend may well be reckoned the masterpiece of nature.

—Ralph Waldo Emerson

WE TELL OUR friends secrets that we wouldn't entrust to anyone else; we cry on their shoulders when things have gone wrong and we toast them when they've succeeded; we talk to them about our significant others, our kids, our parents; we go on adventures together; and we laugh over each other's imperfections. What would we do without our friends?

I know I couldn't live without mine.

We feel better when we're with our friends—even knowing they're there for us can make us happy. And research has begun to back up the magic of friendship and its connection to our health. Having friends improves our immunity, promotes healing, lowers blood pressure, and makes us feel less depressed—it even makes us live longer.

But sometimes, our friends can behave in strange and mysterious ways—they may act jealous or unfeeling; they may undermine us or, even more seriously, they may cause us to break up with them, permanently. At the same time, other friends will go on being supportive, kind, and caring. What makes women behave in these ways? I've had my own friend breakups in the past, and I wanted to understand why they happened. As I started talking to my current friends about my experience, I realized that I wasn't alone. Many of them had their own story about the friend that "got away," and most of them were still sad about the loss. But what really struck me, besides the grief, was the sense of confusion. None of us could figure out what had caused a close friendship to turn sour, and that made me curious about the mystery behind these rifts.

I wondered—could there be a scientific explanation for women's behavior with their friends, both good and bad? If I could find an answer to how female friendship worked, could I learn to prevent my own relationships falling apart, and make them stronger, as well as provide useful advice to others? Friends are so important to women, and studies have shown that a breakup with a friend can feel even worse than a divorce.

As a longtime science writer for the *New York Times,* I wanted to investigate the nature of women's friendship. I was curious to find out if there was an evolutionary basis for the way women keep, and lose, their friends. Could the complex social worlds of our primate relatives—especially chimpanzees—help us understand what was going on? *Girl Talk: What Science Can Tell Us About Female Friendship* tries to answer this question, and in researching the book, I talked to evolutionary anthropologists and psychologists. I also interviewed neuroscientists who have studied women and their methods of friendship, and I found out what's behind their behavior, including the latest scientific research on these relationships.

For instance, I looked closely at a recent article suggesting that women have significant misconceptions regarding which of the people they feel close to are their authentic friends. The study revealed that only about half of participants successfully identified their true friends. Insights from evolutionary biologists and neuroscientists about what makes women tick are interspersed here with real-life stories. Women's friendship is a new and exciting area of study, and researchers are just beginning to examine the science behind these relationships.

While friendship is an informal social relationship, many women say they feel closer to their friends than to some of their own family members. On the other hand, male friendships are seldom as intimate as women's, and they rarely go through breakups with their friends. Men can fall out of touch with someone for years and still call him a close friend. While women on the whole find their girlfriends to be more supportive than guys find their guy friends, and women are more inclined to reveal their feelings and emotions with their girlfriends, studies have found female friendships to be more fragile than men's.

Before writing this book, I had noticed that whenever I spoke to my husband about issues I was having with my friends, he didn't seem to understand what I was talking about—he'd never had a rift with another guy, let alone a breakup. It made me wonder: Why are women's and men's friendships so vastly different? This book attempts to answer that question.

As I started to research this book I realized that I also wanted to understand what makes friendships between women work well. Then I read something that resonated with me: It's easy to walk away from problem friendships—but by working through conflict when things go wrong, we have the potential to create deeper, better quality friendships. That stuck with me. I was letting my friendship with one of my best friends from college drift away because I was annoyed that she always seemed to be on her phone whenever we got together—and I saw her only rarely. So instead of ignoring it, I decided to call her and tell her how I felt. She hadn't realized that I'd been bothered by her behavior, and she apologized, promising to change. She also told me that she had a health issue that she was dealing with, and that it had made her anxious about the visit.

I hadn't known this—and it helped me to understand her behavior. Although we don't see each other or talk as much as I'd like to, I still consider her one of my closest friends. Now, I feel like we can be more honest with each other.

Sometimes, the most unlikely women will become friends.

Marilyn Monroe's close friendship with jazz singer Ella Fitzgerald surprised many at the time. *Girl Talk* looks at their relationship, as well as other famous friends in history and literature, such as Gertrude Stein's longtime relationship with Vita Sackville-West, and Susan B. Anthony's lifelong partnership with Elizabeth Cady Stanton as they fought for women's rights in the mid-1800s. *My Brilliant Friend,* a best-selling novel by Elena Ferrante, is about two women who are best friends in Naples and whose lives are forever intertwined. In *Girl Talk* I explore why their story resonates with so many female readers. And I look at other female friendships in recent fiction, such as Claire Messud's *The Burning Girl* and books by Margaret Atwood.

I also compare women's friendships across cultures to understand how they differ and to learn what exactly it is that makes a relationship a friendship. *Girl Talk* examines how social media is changing women's friendship, for the better or for the worse. For instance, is phone addiction making it harder for us to have deep friendships?

I hope that *Girl Talk* will help us understand the science behind women's friendships: what makes them so emotionally supportive, and why they sometimes implode. Writing this book certainly changed the way I feel and act toward my friends, and it has made my friendships stronger. Hopefully, with the knowledge in this book, we can become better friends and enjoy more satisfying and lasting relationships with our girlfriends.

A Note on the Research Study

FOR THIS BOOK, I conducted a survey of women's friendship with my intrepid researcher, Brooke Schwartz, a research coordinator at NYU Langone Health and master of social work candidate at Columbia University. Using MTurk, an online survey tool, we asked more than 125 women questions about their friendships: The women ranged in age from 18 to 74 years old, and they came from various racial and ethnic backgrounds; they lived in 33 different states, and Canada, with the largest proportion from New York, Florida, and California. Most had a bachelor's degree and some had a master's degree or a high school diploma. About 56 percent were married or in a partnership; 31 percent were single, 16 percent were divorced; 89 percent were heterosexual and 11 percent were bisexual. As for their political views, 38 percent were liberal, 18 percent were conservative, and 30 percent were moderate; 17 percent were very liberal and 3 percent were very conservative.

I was curious to know what women looked for in a friendship, so we asked them their top value in a female friend: 22 percent said support; 17 percent cited authenticity; 15 percent, loyalty; 13 percent, success; and 10 percent, good listener; the rest of the answers were under 10 percent, and they were for compassion, intelligence, humor, optimism, and trustworthiness. It's interesting that women found success in a friend to be an important quality, and that compassion and trustworthiness were less essential. When asked how many close female friends they had, the average was five; about 63 percent said they still had good female friends from childhood, and about half found them to be different from the friends they made as an adult—in a good way.

A remarkable 54 percent had experienced a breakup with a female friend, with the highest numbers among the oldest respondents (ages 65–74) and the youngest (18–24); there was no statistically significant difference in the answers when this was broken down by race or marital status. (I look at this more in-depth in Chapter 7.) Only 33 percent overall said that a female friend had helped them professionally, but 70 percent of older respondents said that female friends had assisted them in their careers. (More on this in Chapter 1.) Not surprisingly, most of the women felt that their friendships with women were markedly different than those they had with men.

Social media has become an important factor in our friendships, both good and bad; the highest percentage of respondents (24 percent) had over 401 friends on Facebook, with the next highest having 101–200 friends. Some of the young women that I interviewed for this book had between 1,200 and 2,400 friends on Facebook—and one was only 17 years old! When asked if they had friends from other cultures, most of the women answered yes; what's interesting is that the 18- to 24-year-old age group had the most: 73 percent. Perhaps this tells us something about that generation? Only 15 percent of women in the Midwest had friends from other cultures, the lowest number.

Finally, it has long thought to be difficult to make friends as we age, and my survey results back this up; for those over 60 years old, 32 percent said they found it somewhat difficult to make friends as they became older. It's telling that many of the women under age 25 also found it hard to make new friends (33 percent). Yet 47 percent of the women over 60 reported having the same amount of friends now as when they were in their twenties or thirties. That's promising.

Notes on the format of the study: We gathered responses to a survey we created through a Google form that was posted to MTurk. The survey was in the form of a self-administered questionnaire and it included open and closed-ended questions. The survey was open to anyone identifying as female and was advertised by MTurk and also by us through social media. Participants who took the survey on MTurk were compensated for their participation. Sampling type was nonprobability sampling. We used STATA to analyze data. Survey findings are not generalizable and do not make claims about female friendships in general; the point of the survey was to look at a small sample of female-identifying women, gather some preliminary data, and get qualitative responses to support already established research.

Chapter 1

A History of Friendship
How the idea started

> There is one friend in the life of each of us who seems
> not a separate person, however dear and beloved, but an
> expansion, or interpretation of one's self, the very mean-
> ing of one's soul.
>
> —Edith Wharton

To understand how female friendship works, it's important to
go back in time to look at how it began. It may be hard to believe
today, but in Ancient Greece, great thinkers and philosophers such
as Aristotle thought that only men were capable of forming strong
connections and making friends.

Since men wrote all of the historical documents about friendship in the first two thousand years of Western history, women were
rarely included. They were thought to be weaker than men and un-
suited to the loftier concept of friendship—especially during the
time of the Greeks and Romans.

Today, more scholars are recognizing the important place that
women have held through the ages. And by taking a long view of the
history of female friendship, we can come away with a greater understanding of not just female but human behavior, and what makes
our lives meaningful. Benefiting from a historical perspective,

scientists around the world—biologists, sociologists, physiologists, and more—are beginning to understand the influence of women's friendship on the evolution of culture as well as, more immediately, on women individually.

Within the classical philosophical tradition, women were historically judged to be without the passion, sense of individuality, and capacity for thought that makes for a good friendship. So impressed were the Greeks with the manliness of friendship and its power to prompt men to heroic action, they set the love of male friendship above even the love of man for woman, according to Janice Raymond, a professor emerita of women's studies at the University of Massachusetts, Amherst.

"It has always been difficult for women to become friends, both because of patriarchal norms in every society, and because women have internalized these norms," said Raymond, the author of four books, including *A Passion for Friends: Toward a Philosophy of Female Affection.* "Women's friendships are a challenge to this tradition."

Until the 1960s, there was little research done on women's friendship in history, as females had been subordinate in society for so long. Studies of women were seen as less vital than and not as interesting as the traditional studies of male areas, such as politics. For instance, there are thousands of books on leaders such as George Washington and Franklin Delano Roosevelt, but very few on the women who lived during those times. During the feminist movement, academics and historians started putting women back on the record, bringing more attention to their accomplishments.

Looking back on the history of women's friendship, it's evident that the classical ideal of men's friendship was ultimately rejected by women, who found that their relationships with women offered them the support and affection that they sometimes didn't receive from their husbands. Of course, one chapter cannot encompass all the history of women's friendship, but it can provide an overview of the shifting attitudes that women experienced over time, and how those relationships influence us today.

One of the earliest accounts we have of female friendship is the story of Ruth and Naomi from the Book of Ruth in the Hebrew Bible. Their account is one of the rare places in the Bible where women speak to each other; while women are represented in various books of the Bible, we seldom find them talking to one another. Thus, according to Wendy Amsellem, a teacher at the Drisha Institute for Jewish Education in New York, the Book of Ruth is a unique celebration of female friendship.

In the beginning of their story, Naomi does not see the value of friendship with Ruth, a younger woman. Naomi has no sons to offer Ruth in marriage and she believes her worth as a woman is simply as a matchmaker and eventual mother-in-law. In contrast, Ruth values Naomi for herself, not for any potential suitors that she may provide. In one of the most powerful and eloquent statements between women in the Bible, Ruth declares her devotion to Naomi:

> Entreat me not to leave thee, or to return from following after thee: for whither thou goest, I will go; and where thou lodgest, I will lodge: thy people shall be my people, and thy God my God: Where thou diest, will I die, and there will I be buried: the Lord do so to me, and more also, if aught but death part thee and me. (Ruth 1:16–17)

Naomi can't fathom that she has anything to give to Ruth, since her sons are all dead.

But Ruth convinces Naomi that she just wants to be with her— forever, until death separates them.

"Through Ruth's love and devotion," said Amsellem, "Naomi has been redeemed and made full."

Classical Ideals of Friendship

Friendship was an important concept in the time of classical Athens; philosophers debated its social importance and its ethical demands. The philosopher Aristotle said that friendship was essential to a well-lived life, and he believed there were three types of friendship: utility, pleasure, and the good. In utility, people are friends with each other based on what they can do for one another, such as business associates or classmates. These friendships aren't permanent, because once the benefit of being friends ends, so too does the friendship.

The second type of friendship is one of pleasure: "We enjoy the society of witty people not because of what they are in themselves, but because they are agreeable to us." As with utility, in the friendship of pleasure, people love their friends not for the sake of the friends, but for the sake of the pleasure received. But these friendships are also tenuous, as they can change or end as quickly as the pleasure received can change or end.

The good or "virtuous" friendship was the rarest form but the most valuable. Aristotle observed:

> Such friendship is naturally permanent, since it combines in itself all the attributes that friends ought to possess...it is between good men that affection and friendship exist in their fullest and best form. Such friendships are of course rare, because such men are few. Moreover, they require time and intimacy...people who enter into friendly relations quickly have the wish to be friends, but cannot really be friends without being worthy of friendship, and also knowing each other to be so.

Three centuries later, Cicero, one of the ancient philosophers who wrote most prolifically about friendship, praised its importance, but also questioned some of the problems that might arise in these relationships. In his book, *De Amicitia (On Friendship)*, Cicero wrote of the highest ideal of friendship among ancient Romans—though this did not, of course, include women. His treatise on the subject continues to be relevant to this day. In his book, Cicero says that friends should "share with each other, without reservation, all their concerns, their plans, their aims." His words still resonate:

> Even while understanding that friendship includes a great number of important advantages, it must be said that it excels all other things in this respect: that it projects a bright ray of hope into the future, and upholds the spirit which otherwise might falter or grow faint. He who looks upon a true friend, looks, as it were, upon a better image of himself. For this is what we mean by friends: even when they are absent, yet they are with us; even when they lack some things, still they have an abundance of others; even when they are weak, in truth they are strong; and hardest of all to say, but also most deeply felt: even when they are dead, in truth they are alive with us, for so great is the esteem of a true friend, the tender recollection and the deep longing still abides with them.

A Nun's Life

Through the ages, women have always been friends with their family members and neighbors, helping each other through births and illness and everything in between. But they were rarely friends with complete strangers. That started to change during the Middle Ages, when some early Christian communities allowed nuns to live in a separate part of monasteries, where they were able to live secluded from society and could dedicate themselves to their religion. These medieval nuns were able to form close, lifelong friendships with other women. Because Christianity consistently cast aspersions on women's independence, there were few outlets for women to have significant intellectual, political, and social power. Early religious communities of women became the refuge of many women who craved influence and independence. They offered opportunities undreamed of by most women, especially during that time. Convents allowed women an education that was better than that enjoyed by most women and many men outside their religious community.

These convents also provided an environment in which female friendship prevailed. Women spent their lives primarily with other women, giving them their attention and energy, and forming powerful ties with one other.

"I was surprised to find ample records of the friendships between nuns, going back to the Middle Ages. How these women supported each other with loving friendship was a revelation to me," said Marilyn Yalom, author of *The Social Sex: A History of Female Friendship*.

The female "monastery was, in those days, anything but an isolated and strictly meditative community. It was a busy and active unit of society with its own economy and an outward thrust of service to the community," said Raymond in her book *A Passion for Friends: Toward a Philosophy of Female Affection*.

According to Raymond, the convent was a community of spiritual friends who could do great things.

Convents were a welcome respite for women who did not want to marry—especially in an age when men had the power to mistreat their wives at will, without penalty. These places held an attraction for women who wanted to be somewhat independent, creating the conditions for women's friendships to thrive. Segregation of the sexes had the virtue of "introducing women to the great joys and rewards of friendship with one another," said Jo Ann McNamara, author of *Sisters in Arms: Catholic Nuns Through Two Millennia*.

By the seventeenth century, the salons of Paris had begun to create a new kind of friendship between women. It was during these literary rendezvous that women could talk about literature and music and, with some independence from their husbands, befriend other women. In her book, Yalom described these meetings as foretelling the philosophy of the feminist agenda, allowing women to discuss cultural subjects that had previously only been touched on by men, and enabling them to befriend men as well. She suggested that these salons may have even augured the women's clubs that came into fashion in later years, including the book clubs, garden clubs, and the Junior League organizations of today.

New World Friendships

By the late seventeenth and early eighteenth centuries, there were important cultural, economic, and political changes that started to strain British society. What's more, all of the European countries that created colonies in the "New World" of North, Central, and South America, including Spain, France, Portugal, and the Netherlands, were feeling this pressure.

Families were also emigrating to America to start a new life. Dr. Amanda Herbert, author of *Female Alliances: Gender, Identity, and Friendship in Early Modern Britain,* said that through their friendships and alliances, women were able to bring their families and British society together while helping to build the colonies in the New World.

"When Europe began to expand so rapidly into the New World, many people became worried that the fabric of society would snap. They looked to women to maintain those social networks and the cohesiveness of European society," said Herbert. "When most people imagine early modern Britain, the British Atlantic, and colonial America, they think of what men did; the laws they created, the colonies they built. We tend to overlook the important behind the scenes work that was done by women. It's gone under the radar."

That's probably because women were thought to be more vulnerable and lesser than men; they were considered to be more emotional and more easily manipulated. While men relied upon women to do important work—such as taking care of the children and the household—they still made sure to carefully monitor their wives.

Transatlantic travel, enslavement, and emigration brought huge changes in seventeenth-century women's lives, bringing them to a strange world across the ocean and into contact with unfamiliar people, who came from many different races, cultures, and backgrounds.

"Emigration, whether it was voluntary or forced, created a sense of terror as well as wonder, and thinking about the way that people in the past encountered, adapted to, and tried to survive these challenges offers us some important lessons on friendship: How do we work with people who are unlike us? How do we perceive difference?" said Herbert.

Women—and especially enslaved women, who had no legal protections—were easily taken advantage of in these colonial American times. Those who went to live in the colonies had to work with other women of different backgrounds and cultures. Sometimes they forced themselves to get along in order to survive: making, selling, and sharing medicines that kept people healthy; and growing, harvesting, and circulating food to keep people from starving. As a result, friendships between women were formed, sometimes out of obligation, sometimes out of necessity, and other times out of mutual affection. If they were able, women also maintained ties with female friends back at home, in the hopes that their old friends would have supplies shipped to them.

"In the early modern British world, friendship was an important part of women's survival. It wasn't easy or perfect, but they needed one another, and their families needed one another. They were forced to rely upon each other," said Herbert.

Yet women weren't always trusted to manage their friendships on their own. Men kept tabs on their wives' relationships with other women, worried that the women would become too close and push the men out of their lives. Some of these men felt threatened by women's friendships and relationships; they wanted women to come to them for guidance and believed that women were weak. They wanted to control them.

It was a patriarchal world, and women were subordinate to men. Men had all the power, and women still had little access to wealth, political voice, or legal rights of their own.

According to Janice Raymond, "It was expected in the past, and still in the present, that every woman's most meaningful and most satisfying relationship was with men. This is the patriarchal ideology that woman is for man. In this world, female friendship is regarded as second-rate, insignificant and often as an adolescent phase in female life."

A Novel Approach

Society expected women to behave a certain way, but that began to change when novels became more popular.

As more women became readers, books began to be written for female readers about their lives and experiences. These novels actually helped women to see themselves as the protagonists of their own stories. They didn't just "reflect" their lives, but helped to "shape" their experiences by giving them expectations about human behavior and relationships.

When the first modern English novel, *Pamela*, by Samuel Richardson, was published in 1739 (some people give the honor of the first modern English novel to Daniel Defoe's *Robinson Crusoe* in 1719), those who read it began to understand the suffering of someone else—someone with whom they were not related. And that changed how people began to recognize other people and their relationships in the real world, said Ana Schwartz, a professor of English at Montclair State University. "Novels helped shape women's experience of how other people lived, and how they saw themselves in their community." Schwartz suggested that the enduring popularity of female friendships in novels came from women enjoying the chance to read about these different experiences. Since novels can help to shape how we understand the ways we gain emotional satisfaction from a relationship, that knowledge consequently shaped what women expected from their friends. Stories of women's friendship were a result of increased attention on women's lives in general. The number of published female writers also grew. At the same time, as England became wealthier in the eighteenth century through trade, there was a bigger middle class, and more women had leisure time to read.

Pamela is an epistolary novel; the entire story is structured as a series of letters written by a young maid, Pamela. She is a servant in the house of a rich and evil man who is trying to seduce her while she struggles to keep her purity. Eventually, her master stops pestering her, changes, and marries her. In the book's introduction, the author said he wanted to teach readers not only how to write elegant letters but "how to think and act justly and prudently in the common concerns of life."

Quaker Women: Brave Souls

For Quaker women, friendships were an important way for them to spread the word about their faith.

In the late 1600s, Quaker women undertook vast journeys in their quest to spread their message. Traveling only in pairs, these brave souls journeyed by ship, horseback, and on foot all over the world to enormous distances with little or no protection or help. They were roaming preachers and called themselves "yokemates." The women traveled by ship to islands in the Caribbean, where they preached to enslaved and free people, and all over the British Isles, including England, Ireland, Scotland, and Wales. They voyaged up and down the East Coast of North America for years, preaching the religion of the Society of Friends.

"They were some of the worldliest, most experienced travelers that existed in the 17th and 18th centuries," Herbert stated. "Trans-Atlantic travel was dangerous and difficult, but some of these Quaker women made this journey over and over again during their lifetimes."

Friendship was essential to these Quaker women; many were poor and uneducated, and they relied on each other and their faith to survive. They wrote of their travels, which they called "the sufferings," and which they undertook for Christ. These women valued female companionship and said their friendships sustained and intensified their religious experience. They were convinced that the physical suffering they experienced during their travels brought them closer to Christ.

Witches

But there was a darker side to the singularity of women's relationships.

In the early modern period, from the late fifteenth century to the late eighteenth century, there was speculation that groups of women who were friends could be witches.

In the spring of 1692, a group of young girls in Salem Village, Massachusetts, began having fits, wild contortions, and uncontrollable screaming. They claimed to be possessed by the devil and accused several local women of being witches. Hysteria spread through the colony, and a special court was called to hear the Salem Witch Trials. Nineteen women were convicted and hanged for being witches, and more than 150 men, women, and children were later accused of witchcraft.

The trials tore the community apart, with neighbors and friends accusing each other of practicing the occult. The people who became the victims of the witch hunt were those who were most vulnerable: girls and women—especially older women who were isolated.

Scientists later discovered what they believed to be the cause of the girls' hysterical fits: A study published in *Science* magazine cited the fungus ergot (found in rye, wheat, and other cereals) as the probable cause (although some academics don't believe this theory). Ergot can cause symptoms such as delusions, vomiting, and seizures.

Victorian Women and the Cult of Friendship

Fortunately, during the time of Victorian England, women's friendship began to become more acceptable and less threatening to men. They also became romanticized; women were more affectionate with one another and spoke about their friends using words usually reserved for lovers.

This development was called a cult of friendship.

The literature at the time encouraged women to be expressive in their emotions and in their feelings for each other.

In her book *Between Women: Friendship, Desire and Marriage in Victorian England,* Sharon Marcus argued that women's relationships were central to Victorian society. Unlike other eras, women in the Victorian age were able to create strong bonds with one another, and were not defined only in relation to men. But the term "friend" during Victorian times had a different meaning than it does today. In earlier times, "friend" could mean a relative or a romantic or sexual partner, but Marcus posited that by the turn of the nineteenth century, the word was all-encompassing and included relatives, patrons, neighbors, and spouses, as well as confidants. For Victorians, the term referred to a close relationship with someone who was not a relative, and it could also refer to a lover.

Victorians accepted and even encouraged friendship between women because they believed it made them into good wives. Female friends called each other "sister" and their friendships were considered useful, as they helped to arrange courtships and marriages. For women, friends were people they could love without the responsibilities connected to family life. It was considered a luxury for a middle class woman to have a close friend, someone she could spend time with just for the sheer pleasure, someone she could lavish with affection.

Much can be gleaned from the writings of women during this time. They were prolific in their diaries, letters, and memoirs, and their understanding of friendship was very different from their predecessors'. The period between 1830 and 1880 was the peak of sentimental friendships, with women writing lovingly to each other of their affection. They often used the word "love," and were passionate and sometimes obsessive about each other, frequently using the language of physical attraction to describe their feelings for their girlfriends. Some of these women were lesbians, but many were not. In fact, at the time, Queen Victoria made a famous pronouncement that exempted women from anti-homosexual laws because she didn't believe that women could be gay. This exemption reflected the general belief at the time that women's friendships of all kinds were beyond sexual suspicion.

Ann Gilbert, who co-wrote the poem now known as "Twinkle, Twinkle, Little Star," wrote of her friendship with another woman as "the gathering of the last ripe figs, here and there, one on the topmost bough!" In another poem that she sent to a childhood friend, she wrote,

> *As rose leaves in a china Jar*
> *Breathe still of blooming seasons past,*
> *E'en so, old women as they are*
> *Still doth the affection last.*

During this period, friendship was considered a complement to a woman's family life, and many kept these close relationships throughout their lives—even after marrying and having children. One historian said that these women invented a newly self-conscious and idealized version of female friendship. Marcus noted that these relationships were considered essential because they helped to develop the characteristics that women were encouraged to exhibit to their husbands: loyalty, selflessness, empathy, and self-effacement. But some historians suggest that the ideology promoting friendship between women at that time was merely a way for men to confine women to a female world.

In my interview with her, Marcus didn't agree: "I don't think that people encouraged female friendships in order to confine women to typically feminine roles, but I do think that few people saw any serious conflict between female friendships and typical feminine roles."

Despite the romantic version of women's friendship in nineteenth-century America, there was still separation of the sexes, which meant that women still did most of the work involved with taking care of the children and the household. Historian Carroll Smith-Rosenberg suggested that this dichotomy led to the immense importance of female friends to each other, supporting one another through marriage, childbirth, illness, and death, and providing the emotional support that their husbands were unable to give them.

Virginia Woolf had an intensely close relationship with her friend, the writer and poet Vita Sackville-West; it veered between passionate love, emotional intimacy, and then into a long and steady friendship. Her lover's family inspired Virginia's groundbreaking novel, *Orlando: A Biography,* the adventures of a poet who changes sex from man to woman and lives for more than three hundred years. Considered a feminist classic, it was written as a tribute to Virginia's dear friend.

Virginia told of how she searched for a tradition of female friendship in literature, and described her quest for "those unsaid or half-said words, which form themselves, no more palpably than the shadows of moths on the ceiling, when women are alone, unlit by the capricious and coloured lights of the other sex."

Another intense friendship between two women during the 1800s was so moving that their correspondence later inspired the classic Pulitzer Prize–winning novel, *Angle of Repose,* by Wallace Stegner.

Mary Hallock Foote was raised in a Quaker family in New York. In 1866, she went to New York City to study art at Cooper Union, and it was there that she met the artist Helena de Kay, who would become her lifelong friend.

Mary married a mining engineer and traveled west to live in a succession of mining camps, where she strived to raise their children while continuing to practice her art. She sent back east her pictures and stories about life in the west. Helena married a poet and editor and stayed in New York. The letters between the women chronicled their passionate friendship, which lasted for more than fifty years. They exchanged hundreds of letters, about five hundred of which were saved.

Here is an excerpt from a letter that Mary Hallock Foote wrote to Helena de Kay in the spring of 1869, after Mary had to cancel a planned visit to see her friend:

> I wanted so to put my arms around my girl of all the girls in the world and tell her that whether I go to N.Y. or stay home, whether she signs herself "very truly your friend" or "your ownest of girls" I love her as wives do (not) love their husbands as *friends* who have taken each other for life—and believe in her as I believe in my God—Please don't mind about my decisions—they are not the real thing—It isn't whether we believe in the same thing but whether we believe in each other and, dear Helena, I do believe

in you and have faith in you in spite of the little jeer at "you people of faith"—You are not my "neighbor" but my chosen friend,
chosen deliberately out of all the girls I have known—You believe
that Love has its tides—Well there was a strong ebb tide this
summer—I can't explain to you all that caused it now—many
things combined—but it only shows me how much *you* (not your
opinions, or words or deeds always) but you, the great heart &
soul of you, are to me!

Mary, who was a writer, artist, and pioneer, became celebrated
for her illustrated short stories and novels portraying life during
the turn of the century in the mining communities in the western United States. In the late 1800s, she was one of America's best-
known female illustrators.

Helena was a portrait and still-life painter and writer. She and
her husband, Richard Watson Gilder, helped found the Society of
American Artists, an influential group that included the artists John
La Farge and Louis Tiffany. She studied art under Winslow Homer,
who painted her portrait and was a close friend.

In another letter, Mary wrote to Helena's fiancé, Richard Gilder:

Do you know, sir, until you came I believed she loved me almost
as girls love their lovers—I know I loved her so. Don't you wonder
that I can't bear the sight of you? I don't know another man who
could make it seem "right." You must have been born to make her
future complete and she was born to kindle your Genius.... She is
the most inspiring being I ever saw who was herself so inspired.

These passionate friendships between women were fashionable
at the time, and those who embraced them included writer George
Sand (her real name was Aurore Dupin), who had many female loves
in her life, and Charlotte Brontë, who had a romantic friendship

with a fellow classmate at her boarding school. The English writers Elizabeth Barrett Browning and Christina Rossetti continued their close friendship for more than sixty years and wrote romantic poems to one another. They were considered the female poet laureates of their era.

Upon the death of her close friend, Christina wrote the poem, "Gone Before," for Elizabeth. Here is an excerpt:

> *Earth is not good enough for you, my sweet, my*
> *sweetest;*
> *Life on earth seemed long to you, though to me*
> *fleetest;*
> *I would not wish you back if a wish would do:*
> *Only, love, I long for heaven with you,*
> *Heart-pierced through and through.*

Mrs. Lincoln and a Former Slave Become Friends

An unusual friendship was found between Mary Todd Lincoln, the wife of Abraham Lincoln, and Elizabeth Keckley, a former slave who later became a successful seamstress.

In *An Unlikely Friendship,* Ann Rinaldi describes their unique relationship: Mary was the wife of the president, living in the White House, when she met Elizabeth. The former had been born to wealth and privilege, and was educated throughout her childhood, unusual for girls in that era. But Mary was volatile; doctors later diagnosed her with bipolar disorder.

Elizabeth had been born a slave but was able to buy freedom for herself and her son. She moved to Washington, DC, and set up shop as a seamstress, eventually becoming quite successful through personal recommendations. Elizabeth was brought to the White House to meet with the first lady, who was known for her love of fashion.

She was looking for a seamstress who would make her the extravagant clothes that she liked to wear to state events. Mary took to Elizabeth immediately, and eventually they became close friends. Elizabeth designed and sewed all of the gowns that Mary wore, and served as her personal dresser as well. The first lady confided in her and sought out her advice when she was troubled.

They became so close that Elizabeth was with Mary after Lincoln was assassinated and was even given her blood-spattered cloak and hat from that night. She consoled Mary after Lincoln's death, and comforted her when three of Mary's four children died as well.

But many believe that Elizabeth violated the trust that Mary placed in her when, in 1868, she published a tell-all autobiography called *Behind the Scenes: Or, Thirty Years a Slave and Four Years in the White House.*

In the book, she said that she attempted to place Mrs. Lincoln "in a better light before the world," but, in fact, she divulged private details about the first lady's domestic life, including her anxiety about trying to dress right and her mounting debts. Elizabeth also disclosed private conversations and printed letters that Mrs. Lincoln had written to her. Not surprisingly, Mary was hurt by her friend's betrayal and cut off all contact with her.

The Marriage Resisters

In the 1800s, some young women in China, many who lived in the rural Kwangtung area, effectively kick-started the feminist movement there by refusing to marry and choosing to live with one another instead. If these "marriage resisters" were forced into an arranged marriage, they chose not to live with their husbands. Their resistance to marriage was based on the dire consequences that marriage held for many Chinese women; it's telling that a Chinese word for female is "slave."

According to Janice Raymond, "The marriage resister can be seen as part of the same Chinese women's tradition that spawned the woman warrior. Her battle was against forced marriage, but her resistance went beyond an anti-marriage position to a commitment to female friendship that was long lasting."

Most women in these anti-marriage sisterhoods, also known as Golden Orchid Associations, worked in the silk industry, affording them the opportunity to provide for themselves and often for their families, which was something few other women in China were able to do at the time. Because women in this region had not accepted foot binding to the degree to which women in other parts of China had been forced to, they were physically equipped for hard work and had the mobility necessary for more independent choices.

Girls from the Kwangtung area were literate and were permitted by their families to live in girls' houses, also known as vegetarian houses, at an early age. This early socialization led to young women taking vows of sworn sisterhood in ceremonies that were similar to marriages. They swore never to marry nor part company, and to look after each other throughout their lives, promising each other everlasting friendship.

These women were known as *tzu-shu nü,* "women who dress their own hair."

Some scholars believe these associations were a precursor to the Chinese women's movement. When the Communists seized power in China in the 1950s, the marriage resisters were forced to leave the country—this was after having existed there for more than a century. By then, the silk industry in China had fallen apart, and their jobs had disappeared. Many of the women fled to Singapore, where they set up girls' houses and found work as domestic servants.

A Righteous Friendship

In the mid-1800s, the women's rights movement was starting to gain ground in America. The long-lasting friendship of suffragists Elizabeth Cady Stanton and Susan B. Anthony emphasized how female relationships could be used to achieve one's goals—and other women began to follow their lead.

Marilyn Yalom suggested in her book that "the very long, harmonious friendship between Elizabeth Cady Stanton and Susan B. Anthony laid the groundwork for the suffrage movement and women's rights in the U.S.A."

They were an unlikely pair: When they met, Elizabeth was in her mid-thirties, a married mother of four, and Susan was single and thirty. Elizabeth had just proclaimed "The Women's Declaration of Independence" at the Seneca Falls Convention. Both were committed to women's right to vote, but they also campaigned against slavery and were in favor of abstinence.

Elizabeth said that despite the differences in their family situations (she went on to have three more children, while Susan never married), and their dissimilar personalities, they never fought once.

In her book, *Elizabeth Cady Stanton: As Revealed in Her Letters & Diary*, Elizabeth said:

> So entirely one are we that, in all our associations, ever side by side on the same platform, not one feeling of envy or jealousy has ever shadowed our lives. We have indulged freely in criticism of each other when alone, and hotly contended whenever we have differed, but in our friendship of years there has never been the break of one hour. To the world we always seem to agree and uniformly reflect each other. Like husband and wife, each has the feeling that we must have no differences in public. Thus united, at an early day we began to survey the state and nation, the future field of our labors. We read, with critical eyes, the proceedings of Congress and legislatures, of general assemblies and synods, of conferences and conventions, and discovered that, in all alike, the existence of women was entirely ignored.

Without their friendship, it's unclear whether they would have accomplished all that they did.

Elizabeth said that Susan always pushed and goaded her to work, and that, without Susan's urging, she might have become absorbed in raising a family, as other women had:

> It has been said, by those who know me best, that I forged the thunderbolts and she in the early days fired them. Perhaps all this is, in a measure, true.... In thought and sympathy we were one, and in the division of labor we exactly complimented each other. I am the better writer, she is the better critic. She supplied the facts and statistics, I the philosophy and rhetoric, and together, we have made arguments that have stood unshaken through the storms of long years; arguments that no one has answered.

Together, they edited and published a woman's newspaper, *The Revolution*, and traveled all over the country promoting women's rights. They formed the National Woman Suffrage Association in 1869 and continued to fight for women's right to vote, as well as equal rights for women, with Susan as the on-the-ground organizer and Elizabeth doing much of the writing.

Years later, in honor of Elizabeth's eighty-seventh birthday, Susan wrote to her:

> We little dreamed when we began this contest, optimistic with the hope and buoyancy of youth, that half a century later we would be compelled to leave the finish of the battle to another generation of women. But our hearts are filled with joy to know that they enter upon this task equipped with a college education, with business experience, with the fully admitted right to speak in public—all of which were denied to women fifty years ago. They

have practically one point to gain—the suffrage; we had all. And we, dear old friend, shall move on the next sphere of existence—higher and larger, we cannot fail to believe, and one where women will not be placed in an inferior position, but will be welcomed on a plane of perfect intellectual and spiritual equality.

Their deep-rooted friendship was very public, but also quite genuine.

Together, they were an inseparable force. They both died before women finally attained the right to vote, with the Nineteenth Amendment in 1920. Elizabeth's daughter, Harriot Stanton Blatch, carried on her mother's work.

By the late 1800s, colleges had begun admitting women, and the social circles of girls started to broaden from relationships mainly with close relatives and neighbors to friendships with classmates. The formation of women's colleges, such as Vassar, Wellesley, Smith, and Bryn Mawr, further engendered opportunities for middle- and upper-class women to achieve a higher education and to have more contact with others who were not their relatives. Working-class girls didn't have the same opportunities to attend university, but they made friends at the factories and shops in which they worked.

A First Lady's Friendships

When Franklin Delano Roosevelt was first elected president in 1933, his wife, Eleanor, turned to her many friends for the love and support she needed in her new position as first lady. She'd discovered that her husband had been having an affair with her personal secretary for two years. They decided to live separate lives but remain married, and so Eleanor surrounded herself with her own group of loyal women and men. She continued to be a helpmate to her husband's political career while pursuing her own interests and causes.

Eleanor's devoted friends included Isabella Selmes Greenway, whom she met before she married Franklin. Isabella later ran for Congress and served for two terms, and she supported Franklin when he ran for office. Isabella helped Eleanor after the death of her third child, Franklin, from influenza, and the two remained close throughout their lives.

Eleanor had many other close female friends in her life, but one of the most important was probably Lorena Hickok, known as Hick, a journalist who covered Franklin's first presidential campaign. The two women were devoted to each other and exchanged thousands of letters with many of them affectionate and loving. Their friendship turned into a love affair that continued for twelve years, with Hick largely living at the White House with the Roosevelts. She became Eleanor's emotional anchor, and an adviser in dealing with the press. She even gave Eleanor a ring that she wore constantly. Hick wrote to Eleanor: "I want to put my arms around you and kiss you at the corner of your mouth." And Eleanor penned to Hick: "I ache to hold you close. Your ring is a great comfort, look at it & think she does love me, or I wouldn't be wearing it!"

Eventually, their relationship began to unravel as Eleanor's feelings for Hick changed, but they remained friends for years afterward.

Sisterhood Is Powerful

In the 1940s and 1950s, women were meant to stay home to take care of the kids and the house, while their husbands went to work and made friends there. Women in the suburbs became friends with other women they met through their children's schools and activities.

But by the 1960s, things started to change dramatically with the advent of the women's rights movement.

Betty Friedan's groundbreaking 1963 book, *The Feminine Mystique*, challenged the belief that "fulfillment as a woman had only one definition for American women after 1949—the housewife-mother." Friedan talked about "the problem that has no name"—the widespread unhappiness of women in the 1950s and early 1960s, such as the housewives who despite being married with children and living comfortable, middle class lives, were unfulfilled.

The book is widely credited with sparking the beginning of second-wave feminism in the United States.

Friedan went on to help found the National Organization for Women and to become a leader in the women's rights movement. As a result of debates about women's liberation, many women started consciousness-raising groups that helped to upend the conventional male-dominated wisdom that women should do what their husbands told them to do and that they had to conform to gender stereotypes.

Feminist literature emphasized the "sisterhood of women," as Robin Morgan phrased it in her 1970 book, *Sisterhood Is Powerful*. Both Friedan and Morgan's books empowered women to join the women's movement and to try to change society. "Sisterhood" became the catchword for female friendship, and women used the term affectionately with their friends.

During the women's rights movement of the 1960s and 1970s, Hedva Lewittes, a psychology professor at SUNY Old Westbury, who is now 71, and many others who became involved met some of their closest, lifelong friends through the feminist groups they joined.

"I wanted to have a political commonality with women and to fight for progress. The friends of mine who've lasted have a much stronger commitment to being connected to other women. I think feminism is really about valuing your connection to other women," said Lewittes, adding that many of the friends she made through these groups ended up later helping her in her career as a professor.

WHILE THE IMPORTANCE of women's friendships may have been downplayed by society early on, the state of affairs for women running for higher office has changed in remarkable ways.

Today, women's alliances are helping women, such as Hillary Clinton and Senator Kirsten Gillibrand and many more, to become elected to positions of power in politics, in corporations, and on college campuses.

Amanda Herbert said that through her work, she wants to draw attention to the sexist assumptions that still exist in women's friendship today: "When women are described as only either 'best friends forever,' or 'mean girls,' the assumption is that they can only experience extreme dichotomies in friendship. These are sexist conventions about women's emotional capacities, rooted in a history that we can reject if we want to. How we create and maintain our friendships should be our own choice, and built according to our own models. We're sociable creatures, and friendship is something that we all need."

Chapter 2

The Science of Friendship

Why we act the way we do with our friends

> I always felt that the great high privilege, relief and comfort of friendship was that one had to explain nothing.
>
> —Katherine Mansfield

Friendship between women can be a complicated psychological dance. We love our friends, but we can also feel conflicted about them. Even Katherine Mansfield, who is quoted above, found her relationship with Virginia Woolf to be fraught, and they were considered bitter rivals. Virginia's first impression of Katherine was scathing: She likened her to "a civet cat that had taken to streetwalking." But it turns out that the literary pair considered themselves dear friends who read each other's work and exchanged gifts of bread, coffee, and cigarettes.

Yet Virginia was hurt when Katherine wrote a damning review of her second novel, and she fretted when her friend didn't respond quickly to her letters. References to her friend are scattered throughout Virginia's journal, and she once wrote, "I was jealous of her writing—the only writing I have ever been jealous of."

Katherine Mansfield died at the age of 34 from tuberculosis, and long after her death, Virginia Woolf described being haunted by her friend in her dreams.

The friendship between these two literary geniuses was intense, troubled, and intimate.

Why are our closest friendships sometimes beset with tension and jealousy? It's a question that has baffled many women, myself included, over the years.

While it's not uncommon to be envious of our friends or to resent them when they are more talented, successful, or richer than us, this envy can lead to a type of social aggression that makes women or girls behave in ways that intentionally hurts their friend's social status or self-esteem. And that can seriously damage a friendship.

For instance, Sue's roommate in college, Alex, was funny and smart and always great to talk to. They were close. But sometimes there was a negative side to their relationship—Alex was competitive. If they went out to a bar and a cute guy talked to Sue instead of her, Alex would get jealous and make cutting remarks to Sue. Alex seemed to be threatened by the fact that Sue had more money than her, and she would borrow money and never pay her back. Alex would take Sue's designer clothes, then leave them crumpled in a pile on the floor.

"She was jealous of me. She thought I was prettier than her and had more money. She struggled in college. If I got an A in class and she got a B, she'd get mad. I'm sure she was badmouthing me to our friends," remembered Sue.

Finally, Sue was so fed up with her friend's behavior, that she called Alex during summer break and told her off. She said that she was done with their friendship—and they haven't talked since. While Sue is sad about the breakup, and sometimes misses her friend, she is convinced it was for the best.

Female Aggression

Scientists say that much of the behavior that Sue experienced from her friend has to do with the aggression that is fundamental to being human.

If you strip away the veneer of society, one of the primitive behaviors found in humans is aggression. Scientists believe that this conduct may have evolved because it increased the chances for an individual to survive or reproduce. While humans are considered the most altruistic and empathetic of all species, we are also among the most violent.

But while we're often unsurprised by aggressive behavior in men, women are not "supposed to" act this way—and when they do, they're called "mean girls"—or worse.

In my interview with Agustín Fuentes, an anthropologist who studies cooperation and bonding in human evolution at the University of Notre Dame, he said that human aggression mainly happens between people who know each other, and it's usually between those who are competing for the same resources or who spend a lot of time together. Much of the aggression seen in women is indirect aggression, or "bitchy" behavior, while men continue to just act, well, aggressively. Fuentes said that before the age of 7, boys and girls both act equally and directly aggressive, but as they grow older, it becomes less socially acceptable for girls to be outright aggressive— since they're socialized to be sweet and nice. That's when the indirect, low-grade aggression kicks in for women.

"People frequently underplay female activity in conflict. We tend to associate conflict with male behavior, but all humans seek power through aggressive behavior. We use aggression to negotiate social challenges," explained Fuentes, who chairs the anthropology department at Notre Dame and is the author of the books *Evolution of Human Behavior* and *The Creative Spark: How Imagination Made Humans Exceptional*. He said that for women "it might be a kind of frustration about their lack of power. Women are taught not to yell or scream or hit when they're angry, so they have to find another, indirect way to deal with it. This way takes longer and requires more intense effort."

A number of studies that tracked hyperaggressive and passive children through preteen and early adulthood years found that by the time the kids hit their post-teen years, the girls dropped way down in terms of aggressive behavior—by more than half, said Fuentes. By then, girls were receiving quite a lot of negative reinforcement about their violent behavior, while generally, boys were not.

Female competition over male attention or popularity can lead to girls acting indirectly aggressive, as anyone who went through middle school can attest.

Girls can be mean, in more ways than one. Some researchers believe that the pressures that young women experience to be "sexy" or "beautiful" according to societal standards is causing some of this subtle—and not so subtle—aggression.

In 2013, Canadian researcher Tracy Vaillancourt, whose work has focused on bullying and popularity, conducted a study that showed how women judge and condemn each other based on appearance. In the experiment, female students were shown into a room at McMaster University in Ontario, ostensibly to discuss female friendship. But when the researchers had another young woman enter the room, their reactions to the stranger were secretly recorded.

In the first encounter, a young, attractive woman entered the room plainly dressed; she wore khaki pants and a T-shirt, with her hair in a bun. The students barely paid any attention to her. When the woman came into the room a second time, dressed provocatively in a tight-fitting top, short skirt, high-heeled boots, and with her long, blonde hair loose around her shoulders, the students immediately reacted with hostility, staring at her, looking her up and down, and rolling their eyes. Once the provocatively dressed visitor left the room, the female students laughed at her and talked about the size of her breasts. One student even asked if the stranger had dressed in that manner so that she could have sex with a professor. Another exclaimed, "What the fuck is that?!" before the woman had even left the room.

Vaillancourt found that women used indirect aggression, such as criticizing a competitor's appearance, spreading rumors about a person's sexual behavior, and social exclusion, as a way to diminish attractive, sexually available young females with whom they may be competing for mates. Other researchers have found that women prefer this kind of indirect aggression because it maximizes the harm placed on a victim, while reducing the risk to the aggressor, because they remain anonymous and avoid being attacked back. This indirect aggression can also make it appear as if the aggressor didn't mean to hurt the other woman. The more attractive a young girl or woman is, the more prone she is to being targeted by other women through indirect aggression, as opposed to direct aggression, including physical or verbal attacks. This kind of indirect aggression probably happens more with younger women, although women of other ages experience versions of it as well.

The "slut-shaming" that is part of this type of aggression is used by women to stigmatize those who they deem promiscuous. And this is done, according to Vaillancourt, because women who will have casual sex undermine the goals of women who want long-term relationships. The motivation for this behavior goes to the heart of females' most fundamental biological drive: the urge to reproduce. Reducing the supply of women who are available to have sex increases female bargaining power with men—even if it means ostracizing and manipulating other women who are deemed promiscuous. As the saying goes, "Why buy a cow when you can get the milk for free?"

But feminist psychology finds a very different rationale for this behavior.

It argues that female competition is determined by society rather than biology. This theory suggests that women internalize the perspective of men, which views women as sexual objects that are necessary to have their babies and further their gene pool. That internalization causes women to fight other women for the attention of men, because they've been taught that they should compete with each other in order to reproduce.

Not surprisingly, the form of indirect aggression that some women use on their friends can ruin a relationship.

In the survey I conducted, more than half of the women who responded had experienced a breakup with a friend. The reasons varied, but many pointed to the kind of oblique aggression that Vaillancourt observed in her research.

Here are some of the responses:

> "I found out my friend was lying to me. She was jealous of the time I was spending with my boyfriend and so she said some things that were not true to try to break us up. I found out the truth and told her that I could not be around her because of her lies."

> "I had what I thought was a good friend until I realized that I was always there when she needed me, which she expected of me, but that she was rarely or never available if I needed help with something or a shoulder to lean on. Gradually she stopped contacting me except when she needed something from me. I did not explicitly end the friendship but I distanced myself from her more and more until we eventually stopped seeing each other or talking altogether."

> "I just distanced myself from someone who seemed to like to cause trouble for no reason. I think she likes to cause trouble to control people."

Alpha Females

What causes some women to be domineering?

Some of them might be what we call "alpha" females. Rather than trying to dominate other women for food or other resources, as primates do, they need to take over their rival socially. Behavioral investigator Vanessa Van Edwards has observed that there are tricks for identifying the female alpha in a group: start by looking down. She said that in groups of three or four females, women almost always point their toes toward the person who is the leader of the pack. Van Edwards also said that women take their social cues from this top dog, holding their bodies like her, talking in the same tone of voice, and even laughing for the same amount of time.

Yet scientists say that human alphas don't really exist; they're just humans who happen to excel in specific areas, such as in sports, in their careers, or in social skills.

Fuentes suggested that Vaillancourt's study and others show how much physical appearance plays a part in the way women react to one another. Like the women in Vaillancourt's study, women will say incredibly vicious things about a rival's physical appearance, and single out females who wear short skirts, low-cut tops, and otherwise revealing outfits; even *looking* promiscuous is enough to be shamed by other women.

So is this aggression driven by evolution or by our culture?

Research has shown that it's impossible to tell apart the brains of little girls and little boys—that is, until they reach adolescence. Then it becomes much easier to distinguish them through brain scans. Fuentes said that this change in our brains as we get older could demonstrate that culture affects the behavior of the different genders.

In another intriguing study, Florida State University researchers found that when women smelled the clothing of young women who were ovulating, their testosterone levels actually increased. The researchers presumed this surge was to prepare them for aggressive competition.

Both Vaillancourt and Fuentes said that by becoming aware of this type of behavior women might be able to change it. Unfortunately, women and girls are encouraged to compete against one another to fulfill society's stereotype that there's a single best way to look and act, especially when they're in a small group of friends. That competition can bring up all kinds of conflict and cause indirect aggression.

Competition between women takes two main forms: self-promotion and disparagement of rivals. Women may promote their own youth and physical attractiveness while putting their opponents down by criticizing their age, appearance, and personality.

It's not a coincidence that these types of conflict are more prevalent among people who are friends. That's because for women, relationships with friends are meaningful and women care about what their friends think. "You'll get a lot more upset about a perceived slight or an injustice from your friend than from someone you don't know. It matters more. In smaller social groups, you've invested a lot of energy and emotions and conflicts count more," explained Fuentes. "You care more because [you invested more and these] people are important to you."

Another reason these relationships can be fraught is because most women are more emotionally sensitive than men, and thus are more attuned to subtle social messages. Women are also more vulnerable to feelings of conflict and stress in a relationship. Research has shown that a woman's sense of self-worth is tied into her friends' opinion of her more than it is for men. A woman's self-esteem can more easily be undermined by a friend's behavior, causing her to be unhappy and stressed.

One recent study examined the nature and complexity of "best" friendships. There are some basic behaviors necessary to maintain these bonds, and they hold true no matter what age you are, according to Marquette University psychologist Debra Oswald, who conducted the research. One quality is intimacy between friends, through self-disclosure. And that self-disclosure has to work both ways; if just one person tells their innermost thoughts and the other doesn't, there's an imbalance that undermines the friendship, and it may eventually end.

Asymmetry can be anathema to friendship.

Social psychologists such as Oswald have also suggested that the closeness between friends must be an enjoyable one; it can't just be about venting to each other. Other key types of behavior essential to having a close friend are supportiveness and interaction—finding the time to meet or talk. Finally, being positive toward one another is important. The more we feel good about a friendship, the more we're willing to expend the energy it takes to keep it alive. That could be why some of my friends' relationships have fallen apart; the negative was starting to outweigh the positive.

In the survey that I conducted with my researcher, Brooke Schwartz, we asked about the principal values that women look for in a friend. The results were intriguing and differed depending on age.

The main quality respondents sought in a friend was being emotionally supportive (ages 25–54), followed by authenticity (ages 18–24) and loyalty (ages 65–74). Surprisingly, success was also a top value that women wanted in a girlfriend, mainly in the 55–64-year-old age group; it was also the number one value chosen for divorced women. Perhaps divorced women are looking for successful female friends to help them with their careers? Funnily enough, none of the respondents chose humor as a key quality.

Here are some responses from the survey to the question "What does friendship mean to you?"

> *"It means having someone special to share my life with, someone who always cheers for me or listens when I need to vent, someone who would do anything to help me. Someone who knows me and gets me."*

> *"Having people close to you, who you feel extremely comfortable with, who you can turn to in hard times, and good. They're there for you, always, and give you advice and try to help you better yourself."*

> *"Support. To me, friendship is my own personal cheerleading group that supports me. Friendship also means people who are honest with me, no matter what the topic is about."*

> *"Both giving and receiving loyal companionship, support and love. It's knowing you never have to go through life's ups and downs on your own. It's being able to have someone tell me when I am unreasonable or wrong and giving me advice."*

Gossip

Sometimes relationships can end as a result of gossip, which some women may use as a way to carry out their indirect aggression toward each other. In a 1980 study of women's oral culture, Deborah Jones found that gossip is part of female speech that illuminates the unity, morals, and values of women's social groups, and they use this informal network to communicate their beliefs. She suggested that as members of a repressed group, women use talking and gossip to gain some of their power back.

Jones divided the types of gossip into four categories: house-talk, scandal, bitching, and chatting. House-talk involves the exchange of information connected with housekeeping, but it can also take on the function of meeting women's need for support and recognition. They may use this kind of talk to share their feelings and attitudes about their roles as mothers and housekeepers.

Scandal is the kind of gossip in which women judge the behavior of others, particularly other females. This type of gossip mainly criticizes sexual misbehavior and can be used to attack the ability of women to find a husband. Women might also use gossip to live vicariously through the behavior of other women.

Bitching is a form of gossip that women use to express anger over their lack of power and status. They don't expect things to change; they just want their anger understood.

And finally, chatting is the most intimate form of gossip and a way for women to talk about themselves with their friends.

Gossip, which is more frequently associated with women than men, has been given a negative connotation by society and is thought to foster aggressive and competitive behavior. Yet some scholars believe that there is a positive aspect to it, as well. Gossip can be a way for women to compare themselves favorably with other women; it can also be the glue that holds a social circle together, similar to the grooming found in primate groups, according to Robin Dunbar, an evolutionary psychology professor and director of the Social and Evolutionary Neuroscience Research Group at the University of Oxford, whom I interviewed.

The term "gossip" comes from the Old English phrase "God Sib," which translates as "God Parent." It was used when female companions who were not family members spent time with a woman who was going through childbirth. The women sat and talked while they waited for the baby to be born. Originally, gossip was used as a noun to describe these female attendants, and the connotation was a kind one. But by the 1500s, the word had taken on a negative hue; Shakespeare's *A Midsummer Night's Dream* was the first literary work to use "gossip." Around the same time, the *Oxford English Dictionary* defined the word as a woman of "light and trifling character," who "delights in idle talk" and is a "tattler." By the 1800s, the word referred to a form of speaking, as well as a person.

Some researchers believe that gossip is an evolutionary adaptation. Why? Our ancestors lived in small cooperative groups, and the ability to read the behavior of others, as well as knowledge of the private dealings of other people, would have been remarkably useful in getting along in these groups. Therefore, people involved in "gossip" about others would have had a better chance of success.

The Brain and Friendship

Another reason why women behave so differently with their friends than men do could be traced to the way our brains are wired.

In one study, it was found that while viewing negative images, women's brains were more sensitive to harmful emotions than men's were. The researchers also discovered that while viewing these images, such as a violent movie, the connection in men's brains actually made them less sensitive, which suggests that men have a more analytical and passive approach to dealing with negative emotions, compared with the emotional approach that women have.

More than a decade ago, pioneering neuropsychiatrist Louann Brizendine, author of *The Female Brain*, embarked on research into how the unique structure of the female brain differed from the male brain. She began her study after she discovered as a Yale University medical student that almost all of the data on neurology, psychology, and neurobiology focused exclusively on men. She went on to found the first clinic in the country to study women's brain function.

According to Brizendine, the female brain has unique aptitudes, such as verbal agility, including a large vocabulary, a talent for reading faces and voices for emotions and states of mind. Women also have the ability to defuse conflict. And we have the capacity to connect deeply in friendship. The differences in the human brain begin during fetal development, when female hormones start to enhance the connections in the speech and communications area of the brain. This area is largely responsible for expressing emotion—as well as noticing others' feelings.

Because of these developments in the brain, women have become extremely perceptive at reading emotions in other people's faces. Men, on the other hand, are not very good at interpreting facial expressions, including any indication that another person might be distressed. That could be why women evolved to become four times more likely than men to cry—sometimes, it's the only way to get men to pay attention to their feelings of despair or sadness. Studies have even shown that newborn baby girls react more to another baby crying than infant boys do. Evolutionary psychologists believe this skill at reading other people's emotions and feeling others' pain developed as a way to give early women the ability to sense when danger was near so that they could avoid it and protect their children.

Perhaps this perceptivity is why women are sometimes referred to as mind readers; I know that I can look at my husband's face or those of my kids and immediately sense their mood or know when something is wrong. (They don't seem to have the same ability—I have three boys.)

But being highly sensitive to other people's emotions can have its downside.

Research has shown that females are more easily startled and react with greater fear in some situations. A study on the effects of watching a scary movie found that after watching the film, women lost sleep more than men did. This could be why I can never watch a violent or frightening movie before bed anymore—I end up staying up all night thinking about it!

Anger Management

There is also a biological and evolutionary necessity for girls to get along and maintain harmony in a group. From a young age, girls prioritize sharing and cooperation, and they tend to adapt to the group's vibe. This, according to Brizendine, makes women good negotiators.

Girls and women are also slower to show their anger than men are. A woman's brain circuitry stops her from expressing her anger immediately, out of fear of retaliation and distress about angering someone else and possibly harming that relationship. In fact, women may even feel physical pain in their brains when they become angry, similar to a seizure, due to a change in some of the brain's neurochemicals. This sensation could explain why so many women that I know will do anything to avoid conflict.

Studies have shown that, when playing a game, girls will stop participating when an argument erupts, but boys will continue to compete, quarreling about who is the winner. Instead of expressing their anger immediately, girls will ruminate over it, often talking to someone else before addressing it with the person in question. But once a woman's anger does burst forth, her increased verbal fluency (compared with men) will allow her to let loose a string of angry words at the other person. Men, on the other hand, can't match that verbal ability and may instead turn to physical forms of anger.

A woman's brain is also wired to experience stress and anxiety more than a man's brain is.

The brain learns about danger when its fear pathways are activated. When the prospect of fear or pain is possible, female amygdalas are more frequently activated, making it harder for women to control their fear, and so they become anxious. In fact, women are four times more likely to experience anxiety than men are, and they also become stressed much quicker. This is also why girls and women are more likely to suffer from depression.

As women age and go through menopause, their brain's wiring changes once again; the flow of impulses to their brain circuits becomes more regular, compared with the huge rushes of estrogen and progesterone to the brain, which the menstrual cycle previously caused. Everything becomes steadier and less volatile. To those close to her, a menopausal woman can seem to change dramatically, caring less about pleasing others and instead, concentrating on taking care of herself. This shift can transform the way she behaves toward her family, since the desire to tend and care for her children greatly dissipates as the oxytocin she used to receive from this behavior is produced less and less. This shift can also change her actions toward her friends, as she is less inclined to take care of others—and might have less patience for those who don't fulfill her needs.

Berna Güroğlu has been studying brain development involved in social and emotional development across childhood, adolescence, and young adulthood—including how friendship develops. A psychology professor at Leiden University in the Netherlands, she also works in the university's brain and development research center.

In a recent study, Güroğlu and her team sought the neurological basis of the development of friendship—and they made an important discovery about why friends are so important to our mental health.

Using magnetic resonance imaging, they assessed brain activity during a task involving social interaction in different types of relationships: with friends, peers, and familiar celebrities. Imaging results revealed that three regions located in the reward center of the brain were more strongly activated when subjects interacted with their friends, rather than with other peers or celebrities. These areas are also known to be involved in empathy and are the parts of the brain that light up when a person experiences pleasure, such as when a person wins money or eats chocolate.

According to Güroğlu, the results showed the role of empathy and feelings of rewards related to friendship. In an important finding, the study may have identified the pathway by which friendships exert such a critical role in development and mental health.

"There's a correlation between interacting with friends and this area of the brain. It could be that if you have many positive interactions with friends and you activate this brain region, in the long term, it might lead to lower levels of mental health problems, such as depression," Güroğlu explained. "There's even the possibility that using this reward area through positive interactions with friends could lift you out of depression in the long term."

Güroğlu said that her findings could provide a neurological explanation for why studies show that positive interactions with other people are good for your mental health, and that people with more friends have lower levels of depressive symptoms.

Further, knowing how the brain develops could help us understand how relationships are formed. That knowledge could be especially important when it comes to adolescents, for whom social interaction is a sensitive area. Güroğlu suggested that if we can recognize how the brain works during these exchanges, we might have a clearer understanding of how adolescents perceive friendships and how they interact with their friends.

"If we better understand the processes that are important for sustaining positive interactions, such as friendship, combined with our understanding of how brain development is related to these, then we can formulate ways of helping or intervening for those who have difficulties in forming positive relationships. And that has an effect on our friendships as we get older as well," she explained. "It might be important for understanding how a person will perceive friendships and understanding how their relationships will unfold over time."

Another study that measured brain activity with magnetic resonance imaging found that showing someone photos of people from their Facebook accounts also produced strong activity in the region of the brain associated with feelings of reward. This could be why some people are friendlier than others—they like the boost they get to the reward center of their brain when they're with their friends.

Social Skills May Be Genetic

Scientists at MIT found that people who are more social may have special genes that make them better at recognizing faces. The results of their study suggested that facial recognition may be separate from general intelligence. Facial recognition is crucial for determining who is a friend and who is a foe, and it makes social interactions possible. There could also be an evolutionary reason for encoding this skill in our genes: it helps us find a partner and fend off enemies. Therefore, it may be that it's actually the genes of people who are social, rather than their personality, that makes them sociable, according to Dr. Lauren Brent.

Social Skills Can Help

For Janice, her friends are part of a family that she doesn't have around her all the time. Her mother lives far away and is emotionally absent, and her father is narcissistic and absorbed in his own health problems. "What I value most in a friendship is when my friends are there for me in a time of need, and I like to do that for them as well. I spend a lot of time as an emotional backbone for my friends, and they do the same for me. I think that's the basis for a strong friendship, more than shopping together or going to lunch. I don't have that many close friends, because that kind of emotional investment takes a lot of time and energy. I value that quiet time that I have with my friends; having a cup of coffee together and talking about the ups and downs of life," she says.

While support and authenticity are important qualities in a friend, being adept at conflict management is one of the predictors of how successful you'll be at making and keeping friends. So are other communication skills, such as being emotionally supportive of your friends and being empathetic.

"People who don't have good communication skills are less likely to be accepted. It's the ones who are more person-centered and who have emotional intelligence who are the most successful in having friendships. They adapt to what is going on in the other person's emotional world, and they try to understand things from their perspective," said Wendy Samter, communications professor at Bryant University in Rhode Island. "For instance, are you interested in the social world and can you read the social world in advanced and sophisticated ways? Do you see another person and understand their psychological traits? If you don't, you might not be capable of reading people's feelings and you might lack emotional intelligence."

The term "emotional intelligence" has become a buzzword recently, and the concept is even taught in schools around the world. It's defined as the ability to identify and manage your own emotions and the emotions of others. In other words, it means being sensitive to and paying attention to other people's feelings and perspectives, and understanding your own feelings as well—and it's an important predictor of social skills. According to Samter, those who aren't good at reading other people's feelings or thoughts may have a tougher time making and keeping friends. Empathy is also important, because if you don't understand or can't share the feelings of another person, how could you give them support or comfort in a time of need?

Nevertheless, while social skills are something that we learn at an early age, we need to continuously work on and relearn them throughout our lives. I understand this well; my oldest son is about to enter college, and I worry that he may have forgotten the social skills necessary to make new friends. His best friends are still the ones he made in kindergarten, and the new friends he's made are generally friends of friends. He can be a little shy and reserved at times, so I'm going to make sure that he relearns these skills before he goes off to school.

Some people are just naturally better at social skills, while others have to work hard to learn them. It starts early: Kids who are good at entering into play with other children, called "peer entry," tend to have an easier time making friends. And the social skills we learn as children are a predictor of the quality of adult relationships that we'll have. "If you're rejected early on by your peer group, that seems to be an ongoing phenomenon that gets worse over time," explained Samter. "It only takes one close friend to buffer the effects of loneliness and isolation. But it seems to be that if there's no intervention, then what's going on in childhood will continue into adulthood."

In fact, women's early childhood experiences may actually dictate how much emotional support they seek from a friend, said Joel Block, a psychologist who specializes in relationships and is the author of many books, including *Women and Friendship*.

"Women who have not received as much emotional sustenance as they required in childhood will crave nurturing as adults," said Block. "They usually do not receive this nurturance from their spouse or minor children, so they will turn to other women to fill this need. Thus, women friends are especially important to each other."

Thus, good social skills can be the key to making—and keeping—friends.

Beverly Fehr, a social psychology professor at the University of Winnipeg, mentioned in our interview that when friends talked to her about their kids who were having a hard time meeting people in college, she offered this advice:

> Make eye contact and show interest in what another person is saying by listening, then responding by saying something related to what that other person just said. Other suggestions: Put yourself in a situation where you'll find yourself in the path of potential friends on a consistent basis. Go to a coffee shop at the same time every day. Attend a Pilates class every week. Strike up conversations with people, and eventually, let them know a thing or two about you.

One study found that students who simply showed up for class were liked more than other students, because the mere exposure of being around others made that person more familiar and easier to relate to.

But start slowly; people who reveal too much right away can make others uncomfortable.

"Some people don't understand that and it can come at a detriment to their friendship. We tend to pull away when people reveal too much too soon. It has to be mutual; first you reveal something a little personal to you, then they respond with something about themselves," explained Fehr, who wrote the book, *Friendship Processes*. "But you have to be prepared to risk vulnerability, and you have to decide if this person is worth risking that vulnerability."

Once the friendship is established, then reciprocity becomes less important. So if a friend is going through a tough time, such as a divorce, it doesn't matter if they're doing most of the divulging, because we know that over the long haul it's going to be a mutual relationship. But when a friendship *isn't* reciprocal, that's when people will start to pull away, because the lack of give and take destabilizes the relationship. If the lack of reciprocity doesn't change, then, according to Fehr, the relationship will operate at a more superficial level, or it will end.

Even when there is reciprocity in a friendship, women's relationships tend to be more fragile than men's. That fragility could be because women have higher expectations of their friendships. If we expect more, then we'll be disappointed more often. And if we're divulging our deepest, darkest secrets to our friends, then we're making ourselves more vulnerable to them, and our relationships can be more easily broken.

Sometimes, we can feel like we revealed too much to a friend and come to regret it.

Over-revealing is a risk of female friendship. In fact, it happened to me: A friend at work once told me that she was being sexually harassed by her boss. She gave me details about their email exchanges, and said that she initially was flattered by the attention, but then was disturbed. I advised her to report him to his boss, which she did, and he was subsequently fired. But afterward, my friend stopped talking to me. I couldn't figure out what I had done wrong, but finally I worked out that she might have been embarrassed by how much she'd disclosed to me. I was sad to see the friendship end.

How Many Friends Do We Need?

Why do some people have more friends than others, and how many friends do we really need? There's an old saying that the number of close friends you have should be the number of fingers you have on one hand, and my survey on friendship backs that up.

Respondents said that they had, on average, about five close female friends, but the numbers varied widely based on age: Women ages 18–24 reported an average of nine close friends, while women over the age of 65 said they had around thirteen close female friends. But 28 percent of the respondents said they had only two close female friends. It could be that younger women have more friends because they are in college, and older women have gathered more friends throughout their lives.

New research also reinforces my study's findings: An analysis by Robin Dunbar and a team of researchers analyzing UK cell phone records from 2007 corroborated the theory that there is a correlation between the size of our brains and the number of people who can play a meaningful role in our lives. It found that individuals called a little more than four people most frequently, on average. This finding supports Dunbar's theory that our social network is layered, and that the inner, most emotional layer, contains about five people, and it suggests that our brains can only handle a limited intimate social group.

Are Friends Like Family?

For many of us, our close girlfriends feel like family; we know they'd do anything for us, and we let them in on our deepest secrets.

That connection to our friends is what Dr. Josh Ackerman set out to understand and define. Ackerman is a psychology professor at the University of Michigan who specializes in decision making—how and why people think, choose, and act with each other.

He conducted a study in 2007 in which he set out to discover whether friendship is akin to kinship. He found that women have interactions with friends that are closely related to our interactions with our families and that we treat them like kin, whereas men treat friends very much like strangers. There are many potential reasons for this finding; one is that our friends share similar properties to our family members, and if we spend a lot of time with them, we begin to understand our friends in ways similar to how we recognize our family members.

Ackerman suggested that because women are more emotionally connected to their friends than men, they typically form friendships that are used for multiple purposes, such as talking and doing different activities together. On the other hand, men have more task-based friends, such as work friends or sports friends.

"When we think about a biological family member, someone we grew up in the same household with, we only see them as people, not as someone having the same genes. The way we understand who is related to us is to look at who is around us—that's a pretty reliable cue to genetic overlap. So if we spend a fair amount of time with our friends, we start to assume that they're genetically related to us," explained Ackerman. "Sometimes we grow up with friends and we have very close personal interactions that involve a lot of sharing. But this is not a tit for tat kind of reciprocity. With good friends, we treat them to things and don't expect something back immediately."

The implication is that the people who women understand to be their family members isn't always based on genetics.

Instead, women rely on the emotions that they feel with other people. The more we have interactions with friends that feel like the ones we have with our family, the more we trick our minds into believing that friends really *are* family. The whole idea of evolutionary psychology is that our mind is a collection of processes that have been developed and defined through evolution. According to Ackerman, by understanding how women feel about those in their social circle, we learn something about the evolutionary history of women's interactions with friends.

Do Women *Need* Friends?

Joyce Benenson, a psychology professor at Emmanuel College in Boston who studies the biological factors that influence cooperation between human beings, said that there are three types of competition among women: veiled aggression toward other women, trying to level the playing field when very attractive women are in their group, and, in some cases, social exclusion of new, attractive women from their social network. The results can be all-out battle among women for male attention.

Benenson said that, from an evolutionary perspective, there's good reason why even females who are close friends aren't more bonded and able to reconcile their conflicts with each other: "There isn't a huge advantage for an unrelated female who has to take care of her own kids to want to help another woman with her kids. She needs her spouse, her mother, or her grandmother. It doesn't make sense biologically speaking to help another woman who isn't in her family. Women might say, as much as I enjoy our similarities and benefit from the emotional support, why invest my energy in repairing this when I can invest my energy in my kin?"

She questioned how much unrelated friends can really help other women.

"How do you define and observe it? Women may help other women who are dying, and that's wonderful. But it's not wonderful if they're leaving their kids at home," explained Benenson.

Perhaps bolstering her point that women don't see any real benefits from having female friends, Benenson admitted that she herself does not have any.

"I've adored them over the years, but I've had constant problems at work with female colleagues. That's how it is for me. I think it's wonderful to have a female friend, and there are probably health benefits. But it's never worked out for me."

Unlike Benenson, many women *do* find that their friends are important. But sometimes they just don't fulfill what we're looking for in a relationship.

Chapter 3

The Evolution of Friendship

How animals make friends, and what it means for humans

An insincere and evil friend is more to be feared than a wild beast; a wild beast may wound your body, but an evil friend will wound your mind.

—Buddha

IN MARCH 1838, the naturalist Charles Darwin decided to pay a visit to the London Zoo. Adventurers to other lands had brought back orangutans, and Darwin wanted to see these unfamiliar creatures up close. So he climbed into the cage with a young female orangutan named Jenny.

Naturalists had noted how similar the creatures were to humans, and some had even proposed that they were our ancestors. At the time, Darwin was struggling to find an explanation for how living things—humans included—became the way they are.

In a letter to his sister, Darwin described his first encounter with the animal:

The keeper showed her an apple, but would not give it her, whereupon she threw herself on her back, kicked & cried, precisely like a naughty child. She then looked very sulky & after two or three

fits of passion, the keeper said, "Jenny if you will stop bawling &
be a good girl, I will give you the apple." She certainly understood
every word of this, & though like a child, she had great work to
stop whining, she at last succeeded, & then got the apple, with
which she jumped into an arm chair & began eating it, with the
most contented countenance imaginable.

Darwin found the orangutan displayed emotions as a human
would and was "decidedly jealous. She would make her jealousy
known by showing her teeth and making a peevish noise. She shook
the cage and knocked her head against the door because she could
not get out—jealous of attention to others."

Through his observations, Darwin became convinced that
orangutans and humans shared similar emotions because they had
a common ancestor. This would later become a central theme of his
theory of evolution. Darwin's theories demonstrated the link between humans and animals, in terms of our behavior and emotions.

So how much can relationships between animals tell us about
our own friendships?

Scientific research into animals supports the concept that
friendship is good for us. It shows that animals are capable of great
depth of emotion and complex systems of social cooperation, and
we know that animals can care for each other as well as for human
beings.

For instance, studies of female primates show that when they
spend time with a small but close group of friends, they exhibit a significant reduction in stress hormones, in the same way that women
experience this same benefit when they're with their friends. Scientists believe that while most animals have acquaintances, only
a few species of animals are capable of true friendship, including
the higher primates—chimpanzees, apes, monkeys, gorillas, orangutans, and baboons—as well as horses, dogs, elephants, dolphins,

and even bats. These animals live in stable, bonded social groups that provide their own benefits, such as protection against predators. This suggests that friendship is a trait that evolved through animals, rather than being solely a human invention.

Dr. Lauren Brent's research focuses on gaining a greater understanding of the evolution of social relationships. In particular, she's interested in why social bonds, or friendship, evolved and what function they serve. She also wants to know why some individuals are more or less social than others.

Brent said that social connections seem to be adaptive in different species, such as nonhuman primates and dolphins. Her research has found a relationship between animals who have social connections and their ability to survive, as well as their reproductive success.

"We're not the only ones that form social relationships—it potentially goes back deep in evolutionary time. A fundamental part of human society is having these relationships. Even in ancient times, in order to be successful individuals and have kids, we had to have friends. That's fascinating to me. It's so pervasive in what we do, but we don't think about it in terms of evolution or hard science. It's a knee-jerk thing. We don't see it as a fundamental thing that defines who we are as a species," she said.

In her research, Brent has focused on a highly gregarious primate, the rhesus macaque monkey. She's discovered evidence of the fitness benefits of sociality, finding that infants of individuals who are more deeply embedded in their social network are more likely to survive, and that females with larger families live longer. Brent has also shown that an individual's position in his or her social network is heritable, confirming that sociality is genetic and is a trait on which natural selection may act.

In the monkeys that Brent has studied, she's found that having lots of female relatives means the animals are more embedded in their social network—and the more social support they have, the more likely the monkeys are to live to the next year. As soon as they reach old age, however, having all those relatives no longer predicts survival. The older females don't seem to need friends as much as their younger counterparts.

This was backed up in a 2016 study that showed that older monkeys became pickier with age and were less social—in the same way that humans seem to be pickier and less social when they get older. The study, focused on Barbary macaque monkeys, showed that there might be an evolutionary "deep" root to this pattern, and that changes in human behavior as we age could have some biological origins. One theory that explains this behavior in humans is that we get more particular with age in order to make the most of the time we have left. However, researchers don't believe this is the case for monkeys.

Dr. Alexandra Freund, a developmental psychologist at the University of Zurich who worked on the study, suggested that monkeys and humans might just lose steam as they get older and become too tired to deal with relationships that are ambivalent or negative. Another theory is that monkeys that age take fewer risks, so they interact less socially—which is what humans do as well.

"Our behaviors that seem very much the result of our deliberation and choice, might be more similar to our primate ancestors than we might think," Dr. Freund told the *New York Times*.

Brent noticed competition for friendship among the monkeys she studied that is similar to the struggles seen among girls in middle school.

This was displayed when two monkeys groomed each other—standard friendship behavior in the monkey world. Brent said they seemed to be thinking, "Do I spend less time grooming you, when my friend is nearby, or do I not care? But my investment in her might not be so important as my investment in you." The primates she observed seemed to be aware that their behavior could affect the other monkeys, and, according to Brent, they were modifying their interactions so that they were equal among all their friends. Some of the animals appeared to be competing for social relationships and seemed jealous of each other. This observation begs the question: Is this where jealousy in humans comes from?

"That has always felt to me like the time in high school when you want all your friends to get along, and your best friend gets jealous when you have a friendship with another girl. It always spoke to me as if they're doing, it too," Brent said. "It's the same behavior as when a bridesmaid doesn't feel recognized enough by the bride."

Cross-species Friendships

We know that animals can be friends, but the idea of cross-species friendship became more popular after the story of Owen, a baby hippo, and Mzee, a 130-year-old giant tortoise, was published in a children's book. The story emerged when Craig Hatkoff's 7-year-old daughter saw a newspaper article about a baby hippo that had been orphaned in the 2004 Indonesian tsunami. Owen was rescued and taken to a Kenyan nature preserve, where he met Mzee, an Aldabra giant tortoise. There were no other hippos for Owen to interact with, so he tried to bond with Mzee, who resembled an adult hippo because of his large domed shell. Incredibly, Mzee adopted the hippo as his own and the two forged an unusual and remarkable friendship that lasted for many years.

Animals can create bonds across species if the need for social contact overtakes their normal biological drive. Quite often, these friendships form when the animals are young and in captivity because they are stressed and they gain comfort from each other. That was the case for a cheetah and a dog that bonded at Busch Gardens. Their friendship was featured in the 2013 PBS film *Animal Odd Couples,* which also profiled various other cross-species friends.

"I think for social animals, having relationships is necessary for good health, so they are sort of primed to have them. It's just particularly interesting when they overlook differences and show a liking for another kind," explained Jennifer S. Holland, a science writer for *National Geographic*, who detailed stories of unusual, cross-species friends in her bestselling series, *Unlikely Friendships*, which includes four books for adults and three for kids.

But are these relationships between interspecies animals really friendship?

Holland said that animals do seem to have some of the same emotions as humans. And she pointed to evidence that mammals can feel empathy similar to the way we do. In some cases, it makes sense from an evolutionary standpoint for these animals to show care and friendship for each other, because they might help one another raise their babies or they might receive protection from predators. These friendships might even get them better access to the food supply.

One of Holland's favorite stories from her books is that of Tarra, an Asian elephant who lived in a sanctuary in Tennessee and became good friends with a dog named Bella, a stray. They had a lot in common, since both animals were smart, friendly, and had good memories. The dog and the elephant started doing everything together, until one day Bella became sick. The sanctuary workers took her to see a vet, and she had to stay indoors for several days to recover. Tarra was very sad and waited outside the building where Bella was recuperating, refusing to leave. When the dog finally recovered, Tarra placed her trunk on the dog to pet her and stomped her feet with joy. The dog wagged her tail and rolled over with happiness.

"These are animals that you might expect to be social and empathetic, because they're also smart. That was such a beautiful story; there was such a bond that happened, beyond any clear benefit they got from being friends," said Holland. "Scientifically, one could always explain it away somehow. My impression is the answer is more along the lines of companionship—social animals will seek it out. We've seen increased stress levels in animals that are lonely."

Many of the animals in the stories that she's recounted were living in captivity and therefore they didn't have to compete for food or to survive—and that left room for a bond to be established that otherwise wouldn't have been there in the wild. On a certain level, according to Holland, these animals could feel a warmth and comfort with other animals that was similar to what humans experience.

One of the more interesting stories that Holland encountered was that of a dolphin who lived in the wild and joined up with a pod of sperm whales in Hawaii. The dolphin had an injured spine, and it was unknown why he was swimming with the whales or why the whales accepted him into their group. Did it benefit the whales in some way? Had the dolphin been cast out of its own pod?

She also chronicled the unusual story of a lioness and a baby oryx, a type of African antelope, that became friends in Kenya. The oryx seemed to have lost her mother. Local villagers saw the lion protecting the baby oryx as if she were her own, walking next to the baby oryx and sleeping next to her at night. But the lion couldn't nurse the oryx, and so eventually the oryx died. Holland believes the relationship stemmed from some kind of confusion that the lioness had—perhaps she'd lost her mother at an early age and wasn't taught how to use her predatory instinct. The lion went on to adopt and care for other oryxes after that first one died.

In a similar story of a predator and prey forming a friendship, a leopard in India was discovered coming into a village at night and lying down with a cow that had been tied up. In the morning the leopard would leave, but every night he would come back and cuddle with the cow—and he never tried to eat it. Eventually, he stopped coming back. The villagers never figured out why he was doing this.

Holland thinks the stories appeal to readers because they already love animals and feel that the animals are more emotional than we give them credit for. She finds it interesting how the animals show that they care for one another even when there isn't an obvious benefit to either of them.

Yet one question remains: How do these animals from different species manage to communicate with each other?

Holland believes that much of it is subtler than we can see, such as using body language: "Animals seem to be so in tune with everything, and they're so much better at reading the situation than we give them credit for. They seem to know when to be afraid and when to be comfortable."

Do these animals even recognize that the other animals are not from their own species? Holland said animals have shown that they can remember each other; for instance, elephants have been known to go back to a place where another elephant from their herd has died to caress its bones. There is a sense of mourning for individuals in their own group.

"I see behaviors in other animals, that sure seem human. One of my dogs is very jealous if I pay attention to another dog. He'll watch and lurk at the edges, like a bratty kid, wanting to make sure he's not missing out on something," she said.

One of her stories recounts the relationship between an ape who was given a kitten as a pet. The primate's behavior was like that of a human—he would cuddle the cat and play with it. It was so reminiscent of a kid playing with a pet that, according to Holland, it was hard not to see the human-like amusement at the kitten and the joy that the ape seemed to get from playing with the other animal. "I see no reason to think animals don't feel joy and sadness and some level of empathy. They may not have the same level of consciousness, and they're worried about their survival, but it seems that individual animals are concerned about other animals. That more than makes sense genetically."

While animals appear to form friendships, do they also show emotions the same way humans do?

Marc Bekoff is an expert on animal behavior and the author of many books on the subject, including *The Smile of a Dolphin: Remarkable Accounts of Animal Emotions*. In the book, fifty leading animal behavior researchers, including Jane Goodall, offer their firsthand accounts of creatures experiencing emotions, such as love, fear, anger, joy, grief, and pride. For example, Goodall writes about the embarrassment of a chimpanzee that fell out of a tree and looked around sheepishly to make sure no other chimps saw him, then strutted off. The book also chronicles a dolphin mother who lost her calf, refused food, and left her group to grieve; and a sea lion who tossed a duck decoy in frustration at a trainer when it failed a task.

He named the book *The Smile of a Dolphin* because their smiles are ambiguous; dolphins actually lack the muscles to smile. It's wrong to conclude by looking at these animals that they're happy since a smile is a natural facial expression for them. The same goes for other animals: A wagging tale on a dog doesn't mean that it's happy—you have to look at its ears and facial expressions, too.

"Animals show a rich array of emotions; they show everything we show. Even fish show a whole range of emotions. Is human joy more complex or richer than a dog's joy or a chimpanzee's joy? Those are nonsense questions. To ask if dogs feel joy or pain is ridiculous. There is research on rats that show they laugh and like to be tickled," said Bekoff, professor emeritus of ecology and evolutionary biology at the University of Colorado, Boulder; a fellow of the Animal Behavior Society; a member of the ethics committee of the Jane Goodall Institute; and cofounder, along with Jane Goodall, of the organization Ethologists for the Ethical Treatment of Animals: Citizens for Responsible Animal Behavior Studies.

"I always say to people who ask me about animals' emotions: 'Have you ever lived with an animal? If you have, you'll see how dogs will mope around and get depressed when another dog leaves your house.' If we have the emotions, they have them. There hasn't been any evidence against it."

Bekoff suggested that animals such as elephants, birds, and chimpanzees can suffer from posttraumatic stress syndrome. Dogs that worked at the 9/11 site to help find bodies suffered from this disorder, as did dogs that had to be rescued after Puerto Rico was hit by a hurricane in 2017. He cited recent data showing that birds and fish are sentient and experience pain and suffering. Bekoff believes that emotions have evolved "as adaptations in numerous species and they serve as a social glue to bond animals with one another."

The takeaway, from Bekoff's perspective, is that since animals do experience emotions, such as being joyful and being depressed, we need to take better care of them. Common sense and intuition also support the conclusion he says, that "at the very least mammals experience rich and deep emotional lives, with emotions ranging from pure and contagious joy shared so widely among others during play that it is almost epidemic—to deep grief and pain."

For instance, according to Bekoff, zoos are notorious for breaking up animal friendships; they'll bring animals together to become friends and then yank them apart to breed at another zoo, or they'll sell them to make money. Sometimes, the animals that have been parted from one another will die. That was apparently the case for two polar bears that lived together for twenty years at SeaWorld San Diego's wild arctic exhibit. The zoo decided to send a polar bear named Snowflake to the Pittsburgh Zoo in order to breed, leaving behind her companion, Szenja, who was born in captivity. While the official cause of death was not known, some, such as members of People for the Ethical Treatment of Animals (PETA), believe Szenja's separation from Snowflake caused her demise:

"Szenja died of a broken heart, PETA believes. After losing her companion of 20 years when SeaWorld shipped Snowflake to the Pittsburgh Zoo in order to breed more miserable polar bears, Szenja did what anyone would do when they lose all hope, she gave up," said PETA vice president Tracy Remain, in a statement.

Bekoff has been asked many times if it could be true that Szenja died because she missed her friend: His simple answer to this question is, "Yes. Nonhuman animals can suffer and die from a broken heart, too." He told me the story of how he once had two dogs, and when one of the dogs died, the other wouldn't eat and was depressed for a long time.

"There's no reason to think nonhuman animals differ in any way in this regard. There are so many examples of zoos trying to force friendships that don't work—they make animals live in cages. They form attachments to other animals and then they're yanked all over the place. They're shipping animals around the world to breed, and these animals are showing signs of stress and depression," said Bekoff.

In fact, Bekoff argues that any social animal can be friends, and that even asking if it's possible is an absurd waste of time. "If you've ever lived with two dogs, what would you call the bond between those dogs, other than friendship? For me the real question is why has friendship evolved? Nonhuman animals form friendships for the same reasons as us: social support, acquiring food, defending their food, and defending themselves against interlopers. It feels good to be with our friends."

How Do We Know That Animals Can Be Friends?

Anne Pusey, a professor of evolutionary anthropology at Duke University, studied female chimps to determine whether they were actually friends with each other.

Among chimps, the males stay with the group they were born into for their entire lives, while females leave their families behind and strike out on their own to join new groups. Recent studies suggest that some pairs of female chimps hang out together more often than others. Pusey attempted to discover if this was intentional; were these chimps, in fact, friends or merely acquaintances?

When a female chimp moves into a new group, she starts at the bottom of the social ladder. The study showed that low-ranking "new girl" chimpanzees seek out and prefer to socialize with other females that have a similar status. This could be because they've found that by teaming up with another chimp, they have better access to food and more protection against predators. The study is part of a larger field of research on the importance of social networks for health and survival in primates and other animals, including humans.

"When you start talking about female relationships, it makes a huge difference if you stay with people you grew up with or you live with people who are not your kin, as happens in agricultural societies," said Pusey. "That's bound to set up very different relationships."

Pusey, whose research involves understanding the evolution of social structure, cooperation, and social bonds in animal species, including humans, is currently studying female social relationships. Social grooming triggers the release of endorphins in the brain, which causes a feeling of relaxation. Pusey found that the baboons she studied spend a lot of time grooming and supporting each other, and that some female–female relationships were closer than others. Not surprisingly, mothers, daughters, and sisters formed the strongest bonds.

In Gombe, where Pusey worked with Jane Goodall on the Gombe chimpanzee project for the past forty years (Pusey also manages the Jane Goodall Institute Research Center), the female chimps seemed to compete more over space and food. When a new female came into the group, the other females were nasty to her and chased her around. Eventually, the new chimps formed their own core area, and they avoided the high-ranking females. This sounds like what happens when a new girl moves into a middle school, and the popular girls are mean to her.

According to Pusey, female blue monkeys, a species of old-world monkey native to central and eastern Africa, stay in the group in which they are born, surrounded by relatives. They groom each other, and together they'll scare off another group that tries to encroach on their territory, acting in solidarity. That's a real benefit to these female relationships.

Pusey also studies lions and has found that female lions raise their cubs together and love to roll on top of one another and lick each other. "If you watch for long, you'll feel like jumping in," she said. "You don't get that feeling at all from female chimps. There's a subtle aggression between them, and sometimes not so subtle. New females get pushed around by resident females."

The lions who live in larger groups do better than those in smaller female groups, because more of them means they are able to protect a larger territory. They benefit from group defense and will also nurse each other's young, and band together to protect their babies from males. Solitary females do badly. There's a selective benefit for these lions to be nice to each other. By being playful and licking each other, they get rid of ticks on one another—which they can't do themselves. Pusey said she sees young girls in Africa grooming each other, and believes there must be some hygienic benefits to that as well.

Robin Dunbar has researched the number of friends an animal or a human can have in his or her social group. He said it takes an intelligent animal to live in a bonded, layered social system because it needs to understand the structure of the whole social network of the group. In other words, an animal needs to know which animal friends will come to her aid when she is threatened, making her aware of the wider social consequences of her actions.

There is also a link between the size and complexity of a species' social group and the size of its brain, because animals need a larger brain to make calculations about social groups. The same is true of humans, and neuroimaging studies of both humans and animals have shown that the size of parts of the frontal lobes in the brain is tied to the number of friends that an individual has. Thus, the more friends you have, the larger these regions of the brain.

In terms of social grooming, Dunbar said he's found that "the bigger the group, the more time an animal devotes to grooming, but the fewer individuals it grooms. This is because as group size increases and group living becomes more stressful, it becomes increasingly necessary to ensure that your friends are reliable and will come to your aid when you need them. You do this by spending more of your available social time grooming core friends. Among female baboons, this has demonstrable benefits—those with stronger friendships produce less of the stress hormone cortisol and produce more surviving offspring."

There might be parallels to humans in that example as well: Do high school girls spend time grooming their friends (doing their nails and hair) to ensure that they'll stick up for them in the event that one day, they might need their help? Perhaps.

According to Joan Silk, who studies baboons and is a professor in the School of Human Evolution and Social Change at Arizona State University, unlike many other primates, female baboons will stay in the groups in which they are born for their whole lives, so they grow up in a world where their mothers, sisters, aunts, and grandmothers also live. Silk is interested in how natural selection shapes the evolution of social behavior in primates; most of her work has focused on behavior and reproduction among female baboons.

The F-Word

The idea of animals as friends wasn't always accepted by scientists.

Silk was the first scientist to use the so-called "F-word" for animals, as in, "friendship." In 2002, she wrote a paper about how primatologists had recently begun to "use the word 'friendship' to describe close, affiliative relationships among monkeys and apes. This seems to be part of a growing backlash against what some researchers see as a narrow-minded preoccupation with the negative aspects of animal behavior, such as competition, conflict, manipulation, coercion, and deception. There is a new emphasis on more positive features of animal behavior, such as coordination, negotiation, reconciliation, and cooperation, that animals use to mitigate conflicts of interest and resolve conflicts."

She said that, in animal species, the ability to form social bonds was an important adaptive strategy, a point of view that spurred scientists to begin using the term "friendship" when describing the social relationships of nonhuman primates.

"Friendship is the F-word; a word that many primatologists have been reluctant to use in print though we may use it freely when we chat with our colleagues about the animals that we study. When we do use the term in academic venues, we feel compelled to cloak it in italics, as if this gives us some indemnity against charges of anthropomorphism or lack of rigor. But lately primatologists have become more relaxed about using the F-word, even dropping the protective italics," wrote Silk in her paper.

Silk also wrote the first seminal paper to show that female baboons that spend a greater amount of time grooming and associating with others have offspring that are more likely to survive at least one year.

"If I describe their close social bonds, it looks a lot like friendship. These relationships that exist mainly between mothers and daughters and sisters tend to be very stable," she said in an interview. "Their mother is their top social partner, and mothers and daughters rarely fight (unlike humans). Sisters fight a lot, but they also engage in a lot of friendly behavior."

Baboons tend to groom each other in a balanced way; the closer their social ties, the more balanced the grooming is. Females will mainly groom close family members. According to Silk, this grooming looks just like friendship, and the females that have these strong social bonds will live longer.

"This matches up very closely with all the data on health effects of high quality social networks. People who have other people they can rely on are much healthier, less stressed, and have better health outcomes. These data (on the baboons) is consistent with that. The difference is who we choose as our social partners; baboons go straight to relatives. When we choose our friends, we aren't limited to our relatives," she said.

Silk said that her work on friendship has resonated strongly with her, perhaps because she knows that having close relationships is important to women and that we're healthier as a result. The emotional support we get from our friends provides for our quality of life, health, and many other things.

"I really value my relationships with my friends; I think they're super important. Academics are funny—you make friends in graduate school, and even though we have dispersed social networks, we're still close. Some of my best friends are those I made years ago," said Silk.

Yet she hesitates to attribute to baboons the same kind of human friendship that we experience.

With baboons, we only know how they act; we don't know whether they *feel* the same way as we do about our friends. There is, however, some evidence: In one study, a number of female baboons were killed by predators, and researchers were able to look at the impact of the loss on the close partners of those baboons. They found that the surviving baboons had higher cortisol levels, which are associated with stress. This finding suggests that the loss of a partner is traumatic for these animals.

In another study, Silk watched two baboons—a mother and daughter—that were very close. When she came back a year later, the daughter had died (probably from a predator), and the mother was extremely lonesome. She would ask the researchers to groom her; Silk said she looked very sad and bereft.

But she sees some big differences between baboons and humans as well; for instance, humans are much nicer to each other than baboons. Baboons are very aggressive toward strange baboons and will compete with each other for food; humans can have a potluck dinner and everyone will share their fare.

"We really care about our friends, and not just in relation to what they can do for us. If you ask people about friendship, some people feel it's about benefiting yourself, but others think of it as an unselfish relationship, in which you care about someone else," she said.

Silk said her work with the baboons made her consider her own relationships with her family and friends—especially her daughter, with whom she has a close relationship.

"I keep thinking how lucky I am to have a daughter," she said.

Do Animals Benefit from Being Social?

Just like humans, some animals are more social than others, and not all individuals are tied to an equal number of social partners; "some have rich, deep ties, while others are loner types and are only tied to one or two other animals in their group," said Marina Cords, an anthropology professor at Columbia University who studies the evolution of behavior, including the development of social relations.

This raises the question—do animals get benefits from being social?

Does being social influence a female's reproductive success? And do females who have more friends have an advantage over their peers? Most of the studies have shown that having strong relationships provide strong fitness benefits, such as better survival rates and greater health for offspring.

Cords, who directs the Kakamega Forest Primate Research Project in western Kenya, has been conducting a long-term study of the same group of arboreal blue monkeys since 1979. She's noticed distinctions among the animals; for instance, a female named Daffy only hangs out with her daughters and her mother, whereas other monkeys her age have lots of friends. Cords suggested that this distinction shows that some animals are more socially oriented than others—just like humans.

Yet, according to Cords, they can be very different from humans: "I have a friend that I met when I was 3 years old. We would do everything for each other. We don't keep up, but if I go to California, we get together and we could tell each other anything. We have memories from long ago that we keep—I'm not sure that nonhuman primates have that."

Cords's main focus has been on conflict management—something that all social animals (including humans) must do. She has observed that female monkeys are more aggressive with other females when they're mating, pregnant, or lactating. This observation made her wonder if much of the aggressive interactions between the monkeys—most of which appeared to be about food or space—were actually connected to mating.

She's also noticed that sometimes female monkeys will band together to protect a female in the group from being harassed by a male; they will take her side and form coalitions to scare him off. If a male comes into the group and tries to kill a young infant, the females will scream like banshees and get him to leave.

Male Versus Female Animals

Researchers have discovered that friendships between males of different species differ from those between females.

One study that looked at the social life of vampire bats found that they shared their food with nonrelatives as a safety net in case their family was not available to help them find food. Another study found that female wild Bechstein's bats preferred to hang out with certain friends while keeping loose ties to the rest of their colony, mirroring human friends. The researchers found that bats were able to maintain long-term relationships, and seemed to prefer certain companions. The species' male bats were solitary, but the females roosted together. "Colony members exchange information among each other about suitable roosts, make flexible group decisions about where to communally roost next, groom each other and profit from communal roosting through warming of each other." Research such as this could help us understand how and why humans evolved to make friends.

How Do Animals Form Friendships?

Just like humans, animals have to actually form friendships with other animals. So how do they do it?

First, they must recognize the other members of their group as unique, and they must know where those other individuals are located in relation to themselves. Then they have to decide when and how to interact with their "friends," and whether they remain friends long term or become enemies. And they must be able to recognize the other animals that are their friends; they do this through smell, sound, and visual cues. For instance, primates and sheep recognize faces, whereas hermit crabs and lobsters use scent to recognize foes. Humans and macaque monkeys use similar regions of the brain to recognize faces.

Animals can remember individuals from the same species; sheep can recall breeding partners from two years before, and dolphins can remember signature whistles from their group for up to twenty years. Female vervet monkeys and chacma baboons can distinguish between the alarm calls of their groupmates versus those who are not in their group. Humans can also remember friends after long periods of being apart. Women, in particular, tend to over include non-kin and treat them as relatives—something that men are less likely to do.

In order to find and maintain friends, animals and humans need social information about others. What is interesting is that both humans and animals connect social information with rewards; human infants will gaze at faces for longer than other stimuli, while monkeys will look more frequently at higher-ranking animals. Social information also activates areas of the brain related to rewards, and some areas seem to be specialized in processing information about others. For example, when rhesus macaque monkeys were asked to choose between juice as a reward or information about others as the reward, they responded more to social information.

Animals that have the strongest social bonds have the most offspring, with more of their young surviving longer, and with more longevity—this correlation is found in female baboons, male Assamese macaque monkeys, and dolphins.

Dr. Brent noted that it's important to first define what we mean by "friendship" in humans and animals.

For her purposes, friends are pairs of individuals that interact frequently and consistently enough that it differentiates them from nonfriends. They cooperate considerably more often, consistently, and over greater periods of time; "spending time together, conversing, vocalizing, grooming, huddling, foraging, and sharing food, as well as forming alliances against others." Animals that are close in age are frequent social partners. But it's also worth noting that, "in many species, the highest ranking male sires the majority of off-spring in a given year, and individuals that are close in age are often paternal siblings."

So how do animal friendships actually form? Not much is known about this, but while many animals choose close kin as their friends, others choose those that are of the same age or social status, or even those with similar personalities or abilities. This is especially true for humans—and as we will see later in this book, many people actually choose their friends based on having similar genes.

Bovine Friends

While we may not normally think of cows as very intelligent animals, Rosamund Young argued in *The Secret Life of Cows* that anyone who spends time with these creatures will realize just how smart they are. The book includes stories about the cows that she and her family raised on their farm, including how the cows have family groups and friends.

Young said that watching cows and calves playing, grooming one another, or being assertive "takes on a whole new dimension if you know that those taking part are siblings, cousins, friends or sworn enemies."

She added that if you know animals as individuals, you will notice older brothers being kind to younger ones, and watch as sisters seek or avoid each other's company. You might also observe some families getting together at night to sleep.

"Cows are as varied as people. They can be highly intelligent or slow to understand; friendly, considerate, aggressive, docile, inventive, dull, proud or shy," she said.

Young, who lived on the farm in England with her family for many years, suggested that everyone who has kept just a few animals gets to know them as individuals, and will probably be able to talk about the idiosyncrasies of their natures. According to Young, farm animals have levels of intelligence that vary just as much as human beings. She argued that forcing animals to live in unnatural, crowded, featureless conditions can cause them to appear to lose their identities—but this doesn't mean that they are all the same or want to be treated as such.

She related the story of a friendship between two calves that were born only a few days apart; her family called them the White Boys because they were both dazzling white bull calves. "The first calf walked over to greet the new arrival and stared at him as if looking in a mirror. They became devoted and inseparable friends from that minute."

The two mothers became fast friends, too, as they were forced to spend all their time together, waiting around to provide milk on request. Young said that the White Boys lived in a world of their own: in the midst of a large herd but oblivious to it. "They walked round shoulder to shoulder, often bumping against each other, and they slept each night with their heads resting on each other."

In *A Talent for Friendship: Rediscovery of a Remarkable Trait*, Dr. John Edward Terrell argued that the ability to make friends is an evolved human trait not unlike our ability to walk upright on two legs or our capacity for speech and complex abstract reasoning. He explained how this trait evolved, examining two unique functions of the human brain: the ability to remake the outside world to suit our needs, and our capacity to escape into our own inner thoughts and imagine how things might and ought to be.

"As an anthropologist who is interested in ethnicity and the definition of self, I'm skeptical about the idea of people coming in tribes. I went to Papua New Guinea, a place of astonishing linguistic and cultural diversity, and thought, is friendship the icing on the cake, or is the cake humanity? These boundaries that we think define groups or tribes don't really exist; they're constructs of the mind," he said. "I came to recognize that the major institution there was friendship, and it's inherited from one generation to the next, and between families that speak different languages. What really connects people there into the larger world is the institution of friendship."

Terrell, who adopted his son, noted that he's also interested in how we create friendships and human relationships, and how we define a family. His research into the nature of friendship has led him to understand that we have friends and social relationships because we need them in order to survive.

Chapter 4

Women Versus Men
Why their friendships are so different

A friend is one that knows you as you are,
understands where you have been,
accepts what you have become, and still, gently allows
you to grow.

—William Shakespeare

AFTER A DISAGREEMENT with a close friend, I was upset. Like most women, I value my friendships, and I found the experience unsettling. But when I talked to my husband about it, he looked at me as though I was from another planet. He couldn't relate to what I was talking about or understand why we were fighting.

When it comes to friendship, men and women come from very different places.

Men tend to take part in activities with their friends, such as fixing cars or watching football, while women reveal their feelings to their friends and confide in them. Men bond through private clubs and sports, while all women really need is a cup of coffee to catch up and connect. Women invest time in maintaining their friendships, while men don't always feel the need to stay in touch with their friends.

Not surprisingly, male friendships tend to be less intimate and may be less supportive than women's, but they also have fewer breakups.

When I asked my husband if he'd ever had a falling out with a friend, he couldn't think of one. When men don't want to be friends any more, they tend to just stop calling each other, and let the friendship fade away on its own. He did remember a time after college, though, when he lived with a group of four male friends and they became angry with one of their roommates for eating everyone's food, failing to do any cleaning up, and for being a general slob. I asked him what happened. Did they sit him down and give him a good talking to? Did they give him an ultimatum? No, they just teased him about it and made fun of him for a while. Eventually, he changed his ways.

I can't help thinking that that scenario would have ended in tears if women were involved. So how distinct are the ways that men and women conduct relationships with their friends?

One study looked at the asymmetries in friendship preferences and social styles of men and women and found that while both genders approached friends based on what they get out of the relationship, they did it from very different perspectives. Men sought large, functional groups of friends, while women looked for small, intimate, secure relationships with other women. Men can fall out of touch with someone for years, and still call them close friends, while that silence would probably mean the end for most female friendships.

In the same study, men were asked to name a good friend they would turn to in an emergency or from whom they would borrow money. Some of the participants named friends who had actually passed away—and they hadn't even known about it!

Evolutionary Behavior

Researchers believe they can explain many of these gender differences based on evolution.

According to Jacob Vigil, associate professor of psychology at the University of New Mexico, women evolved to be more socially skilled because they had to interact with nonfamily members.

In many traditional societies throughout history, once a female found a mate or husband, she typically left her family group and went to live with him and his family. This still happens in many societies, including in parts of Africa, such as Kenya. This relocation often wasn't easy for the women—they had to live with strangers and try to get along. So they learned that expressing a sense of vulnerability and submissiveness with their non-kin was optimal for survival, and this history has informed the way women behave today with other women and with men.

"You're not going to go around boasting to others, if you want to survive," said Vigil. "Women were submissive because they evolved to manipulate their social environment. Females throughout evolutionary history invested in a smaller number of relationships and had smaller social networks, but they invested highly in them so that they could have a more secure social network. Meanwhile, the men were living with their family members, so they already had a high degree of trust with them because they shared their genes."

According to Vigil and others, women are endowed with heightened sensitivity to expressions of vulnerability and suffering, which convey trustworthiness. Making themselves seem vulnerable increased the empathy that they received from this new female group they married into, so women evolved to exhibit heightened expressions of vulnerability. Women use their bodies to manipulate others by demonstrating trust through submissive behavior, and this conduct can be useful within their smaller social networks. This behavior can be seen in the way little girls sit closer to each other and are more likely to touch each other. And this behavior can have other real-life consequences. For instance, Vigil said this submissive style of interaction means that a female nurse may provide better health care than a male nurse.

On the other hand, according to Vigil, men today tend to form larger social networks because they traditionally engaged in male-to-male competition, usually some form of battle. The bigger the social group that men had (and these normally consisted of extended family members), the more effective their group was in winning a war against enemies. Since men stayed with their kin group, they tended to be more confident, because they weren't always trying to win people over and didn't have anything to prove. Larger social groups of men tended to lend themselves to dominant behavior among men, because they were competing against each other to see who might be the strongest fighter. People with larger social networks are also less likely to be sad and anxious, making these groups even more beneficial for men.

Vigil believes that the unique ways that males and females communicate today are a result of these either larger or smaller social networks. For instance, women talk to each other about their intimate lives and will cry in front of their friends. The function of these behaviors is to strengthen their relationships by disclosing vulnerable information, which builds trust. Women also aren't as assertive as men in social situations. In one study, Vigil examined adaptive behavioral differences among men and women. He found that boys exhibited more behaviors that acted on the external environment (such as physical aggression and risk-taking), whereas girls showed more internalizing behaviors that focused on the individual (such as worrying, sadness, and self-blame).

"Women have a firewall of distrust around them. They're more cautious with who they trust and interact with. Once people can overcome that wall, they increase their intimacy with those people," said Vigil.

Because it's so important for women to rely on each other, they don't tolerate breaches of trust well.

It would be intolerable, for instance, for a best friend to repeat a rumor about a friend and spread it around her social network. That would end the friendship for most women—but probably not for men. Women also expect more reciprocity from their friends, so they may feel hurt and angry when they're not getting what they want out of a relationship. Because of this, female relationships are more fragile and they require more maintenance, said Vigil.

For some women, the fragility of their friendships with other women is just too much work; they'd rather be friends with men. That's the case for Kayla, 31, an American woman who now lives in England. She said that most of her friends are men because she finds it easier to be with them.

"There's a lot less drama. With most of my friends who are guys, you can just hang out, and misunderstandings don't seem to happen as much," she said. "With my girlfriends, it's Lucy's mad at me, or I'm mad at her. We have to sit down and talk about that text that I sent her the other day. With guys, I can joke with them. I speak their language. I've had mostly guy friends from the age of 15. We're very jokey, and have the same sense of humor. When you joke with girls, they might think, 'Was that a bitchy comment?' They're always look-ing for an ulterior motive."

Kayla said that she does have some close girlfriends but that they sometimes make hurtful comments to her, such as telling her that she's put on weight or other things that make her feel self-conscious. One friend told her that they could say anything to each other, but Kayla found that what that did was open the door for her friend to say hurtful things to *her*.

When she was at university, she became friends with girls in her dorm, but eventually it became too intense for her.

"The girls at university who were friends, we're not friends anymore. They were emotionally volatile—I found it quite stressful," she remembered. She said that one year, her friend asked if she could stay with Kayla and her family for Christmas. When Kayla told her that it might not work out, her friend didn't speak to her for the entire next semester. "She said, 'Tell me the truth.' But when I told her the truth about why she couldn't come, she got mad. I'm a people pleaser, so I try to avoid conflict. Now I know I shouldn't have been honest with her. Guys take things at face value. I would never say things to make a sly dig at people, like some women do."

While Kayla doesn't have the same emotional connection with her male friends, she doesn't mind. In fact, she has a handful of men whom she knows she could cry to, and they'd listen to her. She said it was easier to be more open about things with them because there wasn't the same element of drama with her guy friends.

Her feelings about her friendships with men versus women match Vigil's findings on relationships among the different genders. According to Prof. Vigil, since men aren't scrutinized all the time, they're more secure in their relationships and can deal with a breach of trust that women cannot. If males are around their family members all the time, they don't have to exaggerate how kind and nonthreatening they are. Men are also more likely to use dominant behaviors to maintain their relationships—exaggerated confidence, aggression, and pride.

To prove his point about these gender differences, Vigil tried an experiment with a class of two hundred of his students at the University of New Mexico.

He asked students to rate themselves on how attractive they were—and he tried this test a few times. Every time, the men rated themselves higher than the women did. But when he asked how kind they were, he got the opposite result; more female students answered positively.

Some of these differences can be detected at birth: Girls look at oval shapes more often than boys, and infant girls are better at detecting emotions at an early age. Even before babies are born, the gender differences are apparent; studies of fetuses in utero have found that female twins will start touching each other in the womb at an earlier stage of life than male twins. Infant girls are better than infant boys at emotional processing—and males never quite catch up. Females are also better lie detectors. But while little girls mature earlier, females never gain the same physical strength as men.

Joyce Benenson of Emmanuel College has been studying sex differences in children and adolescents for years. Through her observations of kids playing, she's found that boys compete more with each other, in the same way that primates do.

"Boys like to spend their time competing on anything; how high they can jump, how far can they throw a piece of paper. Their favorite thing to do is to compete against one another. Boys would rather play anything competitively; that never goes away," she said. "I think this behavior is innate and can be found across every culture."

From an evolutionary biologist's perspective, that competitive drive makes sense, because males that are more successful at competition can theoretically impregnate more females and, thus, reproduce more.

While females are generally considered to be more cooperative with each other, Benenson, who also studies nonhuman primates at Harvard University, disagrees. She said that if you study chimpanzees, our closest living relative, you find that the males compete much more than the females, but they also cooperate more in terms of grooming and sharing food. They form alliances so that they can defeat another community that may be trying to take over their feeding grounds.

Benenson has found that human males also cooperate more; for instance, they can have a terrible fight, and then be friends again. Females have a much harder time reconciling. She recalled a student in one of her classes who told a story about how he and his friend got drunk once and got into a fight. During the argument, his friend stabbed him and the student ended up in the hospital. But now, they're friends again. According to Benenson, women would never be able to get over something like that.

"There is this incredible ability for both chimpanzee males and human males to reconcile in a way that females don't. There are a number of studies that show females have a difficult time with competition and a harder time repairing damage with a coworker or a roommate, for instance. There's a sense of distrust that they can't get past," said Benenson.

This rings true with me, as I've noticed my husband and sons brushing off conflicts with their friends, whereas I've seen women break off friendships over even minor disagreements.

In her observations of young children playing, Benenson found that girls generally engaged in parallel play, such as pretending in a kitchen or with dolls, but they didn't often take part in cooperative play, as boys did.

She detailed these studies and more in her 2014 book, *Warriors and Worriers: The Survival of the Sexes,* which presented a new evolutionary theory of sex differences and explored friendships and relationships from the same perspective. In the book, Benenson drew on her studies to show that boys and men formed cooperative groups to compete against others, while girls and women excluded other females in their search to find a mate—and to keep their children alive. She also believes that, from an evolutionary perspective, friends were more useful for men than for women, because men needed each other to win a battle.

Her theory upends the conventional wisdom that women are more sociable than men and that men are more competitive.

Benenson also said that men will cooperate with each other, even if they don't like the way someone looks—but women won't work together if they don't find the other woman appealing in some way.

This was borne out in research on how genders cooperate—a frequent area of study, since it is central to human existence. In their study, "I (Don't) Like You! But Who Cares? Cooperation and Coordination in Same-Sex and Mixed-Sex Teams," Michael Kosfeld and Leonie Gerhard found that likability played a more important role for women than for men and that the sexes approached social interactions differently. The study had males and females play a game in a lab experiment; the researchers found that, in a group of mixed genders, men were less likely to have friction with others than were women.

Kosfeld and Gerhard also cited Benenson's study of college roommates that analyzed men's and women's thresholds of tolerance for genetically unrelated same-sex individuals. "Tolerance is defined as the acceptance of stresses and strains within a personal relationship. Benenson showed that women are less likely to accept a given level of stress with their roommate than men. This is not only reflected in their answers to the questionnaire, but also in a higher frequency of room switches and relocations within a given period of time."

If males find it easier than females to repair a relationship, as Benenson said, that means that men may be more likely to successfully cooperate in a work environment than women. Failing to get along with someone else could have a negative effect on a team's performance, which could play a part in the gender pay gap.

There are many other marked differences between the genders: Women are better communicators than men, and they tend to focus on how to create a solution that works for a group. They're also better at talking through issues.

Men, on the other hand, tend to be more task-oriented and less talkative, and they can be more isolated. They may have a more difficult time understanding emotions that are not explicit, while women tend to be more intuitive when it comes to feelings and emotional cues. Some scientists call women mind readers, because they are so good at reading other people's faces and emotions. A wife can sometimes tell if her husband is cheating, just by the way he looks at her in the morning, for instance. These dissimilarities can help to explain conflicts in communication between men and women. They also may illuminate why male and female friendships are so different.

Robin Dunbar cited some striking gender differences: Women are much better on social cognition–type tasks, such as mentalizing, than men are. ("Mentalizing" is the process by which we make sense of ourselves and others.) As a result, women have more best friends than men do. This was something that Dunbar and his colleagues picked up by scrutinizing Facebook; while both men and women will post photos of themselves with their partner in a happy state in their profiles, in some cases, women will add a girlfriend as the second person in the picture (rather than a partner). On the other hand, according to Dunbar, while men will sometimes have their girlfriends or a group of men in their profile picture with them, they will almost never have a photo of themselves with a male friend. This signifies that women can manage two very intimate relationships at the same time—a husband or partner and a best friend—while men don't seem to be able to do that.

"Men live in a much less intense social world than girls do. It's a striking contrast. If you move to another town, girls will be on the phone constantly trying to keep that going. Whereas with guys, it's out of sight, out of mind," said Dunbar.

Women are also able to manage the social complexity of their relationships by keeping up to date on the information they need to know about their friends. On the other hand, the male world is much less complicated, so they don't need as much information. This goes back to the very striking difference between the two sexes in the way they build and maintain friendships; girls spend quality time talking with their friends, which enhances the emotional quality of their relationships. With men it doesn't make a difference how much time they spend talking to their friends, because when you're doing things together, you don't need to talk.

Dunbar agrees with Vigil that women have extra-close relationships with other females as a consequence of the tradition of moving from their family group to their husband's family group when they married.

"The problem they have is that they're in a group of strangers. Everyone is related to their husband and they're an outsider," said Dunbar.

He suggested that this explains the difference in the intensity of close friendships between the two sexes. Since women have much deeper relationships, they need to know more about their friends. They can predict how other women will respond if they do or say something. Because men don't live in such an intimate social world, they don't need to know these things, and thus, their relationships are much more casual.

The science of sex differences, however, can be controversial, and researchers seldom agree on the evolutionary basis for the behavior of men and women. Historically, women were thought to be inferior to men, and scientists believed they could prove it with bogus experiments and research—even women's brains were thought to weigh less than men's: Early nineteenth-century neurologists believed that women must be less intelligent because they thought their brains weighed on average five ounces less than men's. Science has made great strides since then in disputing spurious claims of sex differences, but they still continue. For instance, in the past several years, a number of men have been criticized for blaming nature for the failure of women to become scientists.

Larry Summers, the former president of Harvard University, eventually resigned from his position after arguing that biological reasons are to blame for men outperforming women in math and science. And in 2017, a Google software engineer, James Damore, suggested that human nature could explain the shortage of women working in Silicon Valley. He was subsequently fired.

Research has shown that, when it comes to the sciences, the gender differences between men and women is miniscule—in fact, the variations can be attributed to people's motivation rather than their ability.

Cordelia Fine, a British neuroscientist, begs to differ with men who find women inferior. In her recent book, *Testosterone Rex: Myths of Sex, Science and Society,* Fine disputes the argument that evolution has programmed men to be promiscuous and women to be monogamous so that their reproductive success can be assured.

She also disagrees with the notion that testosterone causes men to take more risks, because if we expand our definition of risk-taking to include other activities, such as smoking or drinking or even risky sexual activities, that would shut down this theory.

Fine argues that gender differences can be attributed to the continuing inequities that men and women have, particularly in the workplace. In an interview with the *Guardian* newspaper, she said:

"When we look at the world as it is, and the continuing inequalities that we have—my book looks particularly at occupational inequalities—I think there's some kind of a relief in thinking: 'Well, look, it's not injustice that's creating this situation, it's just naturally ordained.' So you can think: 'Oh well, that seemingly impossible task of creating something more like gender equality—we're off the hook.' I think that's one plausible explanation."

Vigil agreed that taking the easy way out when it comes to explaining sex differences can be problematic.

"It's common to say that girls are more mature than boys, but people are missing the basic point that we are specialized in different ways, and while it's wonderful, it can create real problems. For instance, when males are interrupted, they'll say 'Don't interrupt me'; but when it happens to females, they'll say: 'Oh, you're so right. Go on,'" said Vigil.

Perhaps this explains why men so often manterrupt and mansplain to women? According to the *Oxford English Dictionary*, "mansplaining" is "to explain something to someone, typically a man to a woman, in a manner regarded as condescending or patronizing." We've all been there—your Uncle Steve answers a simple question with a condescending manologue about something you already know. Another definition for mansplaining is "explaining without regard to the fact that the explainee knows more than the explainer, often done by a man to a woman."

As Vigil said, men are more likely to interrupt, frequently in an intrusive manner, and women are more often interrupted—and this behavior goes back centuries.

When women are interrupted, they usually react amiably, with a smile or a nod, probably because they're used to it. To be fair, not all men do this—my husband, for instance, rarely mansplains. (But he does manterrupt me, and he doesn't even realize that he's doing it.)

But while women may just consider mansplaining or manterrupting annoying, these disruptions matter. When two people are talking, it's usually the more powerful person who will interrupt, and a man usually has greater social dominance in a conversation.

This reinforces gender inequality and gender stereotypes, such as that a woman knows less about a certain subject or isn't as smart as a man.

Sometimes this happens when a woman is clearly more knowledgeable about a subject than a man, as in the story of the writer Rebecca Solnit, who had a man try to explain *her own* book to her, even though he hadn't read it. She subsequently wrote an essay and book about the experience, titled *Men Explain Things to Me*. Much of the book is based on an encounter that Solnit and her friend, Sallie, had at a party in Aspen that was held by a wealthy and self-important man who asked them to stay late so he could talk to Solnit about her writing.

He then embarked on a description of the book, *River of Shadows: Eadweard Muybridge and the Technological Wild West*, which Solnit wrote. This is from her essay:

> So caught up was I in my assigned role as ingénue that I was perfectly willing to entertain the possibility that another book on the same subject had come out simultaneously and I'd somehow missed it. He was already telling me about the very important book—with that smug look...

Her friend, Sallie, tried to interrupt him to say, "That's her book." Or she tried to interrupt him. But he kept talking. Until the third or fourth time that Sallie interjected, when he finally stopped and realized that he was speaking to the author of that very book. He was actually describing Solnit's own book to her.

Solnit said the experience made her realize that women in any field find it difficult to speak up and be heard. "It trains us in self-doubt and self-limitation just as it exercises men's unsupported overconfidence."

That lack of confidence in girls can make them more likely than boys to be depressed. Typical teenage girls will express more sadness and vulnerability than boys.

A 2016 study by Swedish researchers found that teenage girls were more engaged in helping their friends and were better than males at developing supportive relationships with girlfriends. But girls also needed a higher commitment in their friendships, and so they were more prone to breakups when they perceived a violation of trust. And that tendency had the effect of making girls more vulnerable to depression.

When I asked Joe, a friend in his early fifties, if he'd ever had a friendship breakup, he couldn't think of one. But he recalled a time in college when he lived in an apartment with a bunch of male friends, including his best friend. One day, Joe made lasagna and told his best friend that he could have some—he just had to take it out of the oven when it was done. But his friend forgot, and the lasagna ended up sitting in the oven for a few days, going bad. No one in the apartment wanted to clean it up, and it was getting more and more disgusting. Finally, one of the guys took the lasagna out of the oven and threw it out the back window of their third floor apartment—and that resolved the issue!

Still, Joe said that his best friend was a slob and would sometimes come home late from drinking, forget where he was, and pee on the floor. The other guys were angry and made him clean it up, but they never had a breakup over it. Joe said that he and his friend drifted apart and don't talk much anymore. But like many men, Joe still considered him a good friend.

Robert, however, did have a devastating breakup with his childhood friend, Henry. (I've changed their names at their request.) They'd been close friends since seventh grade and had moved to the same town halfway across the country with their respective spouses.

They even had daughters the same age, and Robert had been close with Henry's mother.

After moving to the same town, Henry had a career change and became a realtor. In preparation for their pending adoption of a baby, Robert and his husband decided to downsize and buy a fixer-upper shortly thereafter—during a very hot real estate market.

As Robert and Henry explored purchase options in town, it further bonded them. "We had a lot fun together looking at everything available in and out of our price range," Robert remembered. Robert and his husband finally found just the right house, and they proceeded to make the purchase with Henry as their realtor. "Now the pressure was really on to buy low and sell high in order to afford the significant renovations to create a new home for our growing family," said Robert.

But the purchase didn't go as smoothly as they hoped, and Robert felt like there were obvious signs that Henry's inexperience almost let the opportunity slip away, delayed the closing, and hindered them getting the best possible price. Given that experience, Robert and his husband decided it might be prudent to go with a more seasoned realtor for the sale of their home. Since Robert had provided Henry with the opportunity to get his first closing so soon after earning his license, he hoped that Henry would understand his decision to use someone else to sell their original home. Still, they agreed to hear a pitch from Henry and another realtor at his real estate firm who had more experience, to handle the sale.

Robert and his husband needed every penny to put back into the new house, which required quite a lot of renovating. Adding to the financial pressures, Robert had been laid off from his job and didn't know how long it would take to find another position due to a market downturn.

"I hate disappointing anyone. I knew it was going to be a hard pill for Henry because he really wanted to shine at his new agency right off the bat. But we just had too many financial pressures to take a risk with our biggest asset. Our previous realtor was a total shark at the top agency driving over-asking offers and we didn't connect with Henry's choice for co-realtor. Plus, the clock was ticking since we were carrying two mortgages. We didn't have time to think once we bought the new home," said Robert.

He knew that Henry would be upset with their decision not to use him. "I feel like I went overboard to make it up to him and acknowledge that he was feeling like we'd slighted him," he said.

Robert and his husband invited Henry and his wife over for dinner and made overtures to try to patch things up. "We were truly happy with the purchase of our new home—especially after the renovations were complete. I remember genuinely complimenting Henry on finding just the right property for us, but it didn't seem to be enough. I'm not someone that openly processes emotion and feelings, but the decision not to use him for the sale always felt like it hung over us," remembered Robert.

To support Henry's new career, Robert sent an email to everyone he knew in town announcing their move and introducing and recommending his good friend. Robert said he didn't recall Henry ever acknowledging or appreciating that effort. And their mutual friends became aware of the tension and growing rift that began to impact Henry's and Robert's social circle.

Eventually, Henry and Robert stopped talking and drifted apart. The friendship faded away as Robert focused on juggling parenthood and a new job.

"Maybe I should have just used Henry, but it was the right decision for the circumstances at the time and I thought it was something that would eventually get worked out. I've always hated that we parted ways even though our lives are so aligned and we had such a strong connection and deep history. But I don't think I did anything that warranted being permanently cut off," said Robert.

I was able to speak with Henry as well, and his story was slightly different.

"We go back to grade school and his friendship break with me is one of the most significant events in my life. I grew up an only child and consider old friend's bonds sacred. I was shocked when he threw me under the bus 15 years ago," said Henry. "I mean, he was in my wedding party. I was blown away that they wouldn't use me."

Henry was unhappy that Robert decided to use a different realtor, even though they'd been lifelong friends, but he understood why he chose to use someone else. He was more upset that some of their mutual friends decided to go with another realtor as well, and they'd stopped returning his calls. He wondered if Robert had swayed them to use someone else.

But the final blow came when another mutual friend, Cecile, did the same thing. She entertained the idea of using Henry as her realtor to sell her home and even went out with him for two days to look at houses, but then chose to use someone else. Henry was hurt that Robert never called or even emailed to commiserate with him and tell him how wrong Cecile had been in the way she'd treated him.

"I was stunned; I felt like my head was going to explode. That was completely low what she did, and [Robert] never said anything about that. That was the nail in the coffin. This whole storm blew up. He knew I'd have to draw the line in the sand after that. He didn't say 'that sucks,' or 'I can't believe she did that to you,'" Henry remembered. "I could see his reluctance to call me, but sometimes you have to step outside your comfort zone to do the right thing. I think it was the impact of all three at the same time."

Henry never told Robert why he was so upset and stopped speaking to him. For Henry, it was an accumulation of things, and he felt like, as a good friend, Robert should have said something to him about it all.

"I made the decision that I was more valuable than that and I deserved better. It's been 15 years. We bump into each other in town now and then. It's cordial but icy. If it had just been him not using me…but I felt like it was the whole group. And no one said a peep to me; not one thing," he said. "He's the one in the group that I'd known the longest—he was with me and my wife when we went on our first date together in high school! I'd considered him a pretty close friend, and I expected better."

For his part, Robert was very sad that the friendship ended. He couldn't understand why his friend got so upset even though he tried to help Henry find new clients afterward.

Henry said he felt like "the ship has gone too far out to come back in. It would be too weird to be friends again. I was pretty ticked off. I understand it even more now. Some people get spooked about selling their house and they think there might be some advantage to using someone else. Do I miss him? I would like to say yes I miss the guy I knew. I think when the friendship was put to the test it didn't pass. After 15 years what are we gonna do, get together and have lunch? It sounds like a whole bowl of awkward. I think I can do better. I can surround myself with friends who can treat me better."

Bromances

Do men get less from their friendships than women do, since in some ways, they tend to be less close?

One study said that was not the case. While men might not be physically or emotionally expressive, they actually derive great support from their friendships.

Research comparing the strength of boys' friendships with girls' found that, despite having a reputation for not being very skilled as friends, boys were actually as satisfied with their friendships as girls were, and they found their relationships with other boys to be secure and stable. The study also found that boys were just as good at the "social tasks" necessary to be a good friend, such as being a fun companion, being able to handle a friend who doesn't live up to expectations in a relationship, and managing friendship in a positive way when a friend has other friends.

And another study supported this. It said that young men actually got more emotional satisfaction out of their friendships with other men, or their "bromances," than they did from their romantic relationships with women.

The research found that "the increasingly intimate, emotive, and trusting nature of bromances offers young men a new social space for emotional disclosure, outside of traditional heterosexual relationships. Participants state that the lack of boundaries and judgment in a bromance is expressed as emotionally rivalling the benefits of a heterosexual romance. Our participants mostly determined that a bromance offered them elevated emotional stability, enhanced emotional disclosure, social fulfilment, and better conflict resolution, compared to the emotional lives they shared with girlfriends."

The study, which included only thirty young men, found that intimate male relationships with other men, such as the one between Barack Obama and Joe Biden, have become more socially acceptable. Even more remarkable, the study found that many of the young men involved in these bromances had cuddled with their male friend, told them secrets, and at times, even slept in the same bed.

"There was a conclusive determination from the men we interviewed," the study authors wrote. "On balance, they argued that bromantic relationships were more satisfying in their emotional intimacy, compared to their heterosexual romances."

This study was surprising, in that it went against the stereotype that men were afraid of showing their emotions, and found that men *wanted* to have emotional intimacy with their close male friends. It was, however, a very small study group.

But are men truly showing physical intimacy with their friends these days?

My parents are from Argentina, where men openly kissed each other on the cheek and hugged. I remember my father running into male friends on the streets of Buenos Aires when I was a kid, and noticing how demonstrative they were in their affection for each other. It's very different here, and that may be a cultural difference or it may be that times have changed.

So why don't male friends touch in the same way that women do?

Mark Evan Chimsky wrote an essay about this recently for the *Huffington Post*. He noted that he was not referring to the intimacy of lovers, but rather to the physical affection that men once exhibited toward one another. Citing Richard Godbeer's 2009 book, *The Overflowing of Friendship*, Chimsky discussed the physical display of affection that was once common among male friends in the eighteenth and nineteenth centuries, when men would describe "with a swelling of the heart" their friendships with other men, addressing them as "lovely boy" and "dearly beloved," and talking about their ardent affection for each other and their "indissoluble bonds of fraternal love."

This type of warmth between men mirrored the sentimental friendships of Victorian women, and their families, friends, and society accepted their male relationships as healthy and good for everyone. These men once wrote loving letters to each other, and would hold hands in public and even embrace.

"Early Americans," according to Godbeer, "exalted love between men as a personal, public, and spiritual good."

These days, men will occasionally give their friend a bro hug, but that's about it. Has society made men loathe to show affection with each other because they fear people will think they are gay? Do they wish they could physically touch their friends without it being sexualized?

Back in the 1700s and early 1800s, the term "homosexuality" wasn't in use, and people weren't labeled in the same way that they are today.

Do men feel pigeonholed in other ways as well?

Stereotypes in Emotions

For years, there has been an enduring stereotype that women are more emotional than men. The problem is when these gender stereotypes apply to beliefs about the expression of emotion more than to the *experience* of emotion. In one study, participants said that while both men and women experienced most emotions similarly, they thought that women showed sadness, fear, and love more than men, and that men showed anger more than women. These stereotypes even extended to babies—an infant's ambiguous expression was interpreted as angrier when the child was labeled as a boy rather than a girl.

In the study, participants thought that women experienced awe, embarrassment, fear, distress, happiness, guilt, sympathy, sadness, love, surprise, shame, and shyness more often than men. Men were thought to experience anger and pride more frequently. The study also found that both genders were socialized in the emotions that they expressed. For example, boys learned that men should not cry, and girls learned that women should not show anger (except in a maternal role).

Ashby Plant, a psychology professor at Florida State University, who was the lead researcher on the study, said the problem is that we can be influenced by what people say. "If you think of a child trying to learn how to interpret their own experience, it's often not just clear anger or fear that they're feeling. If someone says, 'Don't be so mad,' they may actually be interpreting our sadness or fear as anger.

So you might get confused and think that anger and sadness are the same thing, or you might grow up thinking, 'Oh, this is what I'm feeling,'" she said. "It tells people how they should act. And sometimes, it may not always be clear how to respond in a situation—you may respond with sadness rather than anger if someone is berating you in the office, for example."

Plant said that these stereotypes could interfere with the ability to communicate clearly and to have good, positive relationships. For example, if you're misinterpreting people's expressions, thinking that someone is upset about something when they're not, then you might avoid addressing relatively minor conflicts that could otherwise be resolved.

In fact, my own young son said he believed that stereotypes about boy's friendships with other boys are unfair. He said that society may think that he doesn't care about having friends, or that he doesn't care about his friends, but he really does.

Through Thick and Thin

While men are stereotypically thought to have longer-lasting friendships than women, a recent study showed that that's just not the case. In this study, sociologists from the Centre for Research on Socio-Cultural Change at the University of Manchester found that men were choosier and shrewder about who they should be friends with, while women were considered truer friends and more supportive of their girlfriends during both good times and bad.

According to Dr. Gindo Tampubolon, friendship between women was much deeper and more principled than that of men. And, for women, friendship was more about the relationship rather than what they could get out of it; they didn't mind if their friends lived in the same city or miles apart: "Women tend to keep their friends through thick and thin across geography and social mobility," he said.

The study also found that for women, friendship was a means to "express themselves and form their identity," while men wanted to get something out of the relationship, as in "what's in it for me?" Men were also found to be more inclined to base their friendships on social drinking.

While this study was rather negative about male friendship, it is interesting because it found that relationships were more of a means to an end for men than for women. Perhaps that's one reason why men have a harder time making friends as they get older?

Today, men might be more inclined to get caught up in working, getting ahead, and being good fathers to their children, so that they give up the much-needed time for making and keeping their male friends.

Mike, who is 50 and married with one child, said that while he still keeps in touch with the work friends he's made over the years, as well as a few buddies from high school and college, he hasn't made many new friends since moving to the suburbs of New Jersey—besides a few neighbors. "I consider myself friendly and outgoing, but now I work from home, and I don't have the environment where I'm among people all day. And I haven't gone out of my way to make new friends. My circle of friends here includes my neighbors and the friends that my wife has made."

He noticed the marked difference when he goes to a school event alone versus when his wife also attends—she just knows a lot more people. And while he has kept in touch with friends from high school and college, it's mainly via texting. He rarely talked on the phone with them, and feels that texting is what we're all wired to do now. (There was a happy ending to this story: After I interviewed him for this book, he called his best friend and they reconnected. They're planning to get together soon.)

Mike's story is common; men make lots of friends in high school and college, and then it gets a lot harder for them to do so.

Women are much better at meeting people through their children, and they spend a lot of time cultivating these friendships. (I know I do.) Men, in general, are not very good at developing friendships. If they're married, their wives usually take over their social lives. But a close confidant? For many guys, this is hard to come by.

It gets worse: A 2015 UK study found that 2.5 million British men had no friend they would turn to for help or advice in a crisis. It also showed that married men were less likely than single men to have friends to which they could turn. According to the study, it was much harder for men to have close friendships as they aged, and married men had low levels of support outside the home.

It turns out that even President Donald Trump has few friends. In a *New York Times* column in November 2017, Frank Bruni suggested that Trump needed friends and that his rages and rampages were indications of his friendlessness. Sure, he has a lot of acquaintances, but none of them seemed to have the guts to speak plainly to him, as a true friend would; they all sucked up to him. Bruni said:

> Show me a person who has no true friendships and I'll show you someone with little if any talent for generosity, which is a muscle built through interactions with those who have no biological or legal claim to you but lean on you nonetheless.

Many men who do have friends find it difficult to keep in touch with them, once they have a family.

Steve, 56, who works as a journalist, said he's sad that many of his old friends have drifted apart from him but that he sometimes feels uncomfortable contacting them and trying to sustain their friendship: "Forcing it feels false. I think men can feel sensitive about reaching out to other men because they don't want to seem strange. It's not a macho thing to seem to want a friendship—you don't want people to feel like you need someone."

He sometimes feels awkward making a phone call to an old friend out of the blue, and worries that he might catch them at the wrong time. At the same time, Steve said he feels frustrated with people who only text and never call. It's as if texting brought on a formality between people when it came to making phone calls.

Steve said that while he has a lot of acquaintances, he no longer has many close friends that he sees on a regular basis. Between the demands of work and wanting to be with his wife and daughter, and hobbies such as cycling, he doesn't have much time for hanging out with friends. It was easier if his wife got along with a friend's wife, so that the families could hang out together.

"It's easy to get sucked into your job, your family, your kids. You let friendships of convenience happen, and if you're lucky you'll have the same sensibility with someone, but you're subsisting on superficial interactions," Steve said. "I always thought that if you're a real friend and you need to reach out to them, you can. But if you don't contact them, it can lead to the demise of the friendship if you don't try to nurture or sustain it in some way. I feel like it's missing in my life. I know I'd be happier if I did spend time with my friends. I miss skiing with my friend, Bob, and jamming with him."

Steve said that many of his friendships with men are based on shared interests, such as watching football, cycling, or playing in a band. He also had a policy that he didn't give his friends advice about their relationships, because he didn't believe it was his place to tell them what to do. "It's part of my overly casual attitude toward friendship."

Chapter 5

Famous Friends
Women's friendship in literature

Some people go to priests; others to poetry; I to my friends.

—Virginia Woolf

FROM VIRGINIA WOOLF to Elena Ferrante to Claire Messud—celebrated friendships between women abound in novels from both past and present.

For many women, their female friendships are some of the most significant relationships in their lives. Since the vast majority of readers of fiction are women, it makes sense for novelists to write about the subject. But why do these stories resonate so much with us? And how do they help us better understand our own relationships with our friends?

Laura Miller, who writes frequently about books for *Slate*, believes that we see ourselves in these stories.

"We read fiction to imaginatively test out the paths in life that we can take. For some readers, they feel like they haven't seen their experience represented in fiction, so it feels great to see a fictional depiction of something that you recognize, such as your friendships with other women. It makes you feel less alone, and it gives coherence to our experiences. It makes us feel like we control things. These are all of the reasons why we read fiction," said Miller.

Female friendships have always been popular in literature, but the success of Elena Ferrante's Neapolitan series, starting with *My Brilliant Friend,* may finally be giving the subject the literary attention it deserves. These stories also reveal the psychological dynamics of female friendship and tell us things about ourselves that we didn't even know existed.

Literature expands our minds and gives us a greater understanding of the world around us. And it teaches us about the human experience in a way that can't be learned from textbooks. These insights help scientists understand the implications of their research. Our best writers and poets, such as Shakespeare, understood the human mind and human nature. These concepts are so important that they are studied in literature, as well as by scientists.

"There's a sense that something is sustaining about the friendships that we read about. They last longer and go deeper than ours," said Maria DiBattista, professor of English at Princeton University. "People become captivated by other people's stories. An important part of reading fiction is putting yourself aside and contemplating what it's like to be another person in another world. It's a great self-enlarging experience. Sometimes you don't realize what was in yourself until you read about it."

For many women, the lifelong bond between Ferrante's characters Lila and Elena was captivating; as were the two Afghani women who become friends in Khaled Hosseini's *A Thousand Splendid Suns.* And currently there is a new wave of books about women who are friends; the women who become close friends in Claire Messud's, *The Woman Upstairs* and *The Burning Girl,* and Zadie Smith's, *NW,* the story of two friends and their connection to the neighborhood where they grew up, and her latest book, *Swing Time,* about two women who meet as children and become lifelong friends.

"The subject of women's friendship has been a perennial theme in literature since the 1960s, but now the literary community is taking it a lot more seriously," said Miller. "Hardly any men read Margaret Atwood in the 1970s, but now a lot of them are reading Elena Ferrante. There are also quite a lot of younger female readers who are more empowered now in the literary community, and that helps."

Elena and Lila's friendship in the Ferrante books is complicated and intense; the four novels begin with their friendship as young girls growing up impoverished in southern Italy in the 1950s. Elena is entranced by Lila, the alpha girl in the relationship who is smart and beautiful and goes on to marry a rich local shop owner. Meanwhile, Elena, who is very bright, catches the attention of a teacher who encourages her to continue her schooling. She eventually finishes college and marries Pietro, a boring intellectual from an important family.

The novels trace the pair's turbulent friendship and the way their lives are shaped by the violent, cruel world around them. They also chronicle their jealousy of, and competition with, one another; their class conflicts, their lack of power and equality as women and wives in 1950s Italy, and the role of literature and writers amid a time of social upheaval.

What does the book tell us about women's relationships?

The philosopher Cicero once described friendship as a mingling of souls "as almost to create one person out of two," and that's what Ferrante appears to be doing with her story. In fact, some critics believe that Lila and Elena are actually the same person.

Miller says the novels are, in part, about the choices that women have to make; Lila chooses the more seemingly conventional role of getting married and Elena is educated and moves up a class. While the books are clearly about female friendship, Miller believes they are also about a woman coming to terms with the price she must pay for changing class, as well what it means to leave behind a rooted, traditional, but oppressive way of life. The stories are about being torn between the old way of life and part of your cellular structure, and another, freer way of life that might be less authentic, and feeling like neither alternative is very satisfying.

Upward mobility is another classic narrative that the novels address—these women don't want to remain a member of their class, and Elena aspires for education, but when you change your station in life, you're like Eliza Doolittle—you miss your old world and you feel like a stranger in a strange land.

DiBattista, who loved the novels, said they reveal what it's like being a woman who was brought up in a particular neighborhood in Italy, as well as the shared assumptions about a woman's place there.

"The Elena Ferrante books are both obvious and confused—and subtle. They're about rivalry and resentment and deep attachment," she said.

One of the central motifs in the portrayal of female friendship in Ferrante's novels is to show the different ways that one can be a woman, and to demonstrate that choosing a new way of life means giving up an old way of living. That's a key device in literary fiction, according to Miller. "Ferrante does some new things in her Neapolitan series—she makes it a story of identity in a psychic way; the splitting between these two people, Elena and Lila, it's like two parts of one person. She gives it an epic scale, a literary voice, and a level of literary polish. Unlike her previous novels, it's sweeping, with plot twists and reversals. It has a lot of super entertaining devices of fiction. She gives it epic stature, through her voice and seriousness, and her political engagement."

The books are also about living in a time of extreme social change—Italy, during the upheaval of the worker and student strikes of the 1960s—and what that meant for a woman during that period. While social change tended to be handled flippantly in commercial women's fiction, Ferrante treated the subject much more seriously.

The novels' recurrent theme of boundaries—Lila is visited by traumatic episodes of dissociation, sensations of the borders between objects and people dissolving—is linked to the idea of female identity, a major theme of the books, and particularly to women as potential generators: of meaning, language, children, history.

The first book opens with Elena realizing that Lila has disappeared without a trace, and she realizes why her friend is gone: "She meant something different: she wanted to vanish, she wanted every one of her cells to disappear, nothing of her ever to be found."

The Ferrante books follow the tradition of great novelists who have written about women and friendships, such as Toni Morrison, who wrote about the love of two women in *Sula,* and Doris Lessing in *The Golden Notebook,* which is in part about a writer and her relationship with her friend, Molly. These are novels about women asserting themselves, stirring their readers to change themselves.

Earlier, women's fiction was often represented by the typical paths available to women, such as work or family, and the trade-off involved with choosing either of those. Women's fiction was usually about a group of friends who lived in the same place, and the adventures and challenges they faced, such as the 1966 cult novel, *Valley of the Dolls,* by Jacqueline Susann, about three young women who became friends in the world of Broadway and Hollywood, and who turned to drugs when life became difficult. Rona Jaffe's 1958 bestseller, *The Best of Everything,* changed contemporary fiction when it was released. It was another story of three young women in New York City; this time, they were employees of a publishing company who were trying to make it big.

Margaret Atwood tackled the subject of girls and friendship in the 1980s, but she gave them a slightly evil twist, in *Cat's Eye* and *The Robber Bride,* which Miller said are about "the power of friendship to sustain and (more often) to torment the girls and women enmeshed in them." In Atwood's 1988 novel, *Cat's Eye,* a painter reflects back on her childhood and teenage years, and the trio of girls who first befriended and then bullied her.

"Atwood was grappling with the idea of female solidarity. *Cat's Eye* is about perverse but close friendships among girls. They want to erase her to appropriate her for their cause," said Miller. When the book came out, Atwood was criticized for the way she depicted girls and women as treating their friends in a horrible way, rather than in a nurturing fashion, as feminists at the time believed that women should behave. It was considered politically incorrect to say there was this dimension to girls' friendships. Yet today, that kind of "mean girl" behavior is portrayed everywhere.

When Atwood's books were released, reviewers lauded her for dealing with the negative aspects of female friendship, since women at the time were believed to be more cooperative and supportive of one another.

Atwood was pushing back against the stereotypes of how a woman was supposed to behave, said Miller: "At the same time everyone knew exactly what it was like to have had a 'mean girl' experience. A lot of people thought, finally, someone is talking about this. It was this oppressive thing at the time that women were so much better than men. But there can be a sadistic element in girls' friendships, and the person who dares to say that is seen as brave and everyone is grateful to them. We never seem to be able to get past this weird façade of women's lives that are perfect and blameless. If you look on Instagram, people create this curated collage of what their life is, and everyone else hates them for it. What they're resisting is a more reductive version of the good woman that is either conventional or feminist."

Atwood wrote an essay for the *New York Times* in 1986 called, "That Certain Thing Called the Girlfriend," in which she surveyed the presence of best friends in women's novels, and she drew

attention to the books of Toni Morrison, Alice Walker, Gail God-
win, and Joyce Carol Oates. In her essay, she wrote:

> ...the female relationships seem deeper, more passionate and
> complex. Two recent novels by black women writers suggest their
> scope and central interests. In Alice Walker's, *The Color Purple*,
> for instance, the best, most loving, most enduring relationship in
> the life of the heroine, Celie, is that with her husband's one-time
> mistress Shug Avery.

Atwood suggested that in both *Sula* and *The Color Purple*,

> ...there is a sense that the friendship creates a synthesis, a com-
> pletion, which is larger than each woman separately.

In *Sula*, Morrison wrote about two black women who not only
have to deal with sexism and racism, but with the harm they can in-
flict on each other—and she wanted to show how much these women
could hurt each other. When the novel was published, it broke new
ground by depicting the darker side of these relationships.

After *Sula*, more black writers used women's friendship to tell
their stories, including Gloria Naylor's groundbreaking 1982 novel,
The Women of Brewster Place, in which a group of women lived on a
lower-class, dead-end street; the story was a portrait of women who
coexist with few men present.

In more recent novels about women's friendship, the darkness is
even more apparent.

The Burning Girl, by Claire Messud, is a semi-gothic novel about
the intense friendship between two preteenage girls, Julia and Cassie, best friends since they were small. "I can't remember a time
when I didn't know her," Julia, the narrator says, "when I didn't pick

her sleek white head out of a crowd and know exactly where she was in a room, and think of her, in some ways, as mine."

They are two opposites: Julia is quiet and sensitive; Cassie is the mischievous one. When Cassie's home life is upended by her mother's new boyfriend moving in, she begins to pull away from Julia, and their friendship starts to fall apart. Cassie starts running with a racy crowd, and their class differences become more apparent. Julia questions what happened to their relationship: "Maybe I made her feel trapped like she'd outgrown me. It was like I knew her too well…she wanted to try out a new role and didn't want to be reminded that it was fake."

In the *New York Times* review of the novel, Dwight Garner said Messud "writes with insight about how female friendships dissolve, and about things like how terrifying certain stray glimpses of adult life can be."

Messud, the author of six other novels, said she wanted to write about that time in middle school and high school in *The Burning Girl* because she felt like she experienced it all over again with her own kids when they were that age.

"I was a witness to that world, and I was thereby reliving my own terrible experiences of that time. I found my own memories surfacing and I felt as though my own experiences were yesterday," she said. "I can still blush at something that happened when I was 12 or 13—just thinking about it. I was a witness to this experience of teenagers now, with a slightly different perspective, so I wanted to write about what it's like."

The Burning Girl is, according to Messud, in part, about people who are very close friends and who think they know each other, but realize one can never really know someone.

"All those years we'd been friends we'd used the same words and perhaps meant different things and we'd never known it," says Julia, in the novel. Julia knows how Cassie plays with her hair and what her walk is like, but she doesn't really know anything about her interior life. Messud said she felt that the book was prescient in a way because she later had her own experience with a longtime friend from college who suddenly seemed to not remember important facts about Messud's life—such as that she grew up in Australia and Canada, and went to France every year to visit her grandparents who lived there. Her friend thought of her as a girl from Greenwich, Connecticut, which is where her parents had lived. Messud found the experience unsettling.

"When I think of my closest friends, there are often unacknowledged complications. Some of my friendships are straightforward, and some are fascinating people who I've known for 30 years, and we still have some weird nonsense going on," she said, adding that it often seemed to be hard on her friendships when one of her books is published. Even though friends are supposed to be happy for each other when they have a success, sometimes her friends would become absent around that time. She said it soon passed—and she didn't believe it was conscious. "These relationships are really important to us. They're as complex and as fraught as any of our romantic relationships."

Sometimes women have very different understandings of what the word "friend" means, and that happened to Messud: "It's not someone you just go to movies with—it's someone who will listen to you and try to understand you and be an emotional support. We had a different idea of what a friend is. There's no point asking someone to the kind of friend you want them to be."

Messud says that her novel, *The Woman Upstairs*, is a companion piece of sorts to *The Burning Girl*, in that it's a story about the fraught friendship between two women.

In *The Lullaby of Polish Girls*, novelist Dagmara Dominczyk wrote a coming-of-age novel about three best friends from Poland, starting in their early teenage years through the loss of innocence they later experience. Dominczyk, who was born in Poland and came to the United States with her family when she was 5, said the book was loosely based on her own life.

The novel is about Anna, who immigrated with her parents to the United States in the 1980s as political refugees from Poland. They settled in Brooklyn, yet Anna never quite feels that she belongs there. When she turns 12, she is sent back to Poland to visit her grandmother, and she develops intense friendships with two local girls. Their bond is renewed every summer when Anna returns.

Dominczyk started writing the book when she was in her twenties and the girls in the story are composites of friends she had back in Poland. She wanted to write about girls who were not always pretty and giggly. The girls in her novel start at the same place but end up in very different worlds. They grow apart; one comes to the States and the other two stay in Poland. She said it was important to have a realistic portrayal of these friends.

"Sometimes girls are shitty to each other because they're human. I wanted a picture of three different girls who are drawn to each other—we're always drawn to those who have a quality that we admire and wish we had a little bit of. I wanted a kind of realistic nitty gritty story that did not revolve around boys. These girls have their own drama about the guys in their lives, but men never come between them," she said, adding that that's true for her as well—men have never come between her and her friends.

Dominczyk said that when she reads a book about women who are complicated and human she finds it exciting, and freeing, and it reminds her to go back to her old life and reach out to her girlfriends and appreciate them.

"As we're growing up, our friends are our first step into going outside our family, before we meet a boy; it's like a stepping stone to falling in love. The female friendships I had were very formative before I tried my hand at serious relationships with guys. These relationships with our friends are so deep and meaningful and so fraught with drama. We carve our identities as women through the women we befriend," she said. "There's something so beautiful about female friendship. Women tend to bare their hearts on their sleeves, and their conversations are on a whole other level than men's. There's something so pure about it and wonderful."

WHILE WILLIAM SHAKESPEARE isn't known for depicting female friendship in his plays, there are some female relationships that stand out, and his treatments of them are quite beautiful. In *As You Like It*, Rosalind, the heroine, flees persecution from her uncle's court with her cousin, Celia. They dress up as men and hide out in the Forest of Arden. Celia's love for Rosalind knows no limits and is frequently referred to in the play.

In the forest, they encounter a variety of characters, including the traveler Jacques, who voices many of Shakespeare's most famous speeches, such as "All the world's a stage," "too much of a good thing," and "A fool! A fool! I met a fool in the forest."

In many of Shakespeare's plays, the women who become friends and who support each other are unequal in status, such as Desdemona and Emilia, who are a noblewoman and servant in *Othello*, and their relationships are shot through with issues of power and class and wealth with someone is in someone else's debt. But that is not the case in *As You Like It*, according to Clare McManus, professor of early modern literature and theater at the University of Roehampton, London, who specializes in English and European Renaissance drama, particularly Shakespeare and his contemporaries.

McManus said that with Rosalind and Celia, they're equals. The relationship between them is amazing because they're relying on each other for help. Friendship was incredibly important in that period, and it was essential that friends were on equal footing. In the story,

Celia and Rosalind won't leave each other, so they run away together. Their relationship isn't broken, but it's sidelined by marriage.

In *As You Like It*, it is said that Celia loves her cousin so much that she would have followed Rosalind into exile if she had been banished.

In *A Midsummer Night's Dream*, Helena eloquently chastises Hermia for seeming to forget how close they were as children:

> *For parting us—oh, is it all forgot?*
> *All schooldays' friendship, childhood innocence?*
> *We, Hermia, like two artificial gods,*
> *Have with our needles created both one flower,*
> *Both on one sampler, sitting on one cushion,*
> *Both warbling of one song, both in one key,*
> *As if our hands, our sides, voices, and minds,*
> *Had been incorporate. So we grew together,*
> *Like to a double cherry—seeming parted*
> *But yet an union in partition—*
> *Two lovely berries molded on one stem;*
> *So, with two seeming bodies, but one heart.*

In *A Midsummer Night's Dream*, female friendship is depicted as something beautiful and precious. Shakespeare offers an ideal of the kind of close friendship between women that has been lost, and he keeps coming back to it, says McManus. As a dramatist Shakespeare is more interested in the dynamics of male friendship, but he seemed to know enough about women to write about them—possibly through his relationships with his sisters, mother, wife, and daughters—and their friendships are often the engines of his stories. McManus explained that part of the reason there aren't many scenes with female friends together in Shakespeare's plays is that there were only so many boy actors they could have on stage at the same time.

It would be remiss to talk about novels depicting women's friendship without mentioning the classic books of Jane Austen, Charlotte Bronte, Louisa May Alcott, and Virginia Woolf.

According to DiBattista, Austen's novels, including *Sense and Sensibility* and *Emma,* depict women who have a certain kind of sisterly empathy and understanding of each other, with points of antagonism that are overcome. While most readers believe that Elizabeth and Darcy have the most important relationship in *Pride and Prejudice,* Elizabeth and her best friend, Charlotte, also share a deep and abiding love for each other.

In Charlotte Brontë's *Jane Eyre,* one of Jane's formative friendships is with Helen, who represents a new worldview for her, one of Christian forgiveness and acceptance of the world as it is— something that Jane can't sympathize with, though there's a moral goodness that she responds to. *Little Women,* by Louisa May Alcott, shows that best friends can sometimes be your sisters; Meg, Jo, Beth, and Amy have an unbreakable bond, and their love for each other is unconditional. How many young girls, myself included, dreamed of having a relationship like the March sisters?

In the early 1920s, Virginia Woolf's novels, *To the Lighthouse, A Room of One's Own,* and *Orlando,* were published, and they remain important influences on writers—and on women—to this day. Woolf was a modernist who pioneered the use of stream of consciousness in her work. She was a great advocate for women writers and literature, and her books laid the foundation for women becoming literary critics.

In *A Room of One's Own,* Woolf wrote about the barriers that women writers historically faced, not only in getting published but in having the time and means to write.

In Woolf's work, women like each other. She wrote about the premise of women being attached to each other, of wanting to spend time together. She didn't pretend that their feelings of attachment and influence weren't important. And while in her later novels she was more skeptical of friendship, she's still an important model for other women.

Woolf quietly but insistently made the case for women writers and their literary tradition, said DiBattista, who cited Woolf's novel, *To the Lighthouse,* in her decision to go into the field of English.

"I was born to Italian immigrants, in a farm community. When I went to college and read *To the Lighthouse,* it had nothing to do with anything that I'd experienced. There was something about the style and the emotional delicacy of it and the attitude toward the parents that I understood from my own experience. I was always reading, but I'd never quite made that connection before with a story. It made me think of it as an art form. I was 20 years old, and I knew then that I would become a real reader of novels," said DiBattista, who specializes in teaching about twentieth-century literature and film, the European novel, and narrative theory.

In 1917, Virginia Woolf met the writer Katherine Mansfield, and their eventual friendship helped her tremendously in her work. Though they started out as rivals, Mansfield, who was younger and hailed from New Zealand, won over the more guarded Woolf and became her ideal reader. Mansfield wrote *The Garden Party* and *The Doll's House,* and many other novels.

Woolf's secret literary friendship with Mansfield, as well as those of Jane Austen, Charlotte Brontë, and George Eliot were recently profiled in the book *A Secret Sisterhood,* by Emily Midorikawa and Emma Claire Sweeney. Through letters and diaries that they found, the authors discovered these relationships, which they believe were paramount in helping the now world-famous writers find success.

According to Sweeney, the little-known relationships between these female writers were important, because they reveal to us that these women were producing incredible work with the help of their friends.

"There's been a mythology of female writers as being isolated characters. That's because it's easier to think of a female intellectual as a one-off; Jane Austen sequestered in her village and creating amazing works of literature—as if she wasn't influenced by others and didn't influence others after her. There's been a pernicious myth that if you have two women writers together, and they're ambitious, they must be rivals in a negative way, fighting their way to the top," said Sweeney. "If you think of someone as a genius, then it's not so threatening; there might be one woman writer per generation who is brilliant, so it's not a threat to patriarchal structures. But if you thought they were part of a community of writers, that might be a threat and a force for change."

Katherine Mansfield and Virginia Woolf had a complex friendship, and Sweeney believes their rivalry helped them become better writers. While it was considered acceptable by society at the time for women to need each other in a domestic sense, the idea that women would reach out and seek friends outside of their families for intellectual stimulation went against the concept of femininity at the time. Women were brought up to be accommodating and to hide their light under a bushel—they were not meant to be openly ambitious. Those who sought out success were considered oddities.

Of course, male literary friendships, such as the one between Ernest Hemingway and F. Scott Fitzgerald, were not viewed in the same negative light; while they may have had tension in their relationship, it was presented as healthy sparring.

Many of the early female writers encouraged one another to write, critiqued one another's work, and even helped each other out financially.

Through their research, Midorikawa and Sweeney discovered that Jane Austen was close friends with Anne Sharp, who was the governess to her niece and an aspiring playwright. The two women read one another's work, and Jane even helped Anne find the time to write by arranging for her to have a six-week vacation, which they took together. Virginia Woolf published Katherine Mansfield when she was having a hard time getting her work in print; and at the same time, Katherine helped Virginia by allowing her to publish her work when Virginia was just starting out with her own publishing company—and she needed her first commission to be of a high caliber.

While Charlotte Brontë is historically thought of as a spinster who lived a somewhat lonely existence in the Yorkshires with her sisters, she in fact had a close friend from childhood. The writer Mary Taylor encouraged Charlotte to write, effectively giving her permission to earn her living by the pen. That wasn't considered proper for women to do at the time, according to Midorikawa, adding that Mary's literary influence was undervalued.

"She encouraged her, even hectored her, to write. Sometimes it's wonderful to do that for a friend. Sometimes you need friends, who will say, 'No, you have to get on with it.' You need a friend who will speak the hard truths."

When Woolf wrote about the extreme isolation of female authors who came before her, she was unknowingly mistaken, according to Sweeney; some of them *did* have the support of friends. That's one reason why it's so important to write about the networks of women writers—so that those who come after them will know that they're part of a rich literary history and they don't have to reinvent the wheel, says Sweeney.

Midorikawa and Sweeney first began writing about famous female literary pairs on their blog, *Something Rhymed*. One of the friendships they profiled was that of the poets Anne Sexton and Maxine Kumin, who met through a local writing group in the late 1950s, and attended poetry readings together, encouraging each other's work. They even came up with titles for each other's poetry collections. This is from *Something Rhymed:*

> As well as meeting up in person at least twice per week, [Sexton and Kumin] got into the habit of making regular calls, sometimes talking for hours on end, and even critiquing each other's drafts over the phone.

> During a period when both women had won prestigious fellowships at Harvard, and so were feeling "flush and important," they went so far as to install a secret second phone line. They would sometimes keep their call linked for hours on end, interrupting their poetry discussions to make dinner or hang the laundry, and then they would whistle into the receiver when they were ready to resume. Their illicit phone line allowed them to work together without having to worry about their husbands' disapproval.

> Indeed, the pair kept their mutually supportive friendship intensely private for many years. Kumin, whose formal, reticent poetry won her a Pulitzer in 1973, had been represented by critics as the rival of Sexton, whose wild, confessional style had won her the same prize six years earlier.

> Curiously, the pair felt so "ashamed" of their friendship that they had allowed this myth of rivalry to continue for years before finally announcing that they were actually the closest of friends.

Another literary friendship that was not well known at the time—and still isn't—was that of George Eliot (the pen name for Mary Anne Evans) and Harriet Beecher Stowe. George is the British author of seven novels, including *Middlemarch, The Mill on the*

Floss, and *Silas Marner.* She and Harriet, an American who was well-known for her abolitionist novel, *Uncle Tom's Cabin,* began corresponding with each other in 1869. George's lifestyle—she lived "in sin" at the time with critic and philosopher George Henry Lewes— kept many other respectable ladies from becoming friends with her. Of course, it didn't help that George was a formidable and harsh critic, as could be seen by her essay, "Silly Novels by Lady Novelists." But her reputation didn't deter Harriet from writing to her and making suggestions about her work. That started an eleven-year friendship of two women who were, at the time, the most famous living novelists.

Sweeney said she and her partner kept coming back to why this friendship wasn't better known. Many of the letters that Harriet wrote to George had never been published in full. Harriet's critiques of Jewish stereotypes in novels, such as those by Shakespeare, Christopher Marlowe, and Charles Dickens, even convinced George to write her novel, *Daniel Deronda,* which has a sympathetic rendering of Jewish characters and their nationalist ideas.

"A lot of it comes down to who were the protectors of these writers after their deaths, and was often a male relative. But then you only have one side of the conversation, and that distorts the record," said Sweeney. "Jane Austen's brother and then her nephew wanted her to appear ladylike and unambitious and acceptable to Victorian readership" in the biographies which they wrote about her life.

Virginia Woolf's husband, Leonard, was the protector of her memories, and Katherine Mansfield's husband, John Middleton, wanted to make it seem as if *he* was the one who inspired her work, rather than Virginia Woolf—with whom he had a falling out.

As writers about successful pairs of female writers, it's not surprising that Sweeney and Midorikawa are also close friends who have been supporting each other in their careers since they met sixteen years ago. They've been encouraging each other, sharing their work on a regular basis, and letting each other know about publishing opportunities. They are there to prop each other up when things aren't going well, and congratulate one another on their successes.

"We've both had our fair share of ups and downs," said Sweeney. "But early on in our friendship, we made a promise that any opportunity we found we'd share with each other, even though we were competing with each other. Not only do we want our friend to do well, but it would be better for one of us to do well, than neither of us."

In fact, early on, they both submitted their work to the same competition for unpublished novels, the Lucy Cavendish College Fiction Prize. This was at a time when they were both feeling low about their work. In the end, Midorikawa was shortlisted for the competition and Sweeney was not. But Sweeney was happy for her friend, and she rejoiced when Midorikawa won.

"She was the person who helped me the most on both an emotional and practical level. It was a shared achievement in many ways," said Midorikawa.

They were both able to celebrate, because just before Midorikawa won, Sweeney found out that her novel was going to be published.

Sweeney said she was sad that they couldn't include the friendship of Emily Dickinson and Helen Hunt Jackson in their book, because they were focusing on British authors. The pair had been friends since school days; Emily was a recluse, and Helen was a poet and a social reformer who gave talks to hundreds of people at a time. They seemed like total opposites, but they were actually great friends.

Emily would allow Helen to visit her in Amherst; she was one of the only friends permitted to see her in person. And Helen was responsible for one of her friend's poems to be published during Emily's lifetime—"Success Is Counted Sweetest":

Success is counted sweetest
By those who ne'er succeed.
To comprehend a nectar
Requires sorest need.
Not one of all the purple Host
Who took the Flag today
Can tell the definition
So clear of victory
As he defeated—dying—
On whose forbidden ear
The distant strains of triumph
Burst agonized and clear!

There were many other important female literary pairings: fiercely intelligent women who were friends and who supported each other in their work, such as the American writer Eudora Welty, who hailed from the South (author of the Pulitzer Prize–winning novel, *The Optimist's Daughter*), and the Irish novelist, Elizabeth Bowen (*The Last September, The House in Paris*) who also became friends and influenced each other's work, and the writer Mary McCarthy and the famed political theorist Hannah Arendt. When Hannah died, Mary was her co-executor, and brought her papers to Bard College, where they are now housed at the Hannah Arendt Center.

Perhaps inspired by her friendship with Hannah, Mary later wrote *The Group*, which tells the story of eight female friends from Vassar College who find themselves lacking direction after they graduate. The novel follows the women over seven years as they navigate losing their virginity, having careers, marriage, and children.

The book, published in 1963, stayed on the *New York Times* bestseller list for two years.

More contemporary literary friends include Canadian authors Margaret Atwood and Alice Munro, Ruth Rendell and Jeanette Winterson, and Toni Morrison and Maya Angelou.

The queen of coming-of-age novels about girls and their friends is Judy Blume, who wrote the seminal young adult book, *Are You There God? It's Me, Margaret,* and later, *Deenie* and *Forever.* These books became bibles for girls like me, who were curious about topics that no one would talk about, such as menstruation, teen sex, birth control, and death. Blume said she wanted to be honest, because she felt that no adult had been up front with her and that she and her peers didn't have the information they should have had.

For many, children's literature holds a significant place in culturally defining friendship, and *Harriet the Spy,* by Louise Fitzhugh, was the first book of its kind to truly explore conflicts between friends. The 1964 novel is about an 11-year-old girl who wants to be a spy, and who writes down her true feelings about her classmates and best friends in her notebook. When she loses track of the notebook and her friends find it, they read the awful things she's written about them. Harriet has to find a way to patch things up with them and convince them to forgive her.

In later years, the subject of women's friendship in books became even more popular. Ann Patchett wrote a touching memoir, *Truth & Beauty: A Friendship,* about her relationship with Lucy Grealy, the author of the memoir *Autobiography of a Face.* Lucy's book is about her struggles with living with a distorted self-image and more than thirty reconstructive procedures after childhood cancer and surgery left her face disfigured. The pair met in college, and their friendship defined both of their lives. Ann's book tells the story of their seventeen-year friendship and the obstacles they both faced in their desire to be writers.

In an article in *The Atlantic,* Ann said of her friend, "She was a spectacular person, brilliant and difficult, demanding and talented. She was capable of great love and tenderness, as well as great suffering. She was my best friend for 17 years. I wrote a book about us...a way to memorialize her and mourn her, and as a way of keeping her own important memoir...alive, even as I had not been able to keep her alive."

Chapter 6

Mon Ami

Friendship in other cultures

Wherever you are it is your own friends who make your
world.

—William James

WHEN HE DIRECTED the International Student Center at a
South Carolina university, Dr. Roger Baumgarte often had
students from other countries comment on how welcoming Americans were. Initially, they were charmed by the people they'd meet,
and were excited at the thought that they were already making
friends. But later on, Baumgarte would hear from the same students
about their frustrations—while the Americans gave the *impression*
that they wanted to be their friends, they were just being friendly.
The friendship never took shape.

The reason could be that cultures around the world have fundamentally different ideas about what it means to be a friend.

In some societies, close friends sanctify their relationships with
elaborate public ceremonies, not unlike American weddings. In
other cultures, parents can arrange their children's friendships in
much the same way that marriages are arranged in many countries.

These differences can have a significant impact when you befriend someone from another culture. And while developing

friendships with those of different cultural heritages can be enriching and enlightening, teaching us valuable things about other places, it can also cause unwanted conflicts. Differences in how we value friendship can result in miscommunication, especially if friends expect very different things from each other. This can happen even when people are from the same culture.

Baumgarte, professor emeritus of psychology at Winthrop University in Rock Hill, South Carolina, believes that his students encountered can be explained by the fact that people are either *includers* or *excluders*. In the United States, most people are *includers,* meaning they seemingly treat everyone the same—from the outside. People are open and friendly to others, and smile at them; to outsiders, Americans appear to treat their close friends and acquaintances similarly. But inside, Americans know the difference. Other cultures, such as the French, are considered *excluders;* they change their facial expressions according to who they talk to. They will smile and act friendly toward close friends, but might appear cold and unfriendly to people they don't know very well.

While friendship in the West is defined as a relationship in which one can discuss personal problems and disclose deep secrets, in many places in the world this kind of emotional support is only a minor concern. In some cultures, being close friends means intervening in the other person's life whenever possible, and telling her what she's doing wrong. Yet intervention of this kind would usually be considered overstepping the bounds of friendship in the United States.

On the other hand, there are strong taboos in the United States against lending large sums of money to friends; in many other societies, such financial help can be the basis of a close friendship.

These disparities raise an important question: What defines a friendship? Is it loyalty, shared interests, proximity? Each culture seems to have a very different answer. I've included a sampling of cultures and cultural differences in this chapter.

Daniel J. Hruschka suggested that one value almost all people share no matter where they come from is that it's important to be good to your friends. He also believes that friendship is a special form of reciprocal altruism that is not based on tit-for-tat accounting, but rather on mutual goodwill that is built up along the way.

"Friendship has been incredibly important across human history and evolution. If you think of hunter gatherers, if they came back with no food after being out for three days, they'd have a real problem. You have to have friends around you to help buffer risk," said Hruschka, professor of human evolution and social change at Arizona State University and author of *Friendship: Development, Ecology and Evolution of a Relationship.* "Friendship today isn't given the same rituals and responsibilities that it used to have, and we may not need our friends in the same way that we once did, but we still value them and rely on them."

Becoming friends with someone means that a certain degree of informality is allowed, especially in cultures where there are strict rules about showing family members and elders the proper respect, such as Japan, China, and Korea. Among the Muria tribe of India they say, "When you are friends you can fart together." Many societies use nicknames to connote a degree of informality with each other. These are common in the United States, but also in places such as China, where close friends can call each other *younger brother.*

Miscommunication

In order for friendships to develop and grow, we need to be aware of differences in how we conduct these relationships, and any issues that might arise. Learning about other cultures and how they behave can eliminate negative stigmas, stereotypes, and even culture shock.

Gina Costa, professor of intercultural communication at Bergen Community College in New Jersey, says that most miscommunication comes from a lack of understanding. "We assume that everyone behaves the same way and just don't understand why people act differently. There is a level of ethnocentrism within us, in which everyone thinks their own culture or standard for living is the correct way," she said. "As a result, we tend to measure everyone else according to our own standards and if someone doesn't act like us, we tend to think the other person is wrong. If we took the time to learn and understand why people act a certain way, then we wouldn't judge. We don't need to all agree, but we should understand—with understanding comes appreciation, tolerance and empathy."

Costa also believes that one of the biggest areas of miscommunication between friends from different cultures stems from nonverbal communication, which accounts for about 75 percent of our interactions. Discrepancies over issues such as space and distance, touch, eye contact, appearance, and the use of time can become major problems.

For instance, Asian cultures tend to avoid eye contact as a sign of respect, especially with those of higher status. In the United States people expect others to look them in the eye; if they don't, they think a person is being rude or dishonest.

According to Costa, personal space, known in the field as proxemics, can also become an issue with friends. In the United States, people tend to value personal space and if someone they don't know well gets too close, that person may feel threatened or defensive. In Turkey, men walk hand in hand, stand very close, and often touch as a sign of affection. This behavior would probably make many American men very uncomfortable.

Touch, known as haptics, can also cause conflict. While some cultures are very affectionate and use touch frequently as nonverbal communication (Mediterraneans, Italians, Greeks), others are quite reserved and avoid any physical contact. Most people from Muslim countries will avoid any contact between men and women, especially in public. Very often, the way we are raised within our culture determines how comfortable we are with affection and touch with other people.

Similarly, some cultures are expressive and not afraid to show emotions (Latinos, Italians, Greeks, Hispanics), while others are stoic and reserved in their facial expressions (Germans, Asians). A lack of visible emotion on someone's face may be misunderstood as not caring or disinterest. In the United States, people tend to look at the eyes and mouth to gauge how someone is feeling or what they're thinking, but if a person shows no emotions, this can be confusing .

One person's friendly intentions can be seen as unfriendly to someone from another culture.

The customs associated with affection between friends, similarly, differ dramatically between cultures. In many Asian countries, such as South Korea and China, men and women will hold hands in public with their friends of the same gender. In Thailand, a man sitting at a bar will put his hand on the thigh or knee of the man sitting next to him—and there will be no sexual meaning in this touch.

Italians are extremely physically affectionate; so are Brazilians—men and women in Brazil frequently hug and kiss their friends and walk arm in arm.

Barbara moved to the United States from Brazil eighteen years ago and she has had a fairly easy time making new friends—but she misses her family and friends back home, and their warm, easy ways. She remembers a time when she was home in her native Bahia and found her mother giving lunch and snacks to farm workers who were walking home, past their house. Her mother didn't know them—but she said she knew they must be hungry, so she invited them in for a meal.

"In Bahia, people are very friendly. If you go to someone's house for the first time, they'll hug you and you'll feel like you've known them forever," Barbara explained.

In Brazil, the number of air kisses friends exchange, always from right to left, varies according to which state in Brazil you are in: two air kisses in Rio De Janeiro and most of Brazil; in Bahia, one air kiss; and in Minas Gerais, three air kisses.

According to Barbara, sometimes these kisses seem to take forever; her husband, who is American, said that when he says hello to his wife's friends in Brazil, all the kissing has him afraid he's going to break his nose!

Barbara has noticed some cultural differences between her home country and her new one; when Brazilians say, "let's get together," they'll spontaneously meet up; but when Americans say this, it means they will plan ahead and schedule a time to go out. She finds her friends in the United States more formal in this regard. Brazilians are more open with each other, but she loves that Americans are so transparent. When they say yes or no, they mean it.

But sometimes, Americans are difficult for other cultures to understand. In an amusing chart that's making the rounds on the internet, common words are translated:

What Americans say versus what they mean,
"Awesome," "fabulous," and "amazing" mean **good.**
"Great" means **fine.**
"Fine" and "Ok" mean **bad.**
"Not so great" means **really bad.**
"Challenging" means **driving me completely nuts.**
"For sure" means **probably.**
"Forever" means **30 minutes.**
"Let's get coffee sometime" means **Goodbye; I like you.**
"Let's stay in touch" means **Goodbye; I don't like you that much.**
"My friend" means **a person I know.**
"My best friend" means **a person I know and also like.**

Can't Touch This

The amount of touch that people use with their friends and loved ones varies greatly by culture.

Baumgarte says that if we made a touching scale, the United States would be in the middle, and England and Germany would be at the extreme end for not touching. In Arab cultures, friends may stand very close, with their faces only six inches apart—they know exactly what they each had for lunch that day! This proximity can make those from nontouching cultures extremely uncomfortable. Men in many Arab cultures walk arm in arm or hold hands—and while Westerners may wonder if this behavior means the men are homosexuals, many times they are not. This affection is just part of their culture; it shows that they are friends.

In some cultures, appearance, including the way people dress and the items people choose to wear, can tell a story about who they are. Some people feel insulted if others don't observe their culture's rules on appearance, such as when women fail to cover their hair or bare skin in a Muslim country. Sociologists call these telling signs artifacts. For example, it is possible to determine someone's culture based on if she wears kimono or hijab or to determine her occupation if she is wearing a uniform (such as police or military).

In Germany, friendships typically last a lifetime, but Germans tend to be cautious and aloof when meeting new people, according to Sigrid, who has been living in the States for fifteen years with her husband and two kids. That caution can sometimes be misinterpreted as being purposefully unfriendly. She finds it easier to meet new friends in the United States, but she said people feel more shallow at first; on the other hand, she finds Germans to be more rigid.

For instance, in Germany, if you go to a party and stand next to someone that you don't know, they won't talk to you, they'll just stand there. Sigrid also finds that topics of conversation between women are different between the cultures. She recently went out for dinner in the United States with a group of women, and the conversation quickly turned to sex. Sigrid said she was so embarrassed that she covered her ears and begged them to change the subject. They all just laughed at her. In Germany, women would never talk about sex at a dinner party—to them, that topic is private. Sigrid said she feels that in the United States women talk about sex all the time!

Germans are also more direct than other cultures, and are known for coming right to the point, rather than hinting at the reason for a conversation. The Boas-Jakobson theory about language says that "languages differ essentially in what they *must* convey, not in what they *may* convey." For example, some languages require you to be more specific about things such as gender or tense than other languages do.

The Boas-Jakobson theory was formulated by anthropologist and linguist Franz Boas, who said that the grammar of each language determines which aspects of experience must be expressed. In the 1950s, Roman Jakobson, a Russian-American linguist and literary theorist, elaborated on Boas's theory.

For example, when a German woman speaks English, she may disclose information based on what her own (German) language would offer, or not offer, rather than what an English speaker would disclose. This could make friendship between cultures difficult: Having a chat about something could become confusing if one person thinks the other isn't providing the kind of information that she's used to getting in a conversation. For instance, Germans may use gender when they're speaking about a neighbor, but English speakers may not. In German there's no word for boyfriend or girlfriend; "friend" could mean a love interest or a pal.

And so even the word "friend" can be perplexing.

In many Western countries, the word "friend" is sometimes used informally, and even a recent acquaintance can be called a friend. But other cultures use the word in a much more restrictive way, both linguistically and socially, according to Baumgarte. The use of the word on Facebook makes the concept even more confusing, since everyone you're connected to on the site is called your "friend."

In some cultures, the words used to describe a friend connote what that person will do for you: For example, the translation for the Western Tibetan word for "friend" is "happiness-grief-identical." Some islanders living in Micronesia describe a "friend" as "my sibling from the same canoe," based on the story of two men who became lost at sea and had to share what little food they had, while encouraging each other to survive.

In other cultures, being a good friend means sharing and exchanging food and other material goods—and sometimes, close friends even share their wives. That was the case in some Eskimo and Aleut groups in North America. When the Wandeki people in Papua New Guinea have close friends visit, the best way to greet them is to ask if you can eat their intestines. While the concept might seem rather gory and unpleasant to Americans, to the Wandeki it actually shows their affection and joy at seeing one another.

The proper response? "I should like to eat your intestines, too."

Emotional Support

Providing emotional support to your friends is important in most cultures, but sometimes, it's the *way* you provide it that matters.

A team of researchers was curious to find out if emotional support was equally vital to same-sex friendships for Euro-American, African-American, and Asian-American women. Wendy Samter and her colleagues at Bryant University studied nearly two hundred female students and found some differences in the way they cared for their friends.

On the whole, Samter and colleagues found that, when they're dealing with minor hurts and disappointments, young women turn to their friends for emotional support far more often than older women do: "Young adults expect same-sex friends to 'be there' in times of emotional distress, to 'help out' when traumatic events occur, and to 'listen and work through problems.'"

But there were some subtle differences: Asian-American women spent less time comforting their friends one-on-one. This could be because many Asian-Americans come from collectivist cultures, which emphasize the needs and goals of the group over the desires of each individual. So while these women gave their friends emotional support, they conveyed it through nonverbal cues instead. Or to put it another way, sometimes girlfriends find it best to just be there for each other, rather than talking all the time.

African-American women were also found to rely less on verbal emotional support from their friends than Euro-American females do, for similar reasons.

Intervention

People from various cultures can have very different assumptions about what it means to be a good friend.

"One's friendly intentions can be seen as patently unfriendly by someone from another culture—they simply wouldn't fit with how others think about, feel about, and behave toward their close friends," said Baumgarte, who is also the author of *Friends Beyond Borders: Cultural Variations in Close Friendship*.

For instance, I might consider someone a control freak, but that same person is considered a good friend to someone from another culture. Typically, Americans are very independent in their friendships—they don't feel like they have a duty or an expectation to do certain things for each other. They might say, "I'll listen to you if you're having a problem," or "I'll be there for you if you need me."

But will someone go over to your house and do your dishes or watch your kids if you're sick in the United States? Probably not.

However, in many cultures, it's the reverse. People from some countries are very likely to intervene and do things for you if you're unwell. Their cultural traditions and ways make them feel obligated to help out. Barbara, who is from Brazil, said that when she was home with the flu once, her Costa Rican friend stayed home from work so that she could watch her kids for her. Most Americans probably wouldn't go that far.

Different styles of friendship vary by culture; Americans are *independents* or *individualists,* who value spending quality time with friends, but generally stay out of their business. Then there are the *interveners,* such as Koreans, who are actively involved in their friends' lives; they tell their friends what to do, and when they believe they are making a mistake.

Baumgarte, who lived in South Korea for many years, remembered how his friends there were insistent about telling him if he was doing something wrong—in a way that would have been inappropriate in the United States. Eventually, he realized this behavior was a sign that they were becoming good friends. "For them it's a normal way of conducting a friendship," he said.

Soo was born in South Korea, moved to the United States when she was 8, then moved back to South Korea for a few years to work when she was in her twenties.

She found the concept of friendship very different while she was there.

"There aren't shallow friendships with Koreans. It's definitely not casual. Once you become someone's friend, it's a big thing. It's a deeper connection; like having another sister. They are there for you for anything," she said. "If you get into a fight with someone, they'll back you up and curse the other person—even if it was your fault. If your friend is doing something wrong, you'll point that out to them. Nothing is sugarcoated."

Soo finds that Koreans are highly principled and they will do anything to protect a friend. When she returned to South Korea, she realized just how serious friendship was to Koreans—and that a Korean friend is a friend for life. While there, she met someone who asked her to be his friend; she agreed, but it took her a little while to understand what kind of commitment she'd made to him. For instance, if he called her drunk at three in the morning and asked for a ride home, she'd have to go get him.

"If they're having a breakup, you have to be there for them. If something bad or good happens you have to be part of it," Soo explained. "That's when I realized how different it was. The bond between friends is really strong there. You have to do something really horrible to break off a friendship."

Even when they're far away from each other, Koreans know they can depend on their friends to be there for them. Soo remembered when she found out that a good friend from college who was living in Japan had had a seizure. Soo, who was living in South Korea at the time, immediately flew to Japan to take care of her. "She was always there for me, through any crisis, including breakups. When I broke up with my boyfriend, she came over at 1 am and we stayed up all night cursing him out! Of course I flew out to be with her."

Includers Versus Excluders

Cultural differences can be confusing when traveling to other countries. For example, if you're walking down the street in South Korea, and a stranger bumps into you, he won't say, "excuse me," because if he acknowledges you, then there are social demands about how he treats someone who is older, younger, or female. In South Korea, if someone doesn't know you, then you don't actually "exist" for them; culturally, it's easier to ignore another person rather than figure out what to say to them or how to behave around them.

Baumgarte recounted a time when he was in a movie theater in South Korea and a group of teenaged boys came into his row of seats and actually climbed over him to get to their seats, without saying anything. Angry, Baumgarte, yelled, "Excuse me!" Instantly, the teenagers turned to him and apologized, continuously bowing to him with respect. He found out later that by speaking to the boys, he had made himself "exist" to them, so they had to acknowledge him and show him the respect that was due someone older than them.

In many cultures, including in South Korea, friends can be together in total silence and find it very gratifying. That behavior might seem odd to someone in the United States.

My friend, Julia, lived in Paris for many years and is very friendly and outgoing, but she said it was much harder to make friends with women in France.

"Most of the women who became my friends in France were big travelers, or I met them somewhere else. People are slower to call someone a friend there. We use that term much more casually here [in America]. But once you make the friendships in France, they seem to be longer lasting," she said.

Many of the French people that she did get to know had made most of their friends in childhood or at university, and had remained close to them. They were a very tightknit group and they did everything together; groups of men and women would go away together on weekends, have dinners, and go on vacation. In contrast, in the United States, a person might have friends all over the country, with various groups that one does different things with, rather than just one group.

Julia also found that the subjects she talked about with her friends in France differed from those she chatted about with her American pals: "In the States, you ask a lot of questions. In France, you talk about ideas. You don't share personal information with

French people for a long time. I used to hear that Americans are superficial, that we tend to be so open with people and will talk to any-
body and let people in the door."

Baumgarte agrees that it's more difficult to make friends with
excluders, such as the French, but once a connection has been
formed, these friends treat each other as though they are special. It
would be obvious for an outside observer to tell that they are good
friends. As Julia experienced with her friends in France, excluders
don't exhibit a friendly manner to people they don't know, and they
don't expect people they don't know to be friendly to them, either.

I had this experience when I was living in England; I met people that I liked, and whom I wanted to be friends with, but it wasn't
until I was ready to leave the country two years later that I finally felt
like I had made good friends—that's how long it took for the relationship to form, and for them to trust me.

Cultural Confusion

Baumgarte's students sometimes struggled with these nuances
between cultures, and found themselves frustrated by their experiences with their American classmates.

"They felt like they were getting mixed messages from the other
students, and thought they acted in very superficial ways. Eventually
some people would catch on, and decide they liked our more independent approach to friendship, in which you encourage each other,
but you don't intervene in their lives," he said. "America is dealing
with so many different cultures. We assume that we're running on
the same assumptions about people, but we're not."

For example, in some cultures, if someone has to give a negative
answer—even for something innocuous—they just won't respond.
No response actually means "No."

I realized I had experienced this when I made plans with a few
friends via text to get together for dinner; one of the women, who is

Japanese, never responded, which seemed strange. We all wondered what had happened to her. When I ran into my Japanese friend a few weeks later and asked her why she hadn't come, she merely shrugged her shoulders and said she couldn't make it. At first, I was a little put off by her behavior, but afterward I realized that perhaps she didn't feel comfortable saying she couldn't come. Her decision not to respond meant "No." In fact, the word "no" is rarely used in the Japanese culture.

Apologies can also differ dramatically across cultures—and the failure to apologize can cause all kinds of conflicts.

In the United States, if I promise to do something for a friend and I fail to do it, I apologize profusely. But, according to Baumgarte, in many other cultures the norm is that there is no need to apologize, because saying you're sorry falls flat and friends should have more faith in each other. These cultures believe that an apology comes off as unfriendly, and shows a lack of trust in a friendship.

Instead, someone from one of those cultures might compensate by trying to reinforce the relationship, making clear that you both are good friends. For instance, she might talk about your last birthday and the fun you had, or she will make future plans to get together with you. While this might seem strange to Americans, it's the custom in many other countries. According to Baumgarte, "In these cultures and in the context of a close friendship, apologizing can easily be interpreted as signaling a lack of trust or closeness in the relationship. It's a bit like Shakespeare's Hamlet: 'The lady doth protest too much, methinks.' The friend is left wondering why the apologizer is talking on and on. He/she doesn't need to apologize. We're friends. Apologies can communicate just the opposite."

Yet for many cultures, the failure to apologize could end a friendship.

That's why it's important to realize that people from different cultures have distinct cultural ideas about friendship—and the first step in dealing with any misunderstandings that arise is to realize that they're usually unintentional. It helps to try to understand where your friend is coming from, because that gives you ways to deal with that conflict or misunderstanding.

For a friend who doesn't apologize, you might not confront them, but instead say, "You're an important friend to me; let's make a date to get together," and that would fix the problem.

Conflicts can even be found within the same culture. For instance, Baumgarte said he has an American friend who is an intervener—his friend is constantly telling him how to run his life. Once he understood that his friend was acting this way because of cultural differences, and that he meant well, he could see him as caring and warm, rather than annoying—and he could learn to ignore it. Even among people who are fairly sophisticated, these intercultural relationships can be difficult to understand and navigate.

In a similar vein, in China, many people don't say "please" and "thank you" because it makes them feel uncomfortable. They think that being friends means it's natural that they do everything for each other, so using these niceties is unnecessary.

In fact, America is the exception in many respects when it comes to friendship customs. Most other countries in the world—except for those in Western Europe—are more interventionist than independent. Americans might say they like to help their friends out— but, as Baumgarte says would they truly do it? "America is dealing with so many different cultures. We all tend to think that a friend is a friend is a friend. We make the assumption that we're running on the same expectations, but we're not. It's clear to me that people coming from Asia to the US or Russia to the US are very aware that friendship is different here," Baumgarte said.

On the other hand, Americans are much more likely to self-disclose about their problems or issues to their friends.

Self-disclosure is an important element in friendship to many Americans, who feel like they can tell their friends anything, and still be accepted. They even self-disclose to perfect strangers—something people from other cultures would never do. Curiously, people from some other cultures feel comfortable asking strangers how old they are, or if they're married, whereas Americans rarely ask these things directly. For Americans, the most common question they ask when they first meet someone is, "What do you do?" Those from other cultures probably wouldn't ask that question because their job isn't an important part of their identity.

In many countries, people are careful about what they disclose to the friends they're close to. That's partly because in interventionist cultures, if you tell a friend that you're depressed and you're taking antidepressants, for instance, they will do whatever they can to help get you off the drugs and cure you. Obviously, that's not always easy to do.

Americans also value directness and honesty and speaking up for themselves, which some cultures may find abrasive. But while Americans might be direct in many ways, they are actually the opposite when it comes to close friendships.

"In the US, if a close friend comes to us complaining about conflicts she's been having at work, we tend to be sympathetic and encouraging. We'll offer moral support. We do this even if we know, deep down, that our friend is at least partially responsible for the conflict," explained Baumgarte. "Let's say that, based on our long friendship, we know that this friend can do and say things that are unwise or even inappropriate at work. But in this context, we are unlikely to confront our friend with this reality. In what are traditionally 'face saving' cultures such as Korea, Japan, and China, close friends can be very confrontational, even about very delicate matters. A close friend might come right out and say that these work conflicts are 'your own fault,' then go on to explain how the friend's behavior is unwise or inappropriate."

African Customs

Masela is from Kenya, where female friendship is highly valued and where *everyone* intervenes.

In her homeland, relationships between women are an informal institution, and the ecology of the villages depends on them. The planting season, the harvest season, ceremonies, having babies, and the coming of age of children—what makes these wheels churn is female friendships.

The time that women spend with their friends in Kenya is essential because it's when they share ideas about helping each other.

"Wayward teenagers, how kids should be disciplined, even the kind of food that people thrive on—these are all brought to these circles of women. At a deeper level, it has even changed cultures," said Masela. "We'll discuss the way women relate to their husbands. A woman may say that her husband drinks too much, and for that discussion, other women might have ideas that they've experimented with. If it takes root, it has a magical effect."

Masela explained that friends in Kenya have less distance and fewer barriers than friends in the United States—emotionally, psychologically, even physically. There, she's not scared to tell her friends what's bothering her. People there are more open, and are more likely to reveal their problems. They get involved if they see something troubling: "If I'm walking in the village, and I see a child misbehaving, I'll talk to him or her. Tactfully. People watch out for each other. When you see something, you act as if it's your child— with love and concern."

Much of Kenya is still centered on village life; three-quarters of Kenyans still live in rural areas, and traditional lifestyles there revolve around farming and trips to local markets. In the village where Masela moved to after she married her husband, there are about one hundred houses scattered around. As a woman in that country, you traditionally leave your home once you marry and live with your husband's family.

The women still walk to fetch water each morning; it's a daily chore, but it's an important time for them to talk and exchange ideas. Going to the local market to buy food is another bonding opportunity. As they walk, they chatter about seeds they'll use during planting season, or the amount of help they're getting from family members. Since most families in the villages don't have refrigerators, they must go to the market every day to buy food.

In Kenya, people rarely miss signs of trouble or unhappiness with their friends or loved ones. ("We can smell it in different ways, and you don't even have to open your mouth," Masela said.) There are very few surprises. People there are very good at reading nonverbal cues, and much of the communication depends less on what you say and more on how you behave. Sometimes a friends will walk into your house and not even speak at first.

But when someone wants to tell someone a secret that must be kept, she chooses carefully. In Kenya, there's value in a friend who keeps a secret. People say: If you don't want that thing to be repeated, tell so and so.

There's also a hierarchy to friendship in Kenya: Older people are well respected there, because they have seen things that younger people haven't. The length of your marriage is considered an asset, because the longer you've been married, the more experienced you are with relationships.

Masela said that while she has enjoyed living in the United States for the past fifteen years, she misses her friends back home. "There's something about friendship with other women there; it's the way we value each other, and the depth to our relationships. I miss the common language, I miss walking and communicating without talking. I miss the jokes you can tell. I don't tell my friends here the same things as at home because I think I'll be judged. At home there's trust. In the village, everybody is kin. If something happens in one household, everyone is affected. If a child is sick, everyone is gloomy."

And if bad blood develops between two friends, an older woman will intervene and bring them back together. Older women speak with wisdom.

Masela said her grandmother was one of these women; she died at 102, with her head still clear and with a photographic memory.

Collectivist Versus Individualist Cultures

Social scientists like to divide cultures into either collectivist or individualist; in collectivist cultures such as Kenya's, people are valued for being generous, helpful, and dependable. Japan, China, Korea, Taiwan, Argentina, Brazil, and India are also considered collectivist, because in these countries, people are encouraged to do what's best for their in-groups, essentially their families, close friends, and work or school mates, rather than for themselves. What's important is how they all function together, and decisions are based on the goals of the group and maintaining social harmony.

In individualist cultures, such as the United States and many Western European countries, there's a greater emphasis on independence and assertiveness, which drives many of the decisions people make and how they interact with others. People in individualist cultures strive for creativity and to be different, tend to be competitive, believe in equality, and focus on their own personal goals (sometimes disregarding the aspirations of others). But while individualist friendships may focus on the self rather than the group, Americans and those in Western countries still find their relationships to be meaningful and deep, and they can receive enormous health benefits from them.

The Passenger's Dilemma

In the last five hundred years, governments have largely taken over the basic services that friends used to rely on each other for, such as child care, health care, and mental health counseling. We can travel safely from place to place, rather than depending on someone else to keep us from danger.

We still need our friends—but how far will we go for them? When will we lie for them and when is it best to tell the truth?

Hruschka says that at times, we're confronted with situations where we either have to fib for a friend or throw her under the bus, so to speak.

Take the well-known ethical quandary, the Passenger's Dilemma. In it, a friend is driving down the road and you are the passenger. She is going way over the speed limit and hits a pedestrian; you are the only witness. Your friend goes to court for the crime, and her lawyer asks you to lie under oath and say she wasn't speeding, because then she'll get off with a lighter sentence. The options are: lie to help your friend, or tell the truth.

So why are some people more willing than others to go out on a limb for their friends?

Unexpectedly, Hruschka said the answer depends on the government's effectiveness in a society. When the institutions of a country run well, such as in Switzerland, and its citizens can rely on the government to take care of them, they will generally tell the truth in the Passenger's Dilemma. In fact, 95 percent of Swiss said they would tell what actually happened. But when there is corruption and ineffectiveness in a government, someone will inevitably lie for his or her friend. In Venezuela, the number is nearly reversed from Switzerland; about 70 percent of Venezuelans said you should help your friend and lie. In South Korea, 63 percent also said they would testify in favor of a friend.

While we all share many of the same human values, notions of what is normal and expected in the West are not always in sync with those of other countries. Even using the word "lie" is complicated when viewed cross-culturally. It clearly implies immoral or unethical behavior. Yet, from the Korean or Venezuelan perspective, the moral and ethical thing to do is to support your friend. They don't see helping a friend in this way as lying or doing anything immoral.

"You need to rely on your friends to help you out in those places, so people have more allegiance to their friend than to the impartial rule. That's how you get by in those societies—with strong, loyal friendships. There are a lot of different ways for making a life and making sure we have the things we need in life. In many societies, we accomplish this through friendship and family," said Hruschka.

In Russia, people believe American friendships are insubstantial compared with those in their own country, where there is a much higher expectation from their friends. There, friends act as a safety net.

During the Soviet era, having connections was sometimes the only way to get anything you needed, such as getting your son or daughter into university, or even obtaining meat for your dinner. There's a saying in Russia: "A friend will help you move. But a good friend will help you move a body."

Arranged Friendships and Money

The idea of having your parents arrange your friendships in the same way that some cultures set up marriages is strange for most Americans—but in many countries, such as those in Africa and the Balkans, it's quite common. These arrangements make it publicly clear to everyone that the relationship is a friendship, so people are unlikely to break if off without feeling shame or guilt (we have weddings for similar reasons). These arrangements also mean you can't have many close friends because it's such a big commitment; and the ones you do have become lifelong friends. Sometimes, these arranged friendships are even cemented with rituals, similar to marriage ceremonies, with large feasts and parties.

In a more unusual friendship ritual, the Azande of north central Africa hold a ceremony in which each of the two friends consume the other's blood and then perform a ritual describing their friendship obligations. Sometimes the men carry a blood-smeared lock of their blood brother's hair in a pouch. They believe that if you treat your friend badly in the future, then his or her blood will make you sick.

On the other hand, in the United States, people think of friendship as something voluntary, that shouldn't be arranged. Americans believe that having a friend is something private, between two people.

Some cultures think that friends should help each other with disputes, assist in courtship rituals, and even help with the cost of funerals and weddings, such as in South Korea, where these costs can total up to $7 billion a year.

Before entering a South Korean wedding hall, guests line up to hand cashiers their monetary gifts, which are then registered in a ledger. Some wedding invitations even have the couple's bank account numbers so that those who can't attend can send money. Records are kept by the families so that they'll know how much they should give in return; failure to reciprocate can ruin a friendship. Giving cash is a huge part of the South Korean culture, in which white envelopes, called "greetings" are customary even for a baby's first birthday party.

Likewise, whether or not one should loan friends money is very different for those in the West compared with the rest of the world.

In the United States, loaning money between friends is not frequently done, and it is understood that mixing friends and money could end the friendship. But in other cultures, including parts of China, Arab countries, and Central and South American nations, helping a friend in financial need is precisely what friendship is all about. In many of these cultures, when you loan a friend money, there isn't even a clear expectation that it's ever coming back. Baumgarte interviewed a Mexican man once who said that he liked the fact that his friend owed him money, because that meant he would always be his friend.

In some cultures—especially in countries where bank loans were once difficult to obtain—groups of friends or family band together to create an informal loan club. In South Korea and China the clubs are popular and are referred to as *Hui*. Many immigrant communities in the United States create informal loan clubs, too.

The process works like this: Once a month, a group of people get together and contribute a designated amount of money into a pool. Then each member is allowed to withdraw the entire amount at one time. The money can be used to start a business, for a car or house loan, or to pay for college.

Baumgarte said he had an American friend in South Korea who married a South Korean woman and was very financially successful. In the South Korean culture, the wives tend to take care of the money, so his friend assumed it was being put in the bank or invested. When their son was old enough to attend university in the United States, he was shocked and angry to discover that, in fact, they had only a modest savings account. All the money he'd earned had gone to her family members in their *Hui*. But once their son had enrolled at Stanford University, little by little, all the money came trickling back to them, and they were able to pay for his tuition.

In China and other Asian countries, there's a transactional quality to friendships, in which people use their friends for work contacts or other connections. The Chinese make subtle distinctions between those friends who fall into this category and those who do

not. Sometimes, these friendships can carry over for generations—
"Your father did this for me, so I'll do this for you."

The Chinese value friendship highly and believe a good friend
is hard to find and should be treasured once you find one. An old
Chinese proverb says: "Gold is easy to get; a close friend is harder
to find." When Chinese people develop a deep bond with someone,
they remain friends for a lifetime.

Yan Ge, a novelist, was born in a small town outside Chengdu
in China. In the past, she'd gone abroad from time to time, attending literary festivals or programs as a writer-in-residence. Back then
she didn't notice many differences between her Chinese friends and
Western friends. However, when she moved to Ireland with her husband and baby about two years ago, and started to socialize, she noticed many distinctions.

"My Chineseness became one of the first things that needed to
be addressed and I, in turn, became incredibly awkward or even fake
when I talked to people. I've made a few good friends since I came
to Ireland, but most of them are literary people or a mutual friend
of someone who already knows me well. In Ireland, it's absolutely
amazing how you can just have a chat with anyone, anywhere, under any kind of circumstance. This is something I really love about
Ireland—that people can just talk to each other. My father came to
Dublin for a visit in the summer and he was really impressed by
the warm and friendly atmosphere. He said it reminded him of the
1970s and 1980s in China, the good old days. And he doesn't even
speak English. On the other hand, to develop a friendship is certainly something different."

Chapter 7

The Breakup

Stories of women who experienced the end of a friendship

Don't walk behind me;
I may not lead. Don't walk in front of me;
I may not follow.
Just walk beside me and be my friend.

—Albert Camus

OLIVIA HAD BEEN close with her college roommate for years, but one day, out of the blue, she received an email from her saying that their friendship was over. Her friend said that Olivia hadn't been a good enough friend to her, and that she hadn't made enough of an effort to see her over the years. The email came as a complete shock—Olivia never would have guessed that her friend wanted to end their relationship, or that she'd done anything wrong. They had both married and raised children, and were busy with their lives, living in separate cities. But she thought she'd made an effort to keep in touch. Olivia was distraught. They never spoke again.

"In remembering the whole thing, I think I was struck by our different approaches to friendship. I assumed that an old friendship— one that began when we were so young and in formation—didn't need the kind of maintenance other kinds of relationships require.

I thought we had settled into a comfortable, if somewhat lax, routine. I was always so happy to hear from her, no matter how much time had gone by. And I always felt an intense connection....I was wrong to think that my expectations matched hers—clearly we had different ideas about what makes a good friendship. For me, the best friendships are the ones that feel easy—no drama, no tests. There are times when I miss my old friend. But there's no going back after that kind of confrontation. I still wonder if it is appropriate to force a 'breakup' with a friend—bad relationships die a natural death, while good ones (even if the participants have different ideas of 'good')—can last forever whether they are constant or intermittent," Olivia said.

Experts say that losing our best friend may be even more devastating than breaking up with a lover—that's how significant these female friendships are.

So why do women go through breakups with their friends, while men rarely have the same experience? I wondered if all friendships had a life span: a beginning and an end? Or perhaps it varied according to who you are friends with, and what both of you need at certain times in your lives. There is no language for describing the process of ending friendships. We might use phrases like "breakup," "falling out," and "moved on" to characterize the conclusion of non-romantic relationships. But these don't really describe the pain and heartbreak that can be involved. Is it better to drift apart when that friendship is over, rather than having a clean break?

The Greek philosopher Cicero, who wrote extensively about friendship, said that if it's necessary to break with a friend, the relationship should fade away rather than be stamped out, to avoid creating hard feelings or serious personal enmity. "There is a degree of respect which we must pay to a friendship, even one that has turned sour," he said.

Robin Dunbar told me that he thought women's friendships were more fragile because they're more intense. Women can share quite a lot in common and the relationship can be extremely robust, but if one party pushes it too far, such as not being there when she's needed or not turning up when she's invited somewhere or talking about the other person behind her back, that's enough to break the relationship.

"There comes a point when it breaks catastrophically. And once broken, they break forever," said Dunbar. "Normally you run a profit and loss account. You take some from a friend and you pay them back later. But if it's uneven, if you're not buying your turn at the pub, that can cause the other person to not contact you so much. And that relationship will gradually die, in a way that family relationships don't."

Women are willing to invest heavily in a friendship, which makes friends valuable to them. They'll tolerate some mistreatment, but if there comes a point when the abuse piles up too much, that could end the friendship. Sometimes the fracture is caused by a certain amount of asymmetry in a relationship, where the other person isn't reciprocating in the same way, as Dunbar pointed out.

If someone feels like they are doing all the work and not getting any of the benefit, it can become exhausting. The reasons can also seem trivial, but since there is great intensity, one small thing can tip things over the edge. Guys, on the other hand, are not so invested in their relationships, so they don't have the same fragility, according to Dunbar, who conducted a study on relationship maintenance and decay.

In that study, Dunbar found that "the emotional intensity of friendships is more sensitive to decreases in the frequency of communication and to decreases in the number of activities done together, as compared to kin relations. Thus friendships are more costly to maintain than kin relations, and more prone to decay over time. These maintenance costs may act as a constraint on the number of relationships—and in particular on the number of friendships—that can be maintained at any given level of emotional intensity."

Dunbar also explained that to prevent the decay of a relationship, and to keep it at a particular level of emotional intensity, active maintenance is required. Kin relations, on the other hand, share genes through descent, which may provide the underpinning to create a stable, lasting basis for these relationships, compared with friendships. He also found, not surprisingly, that "well-established friendships may be more resistant to decay than more recently established friendships."

In the survey on women and friendship that Brooke Schwartz and I conducted, the results on friendship breakups were remarkable; more than *half* of all the women who answered had experienced a breakup with a female friend. Women aged 18–24 had the second-highest rate of friendship dissolution: 66 percent. Older women (aged 65–74) had the highest rate, 72 percent; presumably because they've been around longer. As part of the survey, we also asked if the women had personally experienced any mental illness; 35 percent of women who said they had a mental illness had experienced a breakup.

We also surveyed the women based on race, and those numbers came up equal for the number of breakups. Interestingly, marital status did not seem to show different breakup percentages, even though married people have a partner to rely on and could probably "afford" a breakup with a friend more than single women.

Some of the stories that the women in the survey told about their friendship breakups were heartbreaking. Even years later, these breakups were undoubtedly painful and difficult to bear. One woman said, "I don't want to talk about it." Another said, "MY

NOW EX DIDN'T LIKE HER SO I DROPPED HER. I CANNOT
BELIEVE WHAT AN IDIOT I WAS."

Here are more responses from the survey:

*"We were going to live together and I backed out. The
friendship was already in a bad place, so I think the
break-up happened as a result of ongoing arguments and
this big event."*

*"She was just really rude and selfish and I put up with it
for way too long. I got tired of it despite us having grown
up together and let her go. She still tries to contact me but
I refuse to respond."*

*"We were both going through trying times. She had just
had a miscarriage, I had medical problems. Miscommunication and high emotions caused the break."*

*"She ruined my wedding by making a huge scene, talking
about me and my husband behind our backs leading up
to it."*

*"I found out my friend was lying to me. She was jealous
of the time I was spending with my boyfriend and so she
said some things that were not true to try to break us up.
I found out the truth and told her that I could not be
around her because of her lies."*

*"She was someone I met online and we became really close.
I noticed she fought a lot with other people, though. She
would take things highly personally and then lash out in
the worst ways at others. Sometimes she did it to me. She*

was incredibly moody, and had a lot of prescriptions for mental issues. I walked away twice because she would start screaming at me, putting me down. I stopped talking to her for 2 years, and then she found me again and promised that she'd changed. But she had not changed. I knew that she would blow up again, and she did. I was diagnosed with a severe infection in one of my bones, and the treatment was expensive (I had no insurance) and was worried that I would die. I could barely get out of bed each day, I was so sick.

Then, one day I was deathly sick, so I didn't go online for 3 days. Then, my cat became ill and died. I was distraught and stayed away from everyone for a week. While I was gone, she left messages stating I was treating her horribly by ignoring her. Then she just became unglued and said she hoped that my life was hell, that I would be unhappy for the rest of my life. I never replied to her messages, never spoke to her again and never will. I could not believe someone would imagine that me being away was to hurt them, when she knew darn well that I was ill. Not once did she pick up the phone to see if I was okay; she just made it all about her and became unhinged."

Friendship Disruptors

There are many different reasons why friendships can deteriorate, said Beverly Fehr, whose specialty is interpersonal relationships.

"So much of it revolves around situational factors, such as people moving away, your friend at work takes a different job, or one or both of you is going through a life transition, such as having children or caring for an elderly parent. These are situations where you are reducing access to a friend, and that can make a friendship vulnerable to dissolution. Common ground is the glue that holds friendships together. Most people don't explicitly breakup with their friends, although there can be cataclysmic events, such as a friend betraying your trust and stating that the friendship is over. Usually, there's a drifting apart," said Fehr. "If you don't want the friendship to keep going, or you don't want to invest in the friendship any more, then you don't contact that person as often."

Divorce is another major disruptor of friendship.

Often friends are awkward when a marriage breaks up, and if the spouses had a shared friendship network, then the relationships created as a couple will often disappear. However, Fehr said she's found that with lesbians, it's much more likely that the former partner will remain friends with the same people. She felt this was because those from a stigmatized group end up having to create a familial kind of relationship with their friends, so both partners are kept in the "family."

Being at different life stages is another predictor of friendships falling apart.

When you don't have that much in common anymore, such as one person is preoccupied with babies and changing diapers while the other one is checking out the latest nightclubs, then the relationship may fade. Sometimes, we might even get tired of listening to our friend's problems.

Other times, the break can be caused by miscommunication and misunderstandings; that's what happened once with a good friend and myself. She'd taken a new job, had a new boyfriend and three kids to take care of, and was busy. I was also preoccupied with family and work. We hadn't really talked to or seen each other for a couple of months, and it seemed like whenever I asked her to get together, she was busy. So I stopped trying, thinking maybe she was done with our friendship.

A little while later, I was surprised to receive a text from her saying that she felt like our friendship was shallow and that there was too much negativity in it. She offered to talk to me about it if I wanted to. I called her that day and, as we spoke, I realized that we both seemed to be feeling the same way about each other—we felt like the other person didn't want to be friends anymore—but for some reason, neither of us had thought to bring it up. I told her that I still wanted to be her friend, and she said she felt the same way.

We decided that we needed to have at least a weekly phone check-in with each other, to catch up. It helped to talk about how we were feeling, and to work on keeping the connection between us strong. And I was glad that, instead of walking away from the friendship, we decided to resolve the conflict. Now I feel like our relationship is stronger than ever for working through it.

Nearly every woman seems to have a story about a friendship breakup.

And there are countless books on the topic, including *The Friend Who Got Away: Twenty Women's True-Life Tales of Friendships That Blew Up, Burned Out, or Faded Away,* edited by Jenny Offill and Elissa Schappell, in which fiction writers described what happened when they lost a good friend. The essays were full of confusion, sadness, regret, and loss. In two of the essays, close friends chronicled what happened between them when one of their mothers became ill and died while they were in college—telling both sides of the story.

A similar thing happened to Joanne, who said that her relationship with her friend, Sandra, suffered when her own mother died. They had known each other for many years and were extremely close.

"We were very different, but the same in many ways. We even had the same birthday—July 4th. My mother died when I was 37, and I had a very hard time. And when it happened, she wasn't there for me. She just disappeared," Joanne recalled.

Joanne knew that her friend's father had died when she was 11, and she believed that her own mother getting sick was all just too much for Sandra. But she didn't feel the need to talk it over with her girlfriend; they were close enough that she just forgave her: "One of your great fears is losing your mother. I think it was too close to the bone for her; she couldn't deal with me losing my mother. Another friend was appalled about what she'd done, but I understood. There's nothing better than having a close friend, but the other side of that is, sometimes it's too hard. Sometimes women seem to merge their life with their friend's life....I don't need understanding of what happened between us. She's always been a generous, caring friend to me and we're still close."

There is very little research on friendship breakups between women (probably because most researchers are men).

Dr. Katie Jalma, a psychologist in Minnesota, conducted a study on the subject in 2008. She recorded the experiences of fifteen women who had ended a same-sex friendship, and found that the process caused them feelings of grief and loss, as well as feelings of freedom and strength. She found that the dissolution of their friendship was an important experience in the lives of the participants, and many of the women sought counseling because of the breakup.

"I was so shocked that there wasn't more research out there, since this is such an impactful human experience for women," said Jalma. "In my early twenties, I had some very profound female friendships. A couple of them ended, and it impacted me in a way that romantic relationships ending didn't. I started to realize that I wasn't the only one who felt this way. So I thought, let's look at what happens with relational aggression in adults. We talk about cattiness, and hostile workplaces—I was interested in the intimate friendship experience. It was a personal interest; I wanted to know how it happened and why it's so important for women, and why it's so different for men."

While she was in graduate school, Jalma began to look into studying friendship dissolution. Her female professors thought it was a great idea; her adviser, a man, didn't understand the importance of the subject. But she did it anyway.

Jalma says she was struck by the fact that, of the fifteen women she interviewed, fourteen had been the ones who had ended their friendship. That made her realize that it's easier to talk about the relationship that you end, rather than about being left. Some women ended it with friends they'd had for thirty years.

"The amount of pain I bore witness to was striking to me. There was a tremendous amount of emotional investment in these relationships, and there was real grief over their ending," Jalma said. "What struck me was this waking up. Some women experienced relief at being liberated from toxic friendship. A number of women had dynamics in their friendship that were unhealthy, and that surprised them. They couldn't understand how they'd entered into a relationship where their friend was so awful to them on a regular basis."

Women have a need for intimate connections, because they make us feel grounded and safe. It is through connection that we calm our central nervous system—but connection is both a vulnerability and a gift. While we have an inherent need to feel emotionally connected, we may at times overlook pieces of our friendships that may not be a good fit, in order to have this need met.

In her study, Jalma examined aggression within the young female social world and found that it may actually *increase* as young women age. She also found that, surprisingly, women don't always feel sad about a friendship breakup, nor do they always experience grief.

"Perhaps friendship, like most relationships in life, has a time to end. This further suggests that when the time to dissolve a friendship is approached in nonhurtful and communicative interactions, women are allowed to disengage and move into the next phase of their lives with a clearer understanding of themselves," said Jalma.

She believes that being self-aware about why the friendship is ending could help women process the experience in healthier ways.

A number of participants in Jalma's study reported experiencing "red flags" early on in their friendships: warning signs that something ambiguous or negative was afoot within the friendship dynamic:

> "Later it was something that we joked about, like, 'Oh remember when you were jealous of me for no good reason?' I guess I didn't think about it at the time, but it should have been a red flag of what kind of person she was and how she dealt with people."

> "Like in retrospect, that was probably something I should have paid more attention to, but at the time, I wasn't in a place to really pay attention to it. You know? I wasn't feeling good about myself, about my life. I was in a friendship with someone who was at my same level of health, if that makes sense. You know, you find people who are the people that you are sort of equal to emotionally and where I was at that time. That is it. We fit together in that way."

Jalma said that the women's experiences showed that many of them had a sense of intuition that their friendships were in jeopardy. They pointed to various reasons for the breakups, including disagreement with a friend's interpersonal style, aggression in the relationship, disrespect, and an attempt to connect romantically with her partner.

Many of the participants described feeling irritation, frustration, and disagreement with their friend's way of interacting with other people. One woman said her other friends repeatedly commented on the harshness of her friend's interpersonal style; another said she became increasingly frustrated with her friend's tendency to consistently dominate the conversation.

Here's how one woman from the study described her former friend:

> "And then we were in this group. I mean, she has a lot of opinions. This is so hard to explain. I don't even know how to explain it. She read something in the group that offended me. Really offended me. It wasn't about me, but it was about some people that I knew who she had made a judgment about which I thought was totally wrong. And I sat there and I listened to it and when she got through reading it something went off in my head like 'We're done. We are done. I never want to see this woman again as long as I live.'"

Aggression between mothers who meet at their children's schools is a phenomenon unto itself. One participant in Jalma's study talked about the experience of being "shunned" by other mothers from her daughter's middle school:

> "This whole middle school Mom thing—so I'm kind of shunned now by these Moms who are sympathizing with [another woman] and I'm finally going yeah, I don't really want to play. I don't really care if it blows over. This isn't how I function."

Participants were also asked how they knew the friendship was going to end. Here's one response:

> "I didn't. Then my friend called and asked me to get together for coffee because she wanted to 'talk.' I thought,

'I hope everything is okay.' So we met. I got there and I said, 'What's up?' And she said, 'I cannot be your friend anymore.' It was just like that. I was just blown away. It was the absolute last thing I was expecting. I was devastated. We had this whole long conversation. She said that ever since I went abroad and then came back... right around that time, she just kind of decided in her mind that I wasn't really her friend anymore, just more like this cousin that she always had to deal with who was always there. I said, 'I thought you were my best friend.' I couldn't understand this shift that had happened. I didn't even know that she was having all of these problems with our friendship."

Ten years after conducting her study, Jalma said she looks back and realizes that these women really loved their friends; the endings really did feel like breakups. She believes they lost a part of themselves when their relationships ended, and in some ways, the experience redefined how they saw themselves, and how they would handle future friendships.

While these breakups may feel similar to romantic relationships that don't work, Jalma said she was surprised at how few skills we are given to navigate friendships that fall apart—we have a language about ending romantic relationships, but we don't for friendships. That may be because the traditional premise is that you will be friends forever. Jalma believes that we need better training in emotional intelligence to navigate a friendship, as well as to potentially end one—especially for teenaged girls.

"How could we educate kids about what healthy friendships look like, and how you protect yourself and act appropriately mature, so you can get your needs met? How do you appropriately end a relationship when it's not working?" she asked. "Forming friendships and ending them is part of our formative experiences from fifth to eighth grade. If that could be done with more respect and kindness, that could take away from the insecurity and self-doubt that some women feel about themselves. And it could help stop some bullying. Those dynamics still exist; women are still doing those things with each other."

Dr. Laura Eramian, a social anthropologist at Dalhousie University in Canada, is also one of only a handful of researchers looking at the topic of friendship dissolution.

Eramian began studying the subject along with her husband, Peter Mallory, a sociologist at St. Francis Xavier University in Canada. While they found some literature on friendship, they could find very little on what happens when these relationships fall apart. Eramian said they wanted to "find out about the effects of failed friendships on people's lives and sense of themselves, and also what it means to lose a friend."

The couple has been interviewing women and men aged 22–65 in the Halifax area of Canada to find these answers. Eramian found three main themes underlying failed friendships: an imbalance in reciprocity, mismatched expectations of a friendship, and having more than one type of relationship with someone, such as being co-workers or roommates as well, which complicates matters.

"It's an understudied area. Friendship has long been seen as a less important relationship than marital relationships or families. There's an assumption that it matters less to people, but that's not the case at all. These breakups can be just as painful as divorces," she said. "From an anthropological or sociological point of view, we can't understand the self without understanding our relationships. So if we become who we are through our relationships, what happens when our relationships break down?"

What occurs after a breakup is that people begin to have a lot of self-doubt; they question what kind of people they are, and whether there is something fundamentally wrong with them. According to Eramian, both men and women equally had problems in their friendships that they didn't know how to handle. Eramian believes, however, that gender shapes people's response to difficult friendships.

It's difficult to resolve issues in a friendship because, while you're supposed to be able to talk about anything with a friend, there's an unwritten rule that you're not supposed to talk about the actual *friendship,* which is supposed to be a refuge from those relationships that take "work" to sustain. (This is something that I've found in my own friendships—at times, I've wanted to talk to a friend about something that bothered me, but I didn't feel comfortable talking about our relationship with her.)

Eramian says that the men they interviewed were more explicit that they shouldn't talk to their male friends about any issues between them. But when men and women do talk about their difficult friendships, they tend to do it in gender-specific ways; that is, men hang out and don't talk about serious things, while women are generally more talkative and open with each other.

Since friendships are supposed to be stable, dependable forms of support, ones that are purely voluntary, when you're rejected in a friendship, it can feel deeply personal. Eramian believes these relationships involve many contradictions; they're supposed to be solid and steady, but they can also be fragile and fleeting.

My friend, Catherine, had a close childhood friend for many years. This woman was also the daughter of her parents' good friends, so they were bonded through their families as well. But as they became teenagers, Catherine started noticing that her friend, Lee Anne, would subtly put her down whenever they were together.

"We were very close friends, beginning in third grade. Even though I loved being with her, I often felt that she put me down, pointing out things about my personality and appearance that she felt were either problematic or just noticing things—but it made me feel uncomfortable. Over the years I spoke to her about it, that I didn't like how she did this, but she couldn't stop. She was very popular and fun and we had a good time together so I stayed friends with her for a long time. She even introduced me to my husband. But eventually, in my late twenties I had had enough; the relationship was making me feel bad, and I decided to stop being her friend. A challenge was that my parents and her parents had become very close because of our long relationship. My parents had to figure out how to handle the situation, which I'm sure was uncomfortable for them at the time but now—twenty years later, they see each other occasionally."

Catherine said that, in the last five years, a mutual friend reached out to both of them, and today they are reacquainted and things are starting to thaw between them.

"When I see her, I remember what a good time we had together, and I miss her and wonder if I made the right choice. On the other hand, as I look back I feel a little proud of myself for ending a relationship with someone who was often putting me down," said Catherine.

Eramian and her husband also found that friendships are supposed to be based on equality within the relationship, such as time, energy, and material exchanges. "If one friend feels they are giving more in the way of material gifts or emotional support or energy than the other person, that can cause problems," she said. While we're supposed to like a friend mainly for who they are, we also depend on them for usefulness, for their material and emotional support. These contradictions can give rise to conflicts, and then, to breakups. Eramian and her husband were not convinced, however, that difficult people are the cause of friendship problems; they believe these fundamental tensions found in relationships are to blame.

A main source of stress for those involved in friendship breakups is when they don't understand why a friend has exited their lives—it's the not knowing why the relationship failed that really hurts.

Nowadays, we call the practice of disappearing from a friend (or lover's) life, *ghosting,* but people have been disappearing on their friends for a long time. And as my survey results showed, there doesn't seem to be a difference in the ages of people who have suffered a failed friendship; it happens to everyone. Eramian's research also backs this up.

So why is it that some relationships are strong as iron, while others fail?

One study found that most middle school friendships are doomed to fall apart by the time the friends are seniors in high school. The reason? The kids' differences eventually drive them apart. For example, unpopular kids' friendships with popular kids just don't last. Do crucial differences extend to friendships in adulthood as well?

Anthony Giddens, a British sociologist, has talked about the idea of the fateful moment—"when individuals are called on to take decisions that are particularly consequential for their ambitions, or more generally for their future lives." These could be births, deaths, moves, divorce; sometimes they can strengthen friendships, sometimes they can break them apart. They can also be moments of cultural contradictions in friendships that have become more apparent and more problematic.

Respondents to my survey found that an imbalance in the relationship can cause it to end:

> *"I had what I thought was a good friend until I realized that I was always there when she needed me, which she expected of me, but that she was rarely or never available*

if I needed help with something or a shoulder to lean on. Gradually, she stopped contacting me, except when she needed something from me. I did not explicitly end the friendship, but I distanced myself from her more and more until we eventually stopped seeing each other or talking altogether."

Here's another example:

"Maybe not a breakup, but we just grew apart. I got married and had kids and moved to the suburbs. She is single and dating in NY. I sort of feel that she thinks we don't have anything in common anymore. But I'd still have liked to continue the friendship."

While many women have experienced a friendship breakup, as Jalma said there are surprisingly few, if any, rituals for ending a friendship or for moving on. Of the women she interviewed for her study, some women had had no conversations about the breakup; they just stopped communicating with their friend. Others said they'd had a phone call or an email or a talk, but they all experienced pain. Jalma said that, as a therapist, she believes that communicating about the problems in the relationship or the breakup is better than never talking about it. "I think the women who were able to say, 'I described why I changed the boundaries [in our friendship],' had a better understanding of themselves moving forward."

Of her own friendship breakup experience, Jalma said she and her friend never discussed what had happened. The lack of communication left her questioning herself: "Why did it happen? We never talked about it. That's true for any experience of abandonment. We make up a story about what happened, even if the facts are painful. If I hurt someone's feelings, it's more of a shared reality."

Jalma sees many women in her therapy practice who are dealing with friendship issues or breakups; she believes that women are taught to be needy, and when our needs are unmet, we often feel hopeless. Those who are more social and have more friends tend to experience more breakups. In some cases, when women grow up with a needy mother, they seek out friends who also need to be taken care of—because that's what they're used to. She also finds that women are afraid to talk to each other about their friendships and any issues they might have with each other.

"It feels threatening and vulnerable to do this. We are taught to be pleasing and need-less, and as we grow older with one another and our life stressors increase—such as raising children and marriage—there's a greater need to share honest feedback with each other. Are we afraid we'll hurt the other person's feelings? Or are we afraid that we won't be heard, or we'll be left? I have two friends from childhood and we're still afraid to tell each other what we're thinking. It's so ingrained in us to withhold things that could be negative or hurtful. Or we're fearful that the other person could get angry. We're given such mixed messages about befriending other women and withholding."

Jalma said she was drawn to the subject of friendship breakups, in part, because of her own experiences when she was young.

Two of her formative childhood friendships ended when she was in her twenties, and she wanted to figure out what had caused the breakups. She was bullied by the two girls, but she believes she played a role in being the victim in the relationships. While the other two had tendencies to be aggressive, she was vulnerable because she needed their validation. She felt grief and sadness when the friendships ended, but she also felt a sense of taking a deep breath and being more herself again—she said she felt calmer and happier after the relationships were over.

Toxic Friends

There are more than a dozen books on Amazon alone dealing with toxic friendships, and a plethora of articles, such as, "23 Warning Signs of a Toxic Friend," that frequently make the rounds on the internet.

Susan Shapiro Barash wrote *Toxic Friends: The Antidote for Women Stuck in Complicated Friendships* because she wanted to understand why so many friendships went awry.

"I think there are specific gender ramifications to female bonds, and the culture feeds female competition and rivalry," she said when I interviewed her. "This book was fueled by my own lifelong experiences. I'm also the mother of two daughters and a son, and when my girls were in junior high and high school, I watched how it played out. We live in a culture where women are constantly compared to one another. It's really pervasive. I spoke to so many women and it doesn't matter how educated you are or where you live; there's innate competition and sadly, often a lack of trust among friends."

In a study that she conducted about women's friendship breakups, Barash found that at least half of those interviewed said, "Can you believe what this woman did to me?" While the other half said, "What would I do without my female friend?" She also found that these friendship breakups are often a long time coming and that, according to participants in her study, it takes great courage to break up with a friend.

How do you know if you have a toxic friend? They tend to be critical and may look for ways to embarrass you or put you down. They're also good at making you feel bad about yourself. They will lack empathy for you, and might be judgmental about the choices you make in life. These women may also be resentful of your success, or your other friends, and will probably hold a grudge. They can be hard to predict; you never quite know where you stand with them. Bullying and neediness are also signs of toxic friends. Also:

- You don't enjoy hanging out with them, and feel exhausted afterward.
- You feel like you can't be yourself with them.
- You feel like the relationship is unbalanced in terms of how much each of you give.

Barash defined a toxic friend as someone who isn't really authentic and doesn't have your back. She can't be happy for you and separate your success from what she imagines she should have. A toxic friend is someone who would undermine you or steal your job or husband or boyfriend. She'd even steal your ideas. There's a lack of trust between you.

This happened to Emma. She was dating a guy in high school when she found out that her best friend was sleeping with him.

Outside of Emma's hasty, seething rebuke when she found a love letter from her boyfriend to her friend, she actually never even got confirmation that her friend had slept with him. It would have been too hurtful to hear it. Looking back now, Emma thought maybe she should have forced her friend to say out loud what she'd done with her boyfriend, to increase her shame over the betrayal. At the time, Emma felt like she portrayed herself as strong from the outside, even though the whole situation made her feel worthless and ashamed. For Emma, confrontation was intensely awkward and definitely not as easy as it looks on television dramas.

Over time, Emma forgave her friend. After all, they were adolescents at the time. But perhaps because it occurred during such a formative time of her life, the memory of it still rankles her. Or maybe because it was her first experience with betrayal by a trusted friend and a guy she liked. In the end, their friendship bond formed prior to the betrayal won out over her friend's disregard for her. They never really talked about it.

Often women make excuses for a toxic friend, such as, "We share so many friends in common" or "I've known her all my life." Barash said that when you're raised to be a "good girl," it's hard not to have a good friend, so you'll stick with her. By the time you're ready for a breakup, it really *is* like a divorce. Barash believes that life circumstances can have a negative effect on our friendships, such as having a good friend's marriage breakup while you're still married, or having a friend who is single and works long hours while you've moved to the suburbs and had a baby.

According to Barash, there are different types of toxic friends:

The misery lover—she's there when you're down and out;
    say your cat died, your boyfriend left, you lost your job,
    and there she is. But when things start to improve for
    you, she disappears.
The user—you might invite her to get to know your group
    of friends, and then she proceeds to take over and steal
    them.
The gossip—"It's very cruel to be a frenemy. You're really
    speaking against the person in a very unhealthy way.
    They act like they're cheering for you and they're not.
    They're trying to sabotage you."
The taker—Barash cautioned about a friend who is a bla-
    tant taker; she can't be there for you when you need
    her. In times of great sorrow and great happiness we
    often get to see who our true friends are. When the
    behavior becomes most pronounced, that's when
    women will often decide to leave the friendship

Barash said women will give up a bad husband faster than a terri-ble friend. Why? She believes there's a romanticized view of women's friendship—and women really miss the friends they're not seeing.

What should you do if you're in one of these relationships?

Barash recommended having a sincere conversation about what worked or what didn't and how you can both be more respectful of each other and have better boundaries. Sometimes it's hard to break free. You have to ask yourself: What is it about this friend that makes me stay with her? What is going on that the two of us are locked in this dance? What am I getting from the friendship? Barash said we need to ask ourselves the same questions that we'd ask of a love relationship, such as, is this relationship emotionally rewarding?

"Female friendship is riveting. It's profound. We look to our friends for different reasons; these friends fill different parts of our lives," Barush said. "But the toxic friend is so hard to handle, face and fix. They can take our breath away."

Barash explained that it takes a lot of soul searching and courage to end a friendship. We need our female friends, but when one is toxic, it's time to end it.

My friend, Sonya, had two close friends that she worked with at a magazine in New York City when they were in their thirties. They spent a lot of time together, traveling, going to dinner and movies, and just hanging out. But one of the friends, Helen, started at times to withdraw from the threesome. She would make plans with Sonya, then break them at the last minute. And she made comments about the time that the other two were spending together; she seemed jealous of their relationship.

One night, when Sonya and Helen had plans to get together for dinner, Helen called Sonya while she was on her way to meet her and said she'd decided not to go out after all. That was the last straw; Sonya told her friend that she needed a break from the friendship. That was four years ago. "I love her, miss her, and hope the best for her," said Sonya. "But after trying many times to iron it out with her, I finally I had to pull away." She doesn't think she's ready to rekindle the friendship.

"Being in a friendship with someone who makes us feel badly about ourselves is not easy; you're always on a rollercoaster. It's hard to navigate immaturity in adult relationships," said Jalma. "They don't own their negative emotions."

If a friend is ignoring her inability to process her negative experience of the world, she may be using her friendship as a buffer to her own distress. Rather than being vulnerable and saying "I'm so upset that this is happening," or "I feel rejected when you don't say hi to me first," she might become aggressive. For her, your actions seem to turn into a critique of her. It requires a level of maturity for her to process her feelings, and she just may not have this emotional security.

Sometimes, people can use rejection or withholding of an emotional connection to hold a person hostage to do what they want them to do. In marriage, this is called emotional abuse—and it's the same with friends. It can be hard to free yourself from a toxic friendship, but many women say that when they finally do, they feel greatly relieved.

Other times, mental illness can play a factor in toxic friends. For instance, according to Jalma, women who suffer from borderline personality disorder—a mental illness characterized by unstable moods, behavior, and relationships—lack a solid sense of self, and every interaction is a potential for rejection. They tend to be needy and critical and feel frustrated much of the time. Their needs never seem to be met—and they probably suffered some kind of trauma as a child.

"Setting boundaries makes so much sense with these people. That's the control you have in these relationships. But at some point you might have to say, 'I'm not going to tolerate this anymore,'" Jalma said. "When you're close to someone who is mentally ill, it can feel kind of shocking. It's very disorienting."

She likens these relationships to domestic abuse situations, and she gives the metaphor of frogs boiling in a pot. The frogs start in the pot when the water is room temperature, and as the temperature rises and the water starts to boil, the frogs don't jump out because they've acclimated to the water as it heats up. "You start to look around and you're shocked that you can't be yourself with this person."

So is it better to let a friendship fade away, or to have a formal break?

Drifting apart only works if you both feel the same way about the relationship. If you don't, you might have to actually end it. Suzanne Degges-White, the author of *Toxic Friendships: Knowing the Rules and Dealing with the Friends Who Break Them,* said that women should avoid texting friendship breakup messages. She suggested they instead speak to their friend face-to-face about what is going on, even though a conversation of this kind can be awkward and uncomfortable. Being open and honest about your feelings, and using "I statements" when discussing what went wrong is best, such as, "I feel like we've been growing apart for some time now," or "I don't feel like our relationship has been positive for me lately." It's also a good idea to talk about the positive aspects of your friendship, and how much you've valued it.

According to Degges-White, there are different levels of friendship: activity friends, convenience friends, and intimate friends, and they all play an important part in our lives. Sometimes, women may find that they no longer have much in common with the friends they made when their kids were small, for instance. One woman said that while her neighbors were lovely people, she was not sure she would spend time with them if they didn't all have kids around the same age.

Is it unrealistic to think that the friends we have now will be our friends for life? Childhood and college friends can last a lifetime— and they don't necessarily need to be seen or talked to frequently in order to keep the friendship going. That's certainly been the case for me. I know that Denise, my best friend from grade school will always be my good friend, even if we don't see each other for a whole year. And my friends from college will always be in my life, even if we don't talk as frequently as we used to.

But experts say that the friends you make after college will not always last. Sometimes people outgrow each other, or change. Of course, moving away can end a friendship, especially if it was never that strong to begin with. When a friend's values change significantly, and they no longer align with yours, that may also be a sign that the friendship will soon end.

Jalma's study asked participants whether they had any contact with their former friends after the breakup. The majority of participants reported wanting to keep distance and space from them. One woman described a lingering confusion and anxiety regarding how she would talk to her former friend if they were to pass on the street.

> "It [the friendship breakup] was such a profound experience, even to this day. I still have an old address book that has her name and phone number in it and I try to skip past that page as quickly as I can. I don't know if I could say anything to her. What could I say at this point? Really. I search in my mind, what could I say?"

Another woman described the intense feelings of liberation she had after breaking up with a friend. They had been in a hobby group together, and when she announced that she was leaving the group, her friend became upset. This is her description of how she felt after their last meeting:

> "It felt good. It felt good. I thought yep. I know we're done. She knows we're done. It's very clear. And if this is how she's going to get through it that's fine with me. It was fine

with me. *And everybody else was just sociable, friendly, and I mean, it was a little bit weird. But as I say, it was right in my neighborhood. It was about three blocks away and so toward the end of it I left and I just said 'I gotta go' and everyone said 'Oh great, well we'll see you' and they were all people I knew—so it wasn't like I was never going to see them again or anything.*

So I left. I walked out of the house and I was flying. I was gleeful. It was like I was standing back watching myself and I was like 'what is this about' and I'm just going 'Yes! I am out of this!' and I did. I danced all the way home. It was so weird. It was totally weird. And I just felt like I had been released from something. I mean, that again seems weird to me. That whole incident seems weird to me like, Wow! I was feeling way more oppressed than I realized because to feel that kind of freedom from someone. I'm free of her. I never have to speak to her again as long as I live if I don't want to. So strange. So that makes me think that when I recognized whatever it was that was going on I really felt imprisoned in some way."

Chapter 8

Friending and Unfriending
How technology is changing friendship

I fear the day that technology will surpass our human interaction. The world will have a generation of idiots.

—Albert Einstein

WHEN FACEBOOK STARTED up, I was thrilled that I could connect with my old friends from high school, with whom I had lost touch for many years. We excitedly exchanged messages for a few weeks, and talked about getting together, and then...it all just fizzled. Now, we just wish each other happy birthday once a year and occasionally comment on each other's pictures of our kids.

For many of us, the shift to online relationships, texting, and Facebook is changing the way we deal with friendships.

We are more connected to one another than ever before as a result of social media and text messaging, and we might even have three hundred or more "friends" on Facebook (that's the average for typical US teenagers). But advances in technology are affecting these relationships, for better or for worse. In some ways, we are lonelier and less bonded with our friends; that's because social media can make it difficult to create deep, intimate relationships. Social-networking sites let us maintain relationships with those pals who are more peripheral, by messaging or status updates, rather than allowing the friendship to drift apart. But who has time for all that? No wonder we feel as though there aren't enough hours in the day.

"It's instructive to remember that we've been homo sapiens for two hundred thousand years and our biology has adapted to a certain way of interacting with human beings that's based on touch and visual connections as well as on play, and on auditory and visual interactions. The phenomenon of social media is only about fifteen years old—the term wasn't even used until 2004. If you look at this perspective, it becomes clear that this is a rapid shift to a very different kind communication," said Dr. Brian Primack, director of the University of Pittsburgh's Center for Research on Media, Technology, and Health and a physician who is an expert on the effects of media and technology on health. "That doesn't mean that it's always inferior, just that it's an extreme shift. Fifteen years ago, there were zero social media users in the world, and now there are two billion. Twenty years ago, we spent zero hours a day interacting on social media, and now we spend nearly three hours a day."

It's a cautionary tale.

While many people think social media will enable them to have stronger relationships and be more socially connected, the opposite is actually true. Studies show that people who frequently use social media tend to be more socially isolated, more depressed, and more anxious. Which doesn't mean that every person will become despondent by being on Facebook, but the more time spent online, the less time there is for real-world social interactions.

In some ways, we are more disconnected from each other, and in others we are not.

Many people who spend a lot of time on social media are getting a distorted view of the world. When people watch an ad for BMW, they recognize that the person in the ad is an actor and he's getting paid to sell something. But when we see our social media feeds from our friends, we think of them as real people—we don't realize that what they're posting is incredibly curated and created—we just see people smiling at a party or an event together. We don't know that three of the people in the photo are having a miserable time and think the other people don't like them, for instance. We don't appreciate that the person who is posting the wonderful thing that happened to him may actually be depressed.

Teens and Social Media

Primack said that teenagers who go on Instagram and Snapchat and other sites aren't looking at the pictures that they're in; they're looking at the five photos they're *not* in. People think "everyone else is doing great and having a great time, but I'm not." But that's just not true. Kids will say, "Mom, everyone's been invited to these parties but me. See, he's been invited to parties." But this is not a healthy way for kids to feel about themselves.

In one study, it was found (not surprisingly), that people tended to put their best foot forward while interacting on social media, with few displaying emotional weakness or insecurity. On sites such as Facebook, conflicts tended to be concealed or minimized, and the result is that those unreal "status reports" make it difficult to create substantive relationships with others.

Another study found that technology had a negative effect on both the quality and quantity of face-to-face communication and friendship, and had begun to take the place of in-person communication. Experts fear that people are becoming too immersed in the digital world and not present enough in the real world—and this situation is most evident in teenagers.

To combat the negative effects of all this technology, some families have implemented internet "sabbaths," in which no video games, computers, or smartphones can be used. Some restaurants have even banned the use of mobile devices so that customers can enjoy their meals and their company.

Research has found that even the presence of a cell phone can interfere with human relationships; one study found that conversations conducted while a mobile phone was present—but not in use— were reported as inferior and had lower levels of empathy expressed compared with those where a device was not apparent.

Even more troubling were the effects of technology on youth who have grown up with the internet.

These children showed a significant reduction in face-to-face interactions, and a recent study found that this could eventually have "significant consequences for their development of social skills and their presentation of self."

Predictably, a researcher for Microsoft found the opposite was true; he said that digital communication actually enhanced relationships and that "the evidence consistently shows that the more you communicate with people using devices, the more likely you are to communicate with those people face-to-face."

There are, of course, some positives related to being on social media.

It enables us to keep in touch with family and friends who might be far away or in different time zones. It also allows us to share important events in our lives with people that we care about. People might be more open on social media than they would be in real life. And social media could enable you to have more meaningful conversations when you see people because you can use a Facebook post as a jumping-off point.

Still, the study found that "nearly half of survey respondents communicate more frequently with friends and family via technology than in person, indicating that face-to-face interactions have decreased both in quality and in quantity."

Social Networking: Good or Bad?

In my survey on women and friendship, ambivalence toward social media was evident. Strikingly, many of the women surveyed had more than four hundred friends on Facebook. While we can get hung up on the number of friends we have on social media, according to Primack the truth is that having five or six close friends may trump having more than a few hundred Facebook friends.

The answers to the survey question below were decidedly mixed, with more women giving a negative response:

For those who use social media, how does it impact your friendships with women, both positively or negatively, if at all?

Here are some of the responses:

> *"Social media makes me think some women that I am friends with are happier than they actually are."*

> *"Positively: it's easier to keep up with what is going on in each other's lives and interact on a daily basis. You can share news, recipes, photos, interesting articles, memes. Negatively: it's easy to get annoyed with someone if you find their social media habits frustrating."*

> *"I hate it. Aside from my close friends, there are women I was fairly friendly with, but seeing their social media feed showed a side of them I did not know existed. The majority are petty, childish and attention-seeking. I don't deal with that."*

> *"I love social media. I have found a lot of close friends because of social media. It has been a life changer for me.*

I am way more outgoing on social media than I am in real life."

"I'm on a Facebook chat often talking to female friends about work, and we share all sorts of things we are going through. It's nice because you can reach a lot of people at once, rather than being able to only talk to one friend a day."

"It allows me to get closer more easily—I can be a little reticent, but I use Facebook to have a deeper conversation, which I find leads to deeper in-person conversations. Social media has impacted my friends positively, with being able to keep up and congratulate or console a friend no matter where I am, but also negatively, by not liking the type of information/stories/drama that a friend posts."

Primack agreed that there are situations where people can form strong relationships online, if people find the right kind of connection, and if they're honest with each other. This is especially true in cases where people feel isolated, or if they're struggling with something like a rare disease. If someone feels like he's the only person in Cleveland who has his illness, and he is able to go online and connect with someone in another city who has the same experience, then he might feel like he's not alone. Being ill is one situation where the advent of social media can be a wonderful thing.

"The problem is that the kinds of friendships people form online are highly superficial. A lot of people in today's world are friends with people they've never actually met before. On their profile, they like the same bands, or they have the same politics. They might both be alumni of the same college, but they never actually met face to

face. We've found that there are associations between these characteristics and depression," explained Primack.

The Center for Research on Media, Technology and Health has
been studying people's overall happiness and friend composition in relation to social media. It has found that people who used social media
to leverage the friendships they already had—that is, with people they'd
met in person or who they saw day-to-day—were happier. On the other
hand, according to Primack, people who had friends online and used
social media to communicate with those they didn't know—those people were generally less happy, though he added that perhaps they were
already depressed and were trying to expand their circle of friends.

Friendships Fall Apart

The paradox that research has found regarding social media and
technology makes sense.

Social media and technology can be a great way for people to
come together over shared interests—or it can be a way for friendships to fall apart.

Hayley, 25, was excited the morning after she texted five of her
closest friends. *Time* magazine had chosen as its 2017 person of the
year The Silence Breakers—the women and men who came forward
with their stories about pervasive sexual harassment part of the #me
too movement.

"I said, 'This is so awesome! You should all watch the video that
goes along with it, it's amazing!'" she remembered.

But their response wasn't what she expected. One of her friends
said she was sick of all the sexual harassment claims and thought
it was a joke; another friend agreed and wrote "LOL." Hayley was
shaken by their responses; these were two of her closest friends
whom she had known for years—how could their values be so different from hers? How could she be friends with people who were so
ignorant? She was so upset that she immediately left the group chat.

She talked to her best friend about what had happened, explaining how shocked she was by what her friends had said, and their lack of remorse.

"I felt like something had to be said, so I decided to post about it on Facebook—something I rarely do. I felt like if I had texted with them about it, it would've turned into a mundane argument. I wouldn't have been able to get my point across," she said. "But it was a little scary."

Here's what she posted:

Today, after posting the Time Magazine People of the Year article in a group with my friends, one of them responded, "Can I be honest? I'm so over all the harassment allegations. It's absurd— literally a new one everyday it's sort of a joke." To which a second friend responded "Agreed lol."

I very rarely post but the fact that two people I call my best friends can belittle something that I find to be such an issue in our culture today completely shocks me. If they feel this way, I'm sure hundreds of other people I surround myself with do as well.

Privilege. That's all I can think of when it comes to situations like this. Two very privileged white females seemingly blinded by their privilege, completely ignorant to the fact that their family and friends have had to deal with the abuse and harassment they think is "sort of a joke." The lack of remorse, compassion and understanding is disgusting.

I hope if you're reading this and feel the same as these two friends, you take the time to read about the abuse and harassment the women and men in the Time's People of the Year have suffered (as well as so many others.) It's unimaginable.

Hayley received more than two hundred "likes" for this post.

Both of her friends that she referred to immediately messaged her about post. They were mad. They said she hadn't given them a chance to explain and were upset that she'd blasted them on social media. (Hayley never mentioned their names, or any identifying information.)

The friend who wrote the original text message about being so "over" the harassment allegations, sent her another message, saying that she regretted that Hayley had taken it as far as she had. She defended her original message, and said that it seemed like every day there was a new accusation—but that she did consider it a serious subject.

When Hayley and I spoke, she hadn't talked to either friend in more than a month.

"It's been a long time coming. I think we'll be friends again, but I don't think I'll be that close with them. There's been a change in values since we graduated college and I guess this is the icing on the cake," she said.

While that was the most dramatic instance of a social media squabble that she'd experienced, Hayley said that, in her experience, texting is often fraught with miscommunication and mistakes; she feels that even her boyfriend might perceive a tone in a text from her that wasn't there: "He'll say, you used a period in your text—or he'll read it differently than I meant it. I'll tell him, 'if you want to get my tone right, then talk to me over the phone!'"

Hayley explained that sometimes she was typing fast because she was in a meeting at work, so she didn't have time to add an extra word or an exclamation point. Even her roommate has gotten upset sometimes if she texted her to buy toilet paper, for instance. "I feel like I have to add smiley face emojis so people don't think I'm annoyed—I'm just asking!"

By the way, Hayley has 1,267 Facebook friends—that number is actually smaller than the amount she had before she did a major purge of people she wouldn't talk to again, right after she graduated from high school. She told me she's probably on social media about three and a half hours each day; mainly on Instagram, Snapchat, and Facebook, and occasionally Twitter. She's mostly on Instagram now that they added the ability to include "stories" on their site. (This feature allows users to share all the moments of their day in photos or video format, not just the ones they want to keep on their profile. They appear together in a slideshow format as "your story.")

What Did You Say? How Tone Changes Things

As Hayley discovered, misinterpreting tone in a text message or email happens all the time.

The comedians Keegan-Michael Key and Jordan Peele have a very funny comedy sketch about the problem, called "Text Message Confusion," in which Key is texting Peele about getting together for drinks that night. He's frustrated that Peele hasn't been answering his texts:

> *I've been trying to reach out to you all day—are we on for tonight?*

Peele texts back:

> *Sorry dude, missed your texts. I assumed we'd meet at the bar. Whatever. I don't care.*

Key reads the text as though it was written in a snide, flippant tone (which it wasn't), and gets more and more angry as the text exchanges continue. When they finally meet at the bar, Key, enraged by now, shows up with a baseball bat with nails embedded in it; Peele is completely oblivious to any conflict between them.

Their sketch is a perfect example of how people can get the wrong idea about tone. Without hearing vocal inflection and seeing facial expressions when people speak, it's impossible to communicate accurately and understand someone's intention in a message. Even emojis can be misinterpreted. That's why, sometimes, it's better to pick up the phone.

But these days, even making a phone call has changed. I used to call my friends all the time to ask a question, make plans, or just to say hi, but today it feels strange to pick up the phone to do that because people are so used to texting. If I want to call someone, I tend to text first and make an appointment to talk on the phone. When did phone calls become so formal?

Hearing someone's voice on the phone isn't the same as seeing a friend in person, but it's the next best thing. Social media and texting are not.

Stacy's best friend of ten years broke up with her in a text. She told her that Stacy had been draining and exhausting as a friend, and that she couldn't be her best self around Stacy anymore because she irritated her. Stacy was devastated and still can't figure out what she'd done wrong. Since online friends are easier to come by, are we more likely today to walk away from problem relationships?

Social Media and Depression

In a groundbreaking 2016 study conducted by Primack and his colleagues, the link between social media use and depression among US young adults was examined. Keep in mind that 90 percent of young adults in the United States use social media, with most visiting sites once a day or more. They spend 20 percent of their time online on social media and 30 percent when they are on their mobile phones. The researchers surveyed 1,787 adults aged 19–32 on their use of social media sites, including Facebook, Twitter, Google+, Instagram, Tumblr, Snapchat, and Vine.

The study found that social media use was significantly associated with increased depression and that "given the proliferation of social media, identifying the mechanisms and direction of this association is critical for informing interventions that address social media use and depression."

Primack says we should be concerned that, on average, teens spend *forty full days* a year interacting on social media. That's a lot of time. And that kind of focused attention changes all kinds of things—how we think cognitively and how we learn. There are physical changes as well; people have rapid thumb movements that they have developed through texting. Are those movements beneficial in any way? To be sure, social media is probably replacing some of the time we spend with our friends; two hours and forty-five minutes a day has to be taking the place of something. Primack said that the center has studied Facebook interactions versus real-world exchanges and has found that people meeting their friends face-to-face are much happier. We are social beings, and Facebook makes us feel empty.

And in fact, a recent study found that, overall, the use of Facebook was negatively associated with well-being. For example, clicking "like" on someone else's content, hitting a link to another site or article, or updating one's own Facebook status was associated with a decrease of 5 percent to 8 percent in self-reported mental health.

Even the brains of people who have lots of friends on Facebook appear to be different from those with fewer social media connections.

Researchers at University College London found that those with large numbers of friends on Facebook had more gray matter in the brain regions that are associated with social skills. This finding means that either their social media use is changing those brain regions or that people born with more gray matter are more active on Facebook.

According to neuroscientists, brain scan studies looking at changes to brain structure in the future might help to determine whether these changes in the brain are caused by having more on-line social connections.

Foodlike Substances

Primack compared social media and face-to-face interactions with consuming real food versus foodlike substances, as the writer Michael Pollan described them, or an apple versus a highly pro-cessed apple-flavored granola bar. The apple and the granola bar both provide calories and have the flavor of an apple, but one of them has been around for two hundred thousand years and matches our biology better. It provides vitamins and nutrients. The other food item was made in a factory, and chemicals have been added to preserve it. It's a foodlike substance. The same analogy applies when we talk about real social interactions versus social media. There are some similarities—we can communicate with others and tell when something good or bad happens and enable rapid responses. But as a total package, does the social media experience replace face-to-face discussion? That's an important question to ask.

Primack said social media is like food; it would be hard but pos-sible to live completely without it, yet in our society, its use has be-come quite important. For instance, we use it at school as a learning tool, and when applying to colleges. In many ways, social media is crucial in today's society. My oldest son, who is 17, is one of the only teenagers I know who has completely eschewed social media. But then one of his high school teachers gave the students an assignment that needed to be completed via Facebook, and my son was forced to sign on. Fortunately, he hasn't visited the site since.

Primack explained there is a good argument for restricting social media usage by our children. "Just like you shouldn't eat an entire pizza; you should only have two pieces. There are now evidence-based reasons to limit the amount of social media we use, including the total time and frequency. Someone might say, 'Well I only use it an hour a day, total.' But he might do it in segments all day, and that might not be good for his concentration. He could also be on a number of different platforms."

A recent study by his center demonstrated that the number of platforms someone uses is an accurate predictor of depression and anxiety; it showed that people who use between seven and eleven different platforms, compared with those who use two or three platforms, were more than three times as likely to be depressed and anxious. The numbers were the same if they all spent an equal amount of time on the platforms, in total. This may be because each different platform has its own idiosyncrasies and language that need to be learned in order to feel comfortable on them. If you're trying to keep up with Facebook, Twitter, Instagram, and Snapchat, you're becoming very diffuse on each platform, and that might lead you to make a major gaffe on one of them, which could also lead to being depressed.

"It's like trying to be friends with ten different groups of people in high school. If you're only friends with one or two groups of people, then you know what you'll be doing on New Year's Eve," said Primack.

Primack has used Facebook for work and to tell students at Pitt about the programs that they offer, and he's used Twitter about five times. When he gave a TED talk about the subject, he felt like he should have been tweeting it out, but he decided not to. He occasionally uses LinkedIn.

Through his center and the research they do there, Primack hopes to understand social media's influence on mental health, and help to come up with educational interventions to improve people's understanding of the problem. He also wants to help parents decide how to limit social media, as well as teach people how to be more media literate, including ways to analyze and evaluate what they see.

Social Media = Stress

A 2017 study found that social media is stressing people out; researchers surveyed 18- to 22-year-olds and examined how social media impacted their anxiety levels. They found that the more time they spent on social media per day, "the greater the association with anxiety symptoms and the greater likelihood of an anxiety disorder," said Anna Vannucci, co-author of the study and a research associate at Connecticut Children's Medical Center. "We think social media use may exacerbate stress."

Another study found that quitting social media made people happier. The researchers divided one thousand Facebooks users into two separate groups and asked half to take a one-week break from the site. The people who took the time off exhibited large increases in life satisfaction and positive emotions, compared with those who stayed on Facebook. And the more they had used the social media site before their sabbatical, the happier they were.

Disturbingly, kids are starting on social media at younger and younger ages; many get their first phones at around age 10. A 2015 Pew Research Center study found that 24 percent of teens were online almost constantly.

2,410 Facebook Friends and Counting

Sofia Bermack, who lives in New Jersey, is 17 and is on social media around five hours each day; mainly on Facebook, Instagram, and Twitter. She has 2,410 friends on Facebook, and uses her different apps to post different things. Sofia, who is now a senior in high school, has been on Facebook since fifth grade.

"I feel like I'm on social media way too often. I know some people who have a lot of social issues because they have internet friends, but I think I'm good at separating it. When I'm with my local friends, I'm not always on my phone," Sofia said.

A year ago, she started going on meme groups on Facebook, and that became a large part of the time she spent on social media. A meme is an idea that spreads from person to person within a culture—often with the aim of conveying a particular phenomenon, such as doctored photos of President Trump or pictures of Sponge Bob that mock the cartoon character, with funny sayings next to it. Meme groups spring up as a way to share ideas and opinions online.

So far, Sofia has been on seven meme groups, including many that are for specific bands and artists that she likes. One is a sort of fan club for her favorite band, Death Grips, an American experimental hip-hop band from California. Often the memes will be called something that uses a play on words; such as Death Grips Trash Postings.

Through her meme groups, Sofia has met people all over the world, including Matthew, 18, who lives in Scotland. They text and video chat every day. They met about a year ago through a meme group for the TV show, *It's Always Sunny in Philadelphia,* of which she is a big fan. She said they've been quite close for a while now and she considered him her best friend, though they still haven't met in person. She also has good friends online in the United Kingdom, Denmark, and New Zealand—most of these she met through meme groups.

Last summer, Sofia, who is very outgoing and friendly in person, met for the first time nine of her online friends from a meme group. They all drove to Upstate New York and spent the weekend chatting and getting to know each other, in real life.

"We all keep in touch and we talk a lot, about everything. We give each other advice and recommendations on music and movies and we talk about memes and politics. It's interesting to get different perspectives on things from them. It's awesome," she said. "Some things you don't want to talk about to your local friends, and you might need some outside advice from someone who is more experienced. My local friends and I do the same thing all the time, so it's nice to get advice from other people."

Sofia said that when she's on social media she doesn't feel anxious, but when she thinks about how much time she spends online, *that* starts to give her anxiety—and then she gets angry with herself that she's on it so much. Sofia said she knows kids who don't know how to live without social media, who don't know how to have face-to-face conversations. She doesn't feel that way, but she worries—especially about her younger brother, who is 12, and is already on social media.

"I definitely think that we're all being brainwashed by social media. It's an addiction that I don't want to have. Since we're raised on social media it's hard to drop off. There was a year that I deleted it because I was on it all the time. I was 15. Then when I turned 17, I didn't have an iPhone, just a flip phone, and it was a nice break. But I went back because I felt like I was missing out on things and I wanted to get back into the groups. I know kids who can't exist without it; they're impossible to converse with in person. One kid is fine on social media but in person, he'll just sit on his phone and he won't look me in the eye. A lot of kids are like that," she said.

Today Sofia works part time booking bands for a local night club, and she found that she needed to be on social media to promote the groups and the concerts; doing her job was impossible without being online. But she's not on her meme groups as much; she keeps in touch with the friends that she met before, and now mainly spends time on music-streaming sites and looking at art and films that people post online.

Sofia had advice for younger kids, including her little brother, who want to get into social media: She said they should try to balance their social media presence with their real-life experiences. "If your social media usage is outweighing your real life experiences, you're going to forget who you are—and you're going to forget how to exist without the internet."

Families and Social Media

Dr. Sherry Turkle, a social psychologist who teaches at the Massachusetts Institute of Technology, believes social media is straining our personal relationships. Turkle is the author of *Alone Together: Why We Expect More from Technology and Less from Each Other,* which explores the ways online social networks and texting culture are changing how people relate to society, their parents, and friends.

Turkle said that people who spend a lot of time online are more isolated and emotionally disconnected than those who don't. Many are dealing with mental fatigue and anxiety. One of the consequences of having all this technology at your fingertips is that it's easy to check out when you're feeling anxious or uncomfortable in a social situation.

I remember being at a school event with my kids when they were younger, and there was a dad there who I know worked on Wall Street, and he looked very busy and important using his phone. I thought he must be finalizing some sort of important deal, but when I caught a glimpse of his screen, I saw that he was just on Facebook. I realized that he must have been experiencing social anxiety in that situation, and he was looking for a way to escape.

According to Turkle, having lots of friends on Facebook can be a distraction, "providing the illusion of companionship" and causing us to spend less time with our actual friends, face-to-face, in social situations. We give precedence to people we are not with over those we are with—such as texting during dinner with our families, texting when we're out with friends, texting when we're spending time with our kids, and texting while we drive. She's had children tell her that when their parents pick them up from school, they don't make eye contact because they're so busy on their phones.

I've noticed mothers pushing their babies in strollers and talking on their phones or texting, rather than interacting with their child. It's as if there's always someone or something better out there. Turkle has witnessed women who are nursing or giving their babies bottles, texting while they do it. It's hard to connect emotionally with your baby when you're getting tense from reading text messages. She also found that kids were often the ones complaining about their parents' technology usage, and the children she interviewed told her that their mothers and fathers spent more time on their phones than they did interacting with them face-to-face. Unfortunately, technology can make us forget important things in life.

College Kids and Their Phones

Kids going to college are lonelier these days because they're having a harder time making new friends and connecting due to social media.

They stay connected with their friends from high school via texting, and they see what a great time their high school friends seem to be having without them on Instagram, which makes them feel worse. They rarely make eye contact with other college students because their eyes are always glued to their phones. Turkle wrote that we are now "alone together"; we might be there physically with our friends or loved ones, but we are concentrating on someone or something else. And we're paying a price for this in our intimate relationships.

Colleges report that students are arriving on campus feeling anxious, stressed out, and depressed. They sleep with their phones and are constantly on them so that they don't appear to be alone, and are increasingly fearful of face-to-face conversations. One freshman at Cornell University made a short video about her feelings of loneliness and her difficulty in making new friends that immediately went viral; she's obviously not the only one to feel this way.

Turkle and others believe it's important to limit technology for yourself and your children. She has some basic rules: No technology at meals. No technology when she's with her kids or out with friends. And no technology when she's out in nature. She said she's concerned we are losing touch with our physical surroundings.

The Online Breakup

Ilana Gershon, anthropology professor at Indiana University, was intrigued by how new media has affected relationships, as well as the degree to which her students used new media to communicate important information—such as telling a boyfriend or girlfriend that "it's over."

She interviewed a selection of young men and women to find out how they used texting, Facebook, and instant messaging to end relationships, and wrote about it in her book, *The Breakup 2.0*. The book shows the different ways in which media influence behavior, beliefs, and social mores.

Gershon doesn't believe social media is the culprit in making people feel disconnected from one another; the disconnection comes in how people use social media.

"Technology doesn't do things; it's the way people engage with it. In terms of friendships, people report that they're able to stay in touch with their friends regularly, but they have shallower contact with people they may not have been in contact with before," Gershon said. "For some people, it may change the nature of their relationships—allowing them to stay on a slow burn. People also seemed able to stay in contact with high school friends, giving them a more diffuse friendship circle."

Curiously, while the people she interviewed said they found it difficult to have deep intimate conversations face-to-face with their friends, they felt like they could do so via text. According to Gershon's research, different media did distinct things for them: Some college women told her they preferred to use texting to interact with their friends rather than talking on the phone because they felt like they didn't know how to communicate with them by phone, and that it took too much time. With texting, they knew how to signal their feelings to each other.

Gershon believes people have different understandings of what media can do for them and how it can lead to miscommunication. Because they're on a lower bandwidth for communicating via email, texts, and Skype chats, they are more conscious of its limitations.

When it comes to social media, Gershon agreed with Primack that these are "performances" that have been curated for one's peer group and that don't show your true self.

"The weird thing about this is that people were very conscious of their own work at curating and trying to represent themselves on social media, yet they took what everyone else says as the truth. They would never say, 'I'm always curating, so I guess they must be, too.'"

When someone posts on social media, and their friends don't respond, she might say, "You never like things I post on Facebook." What she's actually saying is "What kind of friend are you?" Online posts can create a weird sense of obligation; we might ask ourselves, "Am I supposed to respond?" When does a post call for a response? People have certain expectations on how media is being used, and it's signaling a certain form of affection between friends. People might think that responses are an indication of how much their friends value their friendship, and they are actively interpreting these messages and making demands on each other.

Sometimes, our friends' social media posts might be so cringeworthy that we want to unfriend them—like the come-hither photos they post on Instagram, or the endless bragging about their kids on Facebook. Then what do we do? Unfollowing them is one way around it, or we can just stop reading their posts.

The Selfie Generation

Attention on social media, including selfies and groupies, is a sign of intimacy, and there's pressure to respond immediately to what someone is posting. With closer friendship groups, the rules for social media can be even more intense, especially for women. Similarly, if you text someone and they don't answer, it shows they're not responsive, and for many people, that's not acceptable. There can be social consequences for responding and not responding. However, people can interpret a group text as a signal that they're not required to respond because it's public; they experience it differently if it's addressed to them individually.

Nowadays, when you get to know a new friend, you probably also have to learn their media practices: Is she a lousy texter? Will she never respond on Instagram, but she will on Snapchat? People figure out which ways get faster responses, such as which hours are the best to contact someone. We have to know each other's media practices to understand the best way to communicate; it's a very different way of knowing someone.

Just How Many Facebook Friends Do We Need?

When we do go on social media, sites such as Facebook and LinkedIn encourage us to think of friendship in terms of quantity, and sometimes we wear those numbers like a badge of honor.

Robin Dunbar said that the average Facebook user (of all ages) has between 150 and 250 friends; the site allows up to 5,000 friends—and many users are actually reaching that number. Of course, many of these friends are acquaintances and some are strangers. People with more Facebook friends also tend to have more friends in his or her in-person social networks. Facebook today allows you to sort people into groups based on close friends, family, acquaintances, work friends, or fellow alumni, or you can create your own categories. If you have 1,000 friends, how do you work out who gets which message? Just thinking about it can be exhausting.

What does it signal when you have a lot of friends?

Some people are friend collectors, and they quantify friendship in a certain way. But when you're constantly managing your image for others, it requires a lot of reputation work. LinkedIn is blatant about this, giving you the ability to endorse your friends, based on their skills.

Gershon said that people are conflicted about the way Facebook friends are attached to actual friendships. Some people might say, "We're Facebook friends, but not face-to-face friends," and that would signal something superficial. Or they might say the opposite, and that might mean that they really value that friendship. Who you are friends with across each medium signals what you're saying about each friendship.

Old friends can contact you out of the blue on social media. That's what happened to Gershon's husband; someone from high school friended him on Facebook, and it never went anywhere. They never communicated after that. He found it really odd. I've had the same thing happen to me.

Other times, friends might connect with you when something big has happened in their lives. Gershon said that she and a college friend reconnected on Facebook when her friend's marriage was on the rocks and she began flirting with her college boyfriend.

"We reconnected because of a life crisis. Now we talk on the phone regularly and she tells me she's not sleeping with her college boyfriend, who I knew was a disaster," she said.

So Why Do We Post?

Why We Post is a global anthropological research project on the uses and consequences of social media, based out of University College London. As part of the venture, nine anthropologists were sent to live in nine communities around the world, where they spent fifteen months researching the role of social media in people's everyday lives.

Their mission was to "ignore glib claims that we are all becoming more superficial or more virtual because of social media. What is really going on is far more incredible. Social media is intensely woven into the texture of our relationships." In the study, social media gave the anthropologists intimate insight into the worlds of Chinese factory workers, young Muslim women on the Syrian/Turkish border, IT professionals in India, and many others.

Jolynna Sinanan was one of the anthropologists who took part in this project; she lived in Trinidad, where she found that people there use social media, such as Instagram and Facebook, to post photos and group selfies—they represent their ideals of friendship, and also reaffirm the norms of these relationships. But she said that it is in the back channel apps, such as WhatsApp and Facebook Messenger, where the actual friendships play out. "With women, their usage tends to be volatile and brittle. People will say things on social media that only certain people will understand, such as, 'Don't you hate it when people do this…?' It indirectly alienates people."

The project found that while people tend to regard social media as making us more individualistic and narcissistic, that was not the case; it was actually being used to reinforce traditional groups, such as family, caste, and tribe, and to repair the broken or fragmented relationships created by migration and mobility.

Another discovery from the project was that social media has shifted human communication toward the visual, at the expense of text and voice.

Today a photo can become the core of conversation. For instance, people in Turkey use social media to connect with family members who are physically separated; images can give them the same sense of closeness and intensity as face-to-face communication.

The anthropologists also found that for some people, social media is now "somewhere they live," as well as a means for communication. That's especially true for those who live away from their families; they spend a lot of time on social media and see it as an extension of their social life, rather than as a replacement for it.

Chapter 9

A Friend Indeed

The health benefits:
Why women become friends and
what we get out of it

Good friends are good for your health.

—Dr. Irwin Sarason

WOMEN HAVE LONG instinctively known how essential our friends are to us. They help to shape and define us. They soothe us when we're upset and fill an emotional need that no male, not even a spouse, can satisfy. They keep our secrets, tend our children, and nurse us when we're sick. But they can do so much more.

A new body of research is beginning to reveal some of the scientific secrets to the power of female friendship and the importance of social networks to overall health, and it can help us understand why our friends are so important to us, both emotionally and physically.

A 2016 study by Alexander Miething on close friendship and life satisfaction among men and women of different sexual preferences found that friendship satisfaction was strongly associated with overall life satisfaction for all groups, "corroborating a large body of research that has shown that friendships satisfy many important needs in our lives: the need to bond with someone like us in some ways and unlike us in others, having someone to call on for comfort in times of turmoil, and someone with whom we can share memorable experiences."

In study after study, the importance of good friends to one's health is apparent.

The Nurses' Health Study

In the landmark Nurses' Health Study from Harvard Medical School, which began in 1976 and continues today, it was found that the more friends a woman had, the more likely she was to lead a joyful life and the less inclined she was to become ill as she aged. Women who had close friends were better able to recover from the devastating loss of a spouse than those who did not. In fact, it was found that those *without* friends suffered negative health effects that were as serious as being overweight or smoking cigarettes.

The study followed more than twelve thousand married women who were registered nurses ages 30 to 55 from across the United States. They were chosen because, as nurses, they were able to complete the health-related questionnaires accurately and carefully and they were motivated to take part in the long-term study. The women participated every two years, providing blood, urine, and other samples over the course of the study, which is among the largest investigations into risk factors for chronic diseases in women. It has spawned many offshoots. Now in its third generation, the study has more than 280,000 participants.

Other research has found that people with large circles of friends are much less likely to die from an illness than those with fewer friends. And a 1989 study that looks specifically at the survival rate of women with breast cancer found that those with a strong network of supportive friends lived longer than those who were socially isolated.

Friends Are Good for Your Brain

Studies have shown that women who have strong female friendships have a surprising advantage over the rest of us—and that goes for the brain, as well. Neuroscientists have recently discovered evidence that having close friends can help maintain good brain health, including protecting the brain from developing dementia.

Brigham Young University professor of psychology and neuroscience Julianne Holt-Lunstad was the lead author on a study looking at how the brain's health is affected by friendship. She said the benefits include a lower risk of cognitive impairment as we age, and better brain resilience, which helps protect us from cognitive decline and disease. People with strong social networks also have stronger immune systems and are less likely to succumb to infectious disease. Since having good friends reduces the effects of stress in your life, the result is lower blood pressure, heart rate, and cholesterol as well.

A Harvard School of Public Health study looked at data from nearly seventeen thousand subjects aged 50 and older, over six years. The results found that the subjects who were most socially active and had regular contact with family and friends had less than half the decline in their cognitive function, compared with those in the study who were least socially active.

According to Holt-Lunstad, our relationships can influence our health in a variety of ways, including promoting healthier behaviors and discouraging risky ones. Good friends can encourage you to get more sleep and stop smoking. Strong social networks are also associated with medical compliance—friends might remind you to take your medication and keep your doctor's appointments. And they can help you to be more active.

That's true for me. I regularly walk with my neighbor and good friend, Heidi, a few times a week. Not only is it great for our health, but we get a chance to catch up, give each other advice, and laugh.

Research shows that positive relationships can induce a variety of physiological processes, such as better endocrine functioning (this affects the body's growth, metabolism, and sexual development and function) and better cellular functioning, which affects how quickly we age. On the other hand, negativity in relationships can be a source of anxiety and actually *increase* our levels of stress.

"The question is, do you get rid of these friendships or improve them? Are we better off with negative relationships or no relationships? We haven't been able to answer those questions," said Holt-Lunstad.

One of her studies looked at the quality and quantity of individuals' social relationships and their links not only to mental health but also to both morbidity (disease) and mortality.

Americans are becoming less socially connected and are experiencing more loneliness. Social isolation may represent a greater public health hazard than obesity. Feeling lonely can create feelings similar to physical pain, cause stress, and make us more susceptible to illness.

The Evolution of Being Social

Dr. Lauren Brent studies friendship and social behavior, and said that she's always been interested in the subject, even as a small kid: "I was one of those kids who would play outside in my garden and watch the animals and try to understand them. I got more and more into biology. The study of behavior was an academic discipline that I was interested in because people are so weird. The things that we do are so strange, and social relationships are so salient to us."

As she started to make friends as an undergraduate at university, Brent began to understand that social relationships are a huge part of our lives. "Sometimes something great happens, and sometimes there's great pain. I wondered why we were doing this in the first place?" She began to study animal behavior to help her understand why humans act the way we do. "I can't remember a time when I wasn't interested in social relationships."

Today Brent looks at why social relationships are formed and how they are maintained. She also researches how these social networks impact health and fitness. She said that when we interact prosocially, we get little boosts of chemicals. "We get these good chemicals in our brain when we're with friends. If you're asked to do something stressful like give a speech, your heart rate shoots through the roof. But it increases much less if you're in the same room as your friends." She explained: "We've found that just like in humans, having close relationships or being well connected in your social network leads to female animals living longer. It also leads to them having more babies, with more of their babies likely to survive. All of which suggests that these relationships (with friends) are beneficial and having them is good. They've evolved because they serve a particular function."

Brent believes that evolution has made us rely on our friends, so much so that our bodies react to a lack of friends "as if a crucial biological need is going unfulfilled."

And being with friends is linked to the release of selected neurotransmitters in the brain, as well as the release of biochemicals, such as serotonin. Thus, friendship is driven by a system of reinforcement and reward.

Oxytocin also promotes prosocial decisions, as well as feelings of generosity and trust. Researchers have discovered that endorphins play a part in friendship, too. Endorphins are produced by the pituitary gland and are normally released during exercise; they're linked to feelings of well-being in the brain. Brent pointed to a study performed by Robin Dunbar and his colleagues in which they asked people to row a boat, either alone or in pairs. They measured levels of endorphins both before and after the exercise and found that people who rowed on their own experienced a small spike in endorphins, but those rowing with others had a much bigger spike of endorphins, because they were doing the exercise socially.

The same results were found when people danced alone versus with someone else. Behavioral synchrony, or being in the same place at the same time with friends, can produce more endorphins, making friendship feel good.

From an evolutionary standpoint, it doesn't make sense to become friends with people who don't share your genes, because in this regard, the only purpose of relationships with others is to spread your genes and maximize how many babies you'll have.

It's one of the mysteries of friendship.

One reason could be that if you didn't have any relatives nearby, the only option was to become friends with someone not related to you. Or there could be other advantages to having close relationships with nonrelatives, said Brent, such as gaining information that we need to find jobs or access to resources.

Brent and others believe that genes may play a part in why we are friends with nonrelatives, as well as why we gravitate toward some people rather than others. It's not surprising that we tend to become friends with people who are similar to us, in looks or personality or areas of interest. This tendency for like to associate with like is called homophily, and research by Nicholas Christakis at Yale University has found that people are as genetically similar to their friends (who are not related to them), as they would be to fourth cousins. So maybe our good friends are actually related to us somehow?

Do Friends Share Your Genes?

According to Brent, "You could be picking people to be your friends who are not relatives by descent, but you share enough genes that helping them could actually help your genes get ahead. Wanting to be friends with people who have a similar personality to you, and who like to do the same things, could be a signal that you share the same genes. There are so many combinations of genes that we can have, that it could mean that liking kayaking, for instance, could be linked to your genetic composition."

Genetics could be determining who we choose to be our friends, and choosing friends with a similar personality means they probably share genes with us.

Maybe this is why people are always asking if two of my friends are sisters—they are close friends, look a lot alike, and have similar interests. Maybe they are actually related?

Brent explained that there's still a great deal we don't know when it comes to how friendship affects our brain, including how our different levels of friendship might be differently encoded in our brain. "Are our friends really different from our acquaintances? If you could track what's going on in someone's brain at a chemical level, we could learn so much."

Friends Indeed

Supportive friends were important for Kim, who recently found out that she had a malignant brain tumor. She turned first to her husband to support her and to make sure their children were alright. According to Kim, he was amazingly supportive. But she wasn't sure she could have survived the frightening ordeal without her friends, who flew in from all over the world to be with her.

She was just 47 when she discovered she had cancer. Kim and her husband, Jonny, and their two kids had just returned to Portland, Oregon, after visiting her parents in Nebraska for Thanksgiving. Everything had gone fine during the trip, but in the middle of the night that they returned, Kim felt a strong cramp in her calf. Her husband rubbed and released it for her, and she was able to fall back to sleep. But a few hours later she had a violent grand mal seizure, characterized by a loss of consciousness and intense muscle spasms. It was shocking to both of them—they had no idea what was happening. Kim was rushed to the hospital, where she and her husband were both stunned to discover that she had a stage 3 tumor in the right front lobe of her brain.

This wasn't the first time Kim had grappled with cancer. Just a few years before, she'd been diagnosed with breast cancer. That time, she decided not to tell her friends, and she didn't even let her immediate family know until weeks later. Fortunately, she recovered—though it wasn't easy.

But this time, she didn't really have a choice—she needed her friends to help because she was hospitalized and she couldn't walk or drive or take care of her kids. So her husband called them and told them what had happened. All of them immediately contacted Kim with messages of love and support. They all wanted to help.

"My first friend flew in from Beijing and was here for my surgery. My friend, Catherine, came next. And she had just been here to visit! She came for a week. They all helped with the kids and driving everyone around...It was just incredible. The love...it's hard to talk about. I'm overwhelmed by emotion," she said, as she began to cry.

Kim is upbeat and outgoing and likes to surround herself with friends and family. She loves to cook and throw parties and volunteers for her children's school PTAs. Before moving to Portland, she and her family had been living in the city of Chengdu in southwest China for eight years and, while there, she made five close friends that are still very present in her life. When she became sick, they all came, one at a time, to help her and her family while she was in the hospital and then when she was moved to a rehabilitation facility. By that time, many of her friends from China had moved all over the world—to Sweden, New Jersey, Scotland, and Singapore. If one didn't have enough money to fly to Portland to see Kim, the others pitched in to help pay for it or gave the friend airline miles.

They took turns with Kim's husband sleeping at the rehab facility with her, so that someone was always either with her and with their kids—a son, 11, and a daughter, 14. Kim said she didn't know how they would have done it all without her friends.

"I look at those five women as my family. It's really amazing and overwhelming. They're my true sisters," said Kim. "I definitely think I'm doing a lot better because of their support."

Kim's experience when she had breast cancer was very different; she barely told anyone what had happened to her—at that time she felt like she wanted to have her treatment and get past it. She had also just moved to Portland, so she didn't know many people there. Kim had a lumpectomy and radiation and, looking back, she realized that she had found it difficult to get through the treatments without the help and support of a wide group of friends.

Three years later, with her diagnosis of a brain tumor, Kim and her family had incredible support—from her friends from China as well as from their community in Portland. Kim's friends sent her Lyft gift certificates so that she could go to the doctor (she couldn't drive because she was still having seizures). And a neighbor started taking her dog, a small, white Tibetan poodle, each day to care for it so that Kim and her family wouldn't have to.

Doctors were able to remove most of Kim's tumor, which was very aggressive, and they have given her a positive prognosis. She recently stopped chemotherapy and was undergoing physical and occupational therapy. The removal of the tumor left her with hemiplegia on her left side.

Studies have found that, like Kim, we can attain a longer life span through our friendships.

An offshoot study of nearly three thousand nurses who had taken part in the Nurses' Health Study and later discovered that they had breast cancer, found that women who *didn't* have close friends were four times more likely to die from the disease than women who had ten friends or more. It didn't matter if the friends didn't live nearby or if they weren't in constant contact—just having those friends meant they would live longer.

This phenomenon was documented in the 2009 book, *The Girls from Ames: A Story of Women and a 40-Year Friendship*. In it, Jeffrey Zaslow told the story of eleven childhood friends from Ames, a small city in Iowa, who moved to eight different states but maintained their extraordinary friendships through marriages, divorce, and illness. The story shows how much the deep bonds of their close friendships contributed to their health and sustained them. When one of the women found out she had breast cancer, her childhood friends were the first people she told. They immediately started calling, emailing, and showering her with gifts of food, hats, and pajamas—anything they thought would help. She said her friends' love and support helped her to recover from her illness. Through the strength of their friendships, the women endured the death of a child and the mysterious death of one of the members of the group. The book shows how close female relationships can sustain and nurture women, shaping their lives and their sense of themselves, by supporting each other through good times and bad.

Combating Social Isolation

UK prime minister Theresa May was so concerned about the health effects of isolation that she appointed a minister of loneliness to help combat the problem.

"For far too many people, loneliness is the sad reality of modern life," May said in a statement. "I want to confront this challenge for our society and for all of us to take action to address the loneliness endured by the elderly, by carers, by those who have lost loved ones—people who have no one to talk to or share their thoughts and experiences with."

The appointment came after a study reported that more than nine million people in the United Kingdom often or always feel lonely, and that about two hundred thousand older people in Britain had not had a conversation with a friend or relative in more than a month. The commission challenged the government to step forward and lead a renewed push to tackle loneliness.

The lawmakers said in a joint statement, "Young or old, loneliness doesn't discriminate. Throughout 2017 we have heard from new parents, children, disabled people, carers, refugees and older people about their experience of loneliness."

Holt-Lunstad said that isolation is a problem in the United States as well. "Being connected to others socially is widely considered a fundamental human need—crucial to both well-being and survival," said Holt-Lunstad. "Yet an increasing portion of the US population now experiences isolation regularly."

According to her, living alone, loneliness, and isolation are all significant and equal predictors of risk for premature mortality, and she cited an example of a woman she recently met who had a good social network but who had just lost her spouse. Even though the woman had many friends, she had a profound sense of loss and still felt deeply lonely.

A Public Health Issue

Holt-Lunstad has recommended that more research be done on this subject, and that additional resources be allocated to tackle this public health problem at the individual level as well as at the societal level. She suggested more social skills training for children in schools and said that doctors asking about social connectedness when screening patients would help prevent the problem.

Holt-Lunstad believes that such discussions could have a widespread effect in terms of reducing overall risks for the general population. "We want people to take this seriously for their health. We ought to be discussing this as part of health education—just as we treat other lifestyle factors that influence our health. Having these kinds of discussions and hands-on training in school would be invaluable."

For instance, according to Holt-Lunstad, health education classes in schools already address healthy eating and being active, but they should also teach kids the definition of a healthy relationship. How you make friends, how you become a good friend—these are the kinds of things that could potentially have an important influence in preventing loneliness or isolation, rather than intervening after the fact, when someone is on the fringes of society. One of the peaks of loneliness that people suffer is during adolescence and young adulthood.

"We don't have enough data on the role of technology on younger people," said Holt-Lunstad. "Do they have the kind of face-to-face social skills they need to make friends? Because these aren't really being used when they're communicating via smartphones."

She also recommended developing official guidelines for social connections—just as there are already health recommendations for getting the right amount of sleep or nutrition. With standards in place, people who were curious about how they were doing socially could read the guidelines on social connections and friends. If they thought they might be falling short, they would have an avenue to discover how to make more of an effort. According to Holt-Lunstad, the guidelines could take into account the quantity and quality of relationships, and could be periodically reviewed based on the most current research. Having some kind of general recommendations in place might go a long way in helping people know if they're at risk.

"It's good to have some self-awareness about this, and have people thinking about it more. Sometimes people want to know, how many friends do I need? Just like we may fall short in exercise, we might need to make more time in our schedule to be socially active," Holt-Lunstad explained. "If you find yourself in that position where you recognize you're not as socially active as you should be, think about ways that you can address it. We have lots of ways that help nudge us towards healthier choice, like activity trackers. What kinds of things would nudge us to be more social? Has it been too long since I called my friend that I haven't talked to in a while? People could even start treating their social activity in the same way they do their physical activity. But I'm not talking about just going through the motions—the goal is meaningful social connections. That's what is associated with the health benefits. The quality of these interactions does matter."

Holt-Lunstad said that, on a personal level, she's tried to reach out to her own friends more. Rather than waiting for others to initiate social events, she has been making an effort: "Too often, people wait for others to initiate. If we all did that, no one would get together. I think everyone wants to feel that sense of acceptance and we all live busy lives. It doesn't always mean that everyone will be available when we reach out to someone."

Holt-Lunstad recounted a time when she contacted a friend who seemed uninterested in seeing her. Eventually, she learned that her friend had been going through a difficult time. "She later expressed to me how much it meant to her that I'd reached out. I felt at the time like it was very one-sided—but you never know," she explained.

In recent years, researchers have been able to show how spending time with a close friend can reduce our stress levels and improve our health. They discovered that when women are with their friends, they release the hormone oxytocin, which calms them down. Oxytocin is a normal part of the human body, and for those who have children, the levels rise after they give birth; many experience the hormone's increased level as a warm feeling of love while they nurse their baby.

Fight or Flight?

A landmark 2000 UCLA study, led by psychology professor Shelley E. Taylor, found that women respond to stress with a flow of brain chemicals that cause them to make and maintain friendships with other women. With the release of oxytocin, the normal fight-or-flight response to stress is lessened, encouraging a woman to "tend and befriend"; she tends to her children or gathers with other women instead. When she does this, researchers found that *more* oxytocin is actually released, further reducing stress and producing a calming effect. Strikingly, this calming response does not occur in men, providing physiological proof of how different the genders' friendships are.

The UCLA study found that women are far more likely than men to "befriend" in response to stress. They seek out social contact during this time, by calling friends or relatives or even asking for directions when lost.

Taylor remembered how the study came about:

The project was in response to a researcher who gave a talk on animal responses to stress and he said "we shocked the animals and of course they huddled in the corner." I thought to myself, but that's not what people do; they help and support one another and combat stress collectively. So at the next meeting of my lab group, I pointed this out and we began talking as a group about a model that would characterize human responses to stress. We worked on it collectively over the next six weeks, roughly, draft after draft. Laura Klein and I were in the hallway after that first lab meeting, and I said I thought we should also be thinking about the underlying biology, and we agreed that it would probably be based on oxytocin. Her insights and those of Tara Gruenewald on the biology were very important to the development of the paper.

Until the UCLA study was released, scientists believed that all humans experienced the fight-or-flight response to stress, an ancient survival method left over from the time when we were chased by predators.

Up until that time, very little research had been done on women and stress, because it was believed that men and women responded to stress in the same way. The results of the study have significant implications for women's health; we now know that for women, hanging out with their friends can greatly reduce their stress. Those with lower levels of stress are less likely to develop heart disease and other chronic illnesses, and people with high oxytocin levels have also healed faster from wounds. This could explain why women consistently outlive men.

Researchers believe that, in addition to boosting oxytocin levels, spending time with friends increases levels of serotonin, a natural mood stabilizer. We may have known that being with our friends made us happy—now we have the evidence.

That's how Jane said she feels about being with her friend, Lena. They've been best friends since they were in high school together, more than thirty years. Even though they no longer live near each other, Jane still calls Lena to tell her everything important that was going on in her life. "We have an understanding. We grew up together. She's more satisfying to talk to than my husband," Jane said. "I just feel more grounded when I talk to her." Jane thought her friend understood her on a different level than her husband did. In fact, they have so many shared experiences together, she said she felt like Lena was more like a sister than a friend. "We share a special language. Sometimes we don't even have to say the words, and we know what the other person is trying to say."

Some researchers consider the friends made at earlier stages of life a kind of social insurance for old age, when friends are harder to meet. In the wide-ranging survey of 125 women conducted for this book, the benefits of friendship were evident—especially child-hood friends. In the survey, 79 percent of respondents said they still had close female friends from childhood. The numbers, predictably, went down as the women aged; only 45 percent of older women said they still had good female friends from when they were children.

Said one respondent from the survey:

> *"We grew up in a small town where you knew everyone.*
> *My girlfriends today are my friends from school. They have*
> *been with me and I them—we've married, divorced, hid*
> *one from an abusive husband, been to court, drank until*
> *we fell down and got back up to do it again, we've finished*
> *college, been fired, had children and watched them grow so*
> *now we have grandchildren. The difference is the knowl-*
> *edge, the background, the undying love you have for that*
> *person that the new friends just don't have yet."*

Friends for Life

Kuelli George understands how important friends can be for your health. Her mother, Katrina, was diagnosed with breast cancer in 2005, and Kuelli attributes the love and support of her friends to keeping Katrina alive for much longer than doctors expected her to live.

Originally from Jamaica, Katrina relocated to the United States to attend college. She later moved around the country, then to Japan, and then came back to the United States, where she finally settled in California. Kuelli said that all those moves made it challenging for her mother to create a community for herself.

"She wasn't too social; definitely not a social butterfly. She was somewhat of an introvert. Being social sometimes gave her anxiety. She was in her early thirties when we moved to California in 2000, and we didn't know a single person here. We felt like we were pioneers out here," Kuelli remembered.

Katrina soon became passionate about education reform and started working in the field. It was emotionally draining work, but also rewarding. Five years after moving to California, at the age of 41, Katrina was diagnosed with breast cancer. It was stage 4; she was told she had six months to live. The family was devastated, but Katrina made it her business to understand what was happening to her.

"She threw herself into understanding her care. She'd take her results from the doctor and put them into an Excel sheet. She was this amazing person," said Kuelli. "But my mother found it challenging to know how much to tell her friends. You're trying to gauge your time, and you don't want people to overinvest in you and burn themselves out."

Still, her mother recognized how important it was to have her friends around her. Katrina had built her community in a very thoughtful way—and that's something Kuelli said she learned from her. Kuelli said her mother befriended people who weren't always like her; some came from very different backgrounds or were much older than she was. And many of those friends were the ones who stepped up to help her mother when she became sick.

While she didn't consider herself outgoing, Katrina was still friends with her high school girlfriends from Jamaica, and she had friends from the different chapters in her life from all over the world. She decided to plan one last get-together for herself; she gathered about one hundred family members and friends and took over a resort in Jamaica. It was a farewell party, but everyone felt like it was more of a celebration of her life. According to Kuelli, it was one of her mother's fondest memories.

Even though she'd been given only six months to live, Katrina ended up living for seven years after her diagnosis. Kuelli attributed that to her mother's sheer force of will—and to the love and support of her family and friends.

"She had a band of people around her who were cheering her on. Having people who followed her story and drew inspiration from it helped as well. And my brother, Kaz, was only 21 when she died. As a parent you don't want to leave your child," said Kuelli.

A few years after the first gathering, Katrina was able to organize another large gathering in Jamaica for all her friends. It was wonderful, according to Belinda, one of Katrina's friends from high school in Jamaica.

Belinda remembered her old friend well:

Katrina and I met in first form [sixth grade], our first year at St. Andrew High School for Girls in Kingston. We moved in the same orbit of friends so we were always friendly but not especially close. But she was the kind of person I wanted to know better: She wasn't cookie cutter. I remember a lively mind and a mischievous nature.

For instance, Katrina used to collect old bottles around school— we drank soft drinks from bottles—and return them for five cents apiece. Now that doesn't sound like much of a big deal to an American, but in a class-bound society like ours it was unheard of for any girl who wasn't from extreme poverty to search the garbage and grounds for bottles. I remember the rest of us watched her with something like horror but also with interest. She earned eighty dollars from the bottles and bought herself an Atari game, which at the time was a VERY big deal. We couldn't believe it!

So after that you could see all kinds of girls scrounging around the grounds for bottles. Katrina broke the class taboo. She was a leader that way.

There's more—she roped us into baking laxatives into brownies for a teacher we all detested (it worked); she played soccer, which I had never seen a girl play before; and she had never ridden a horse before when she jumped on the back of an old racehorse, no saddle, and galloped around the field. You get the picture.

When Katrina made it past her three-month death sentence she held the first big party at Silver Sands on the North coast, where she and many of us Kingstonians had grown up vacationing. When she made it to three years she had an even bigger party, and I brought my family to that one. My son still remembers it as one of his favorite vacations because there were so many kids, and of course all of us "old girls" regressed and raced each other on the beach like we were still fifteen.

Even though Katrina was terminal, she took us out to snorkel at the reef in the early morning and she could still dive to the ocean floor. She organized a lot of activities—she must have been exhausted, but I think it was a labor of love, and just bringing together her old school friends with her new ones I think kept her going.

She was always goal-oriented, always working on something. At one point she proposed that all of us old schoolmates write a book! It never got written, but it spurred us to talk about things. Not always nostalgic things either. There were significant class divisions at our old school, and one old schoolmate who still lived in Jamaica told Katrina that she didn't want to attend the beach bash because she was a "ghetto girl" and couldn't afford the cost of sharing a villa. Katrina told her nonsense, you're coming, and worked it out so that she could be there without charge.

Katrina had a deep and abiding sense of social justice and fair play, and was always first in line to speak out when she felt something was wrong. The last time I saw her was in my kitchen in early 2012. We argued about school funding politics. We didn't always agree on solutions, but I trusted Katrina to always try to do the right thing for kids. She looked a lot sicker—she died a few months after—but she never lost her interest in people or politics or life. I think that kept her alive as much as her friendships did. She did have a lot of friends though! I think that being enveloped in her old community was sustaining. Jamaican school networks are very tight.

Katrina passed away in 2012 at the age of 48. While she was sick, she kept a blog of her experience with fighting breast cancer, called *Katrina's Thoughts and Updates*. In it, she chronicled her fight against the breast cancer that would finally take her life. The last entry is titled, "Sad News," and was written by Kuelli:

I am writing to let you know that my mom, Katrina…, died yesterday afternoon after a nearly 7-year fight with breast cancer. I am glad to say that she was at home and surrounded by people who loved her. After weeks of discomfort she finally seemed to have found some peace in the last few days, and the end was quick and came in her sleep. She did become deeply tired near the end but she never stopped being her powerful self. We are mourning her loss and feel sad for the hard struggle she had to go through, but are also fiercely proud of her amazing fight, her strength and her courage, and are grateful that she was able to have the passing that she always said she wanted.

Thank you for being a part of her support network—for growing up with her, raising kids alongside her, working for change with her, laughing with her, pushing her, listening to her, learning from her, and otherwise loving and caring for her both physically and emotionally. In the last 24 hours, we have already received many notes from those of you whose lives my mom touched in some important way, and it has helped to give us an even deeper sense of the enormous size of her footprint on this world. We look forward to getting to hear and share more of these amazing stories over the next few weeks.

The day Katrina passed away, she knew she didn't have much time left. She invited all her friends over and they had one more party so that the women could say their farewells. Kuelli and her father, Wallace, had gone out to give her mother time to spend with her friends. While they were gone, they got the call that Katrina had passed away. They returned to find that her friends had lovingly bathed and dressed her.

"The friends she had with her felt like her family. It was the best way for her to go. That memory I have of those women who had bathed her and clothed her really struck me. They did it so lovingly and were so caring," Kuelli remembered.

150 Friends

Now that we know why our friends are important, and how they can help our health, we might ask; how many friends should we—or could we—have?

Robin Dunbar has tried to answer that question, and the number he came up with is 150. That's the average amount of stable social relationships that Dunbar believes a person can maintain. And that number has been dubbed "Dunbar's Number." It's the number of people who you would strike up a conversation with if you bumped into them in the supermarket—or you wouldn't feel embarrassed if they invited you for a coffee.

Dunbar, whose research is concerned with trying to understand the behavioral, cognitive, and neuroendocrinological mechanisms that underpin social bonding in primates and humans, found an association between primate brain size (of course, we're primates, too) and average social group size. The number he arrived at identified those individuals with whom we could have meaningful relationships, and that includes family members. He believes than an important feature of our behavioral studies has been the constraints that time places on an individual's ability to manage relationships, and the cognitive tricks used to overcome these constraints.

"We're only able to handle so many relationships, and 150 seems to be that number. We've shown with various kinds of data, including Facebook, that this number seems to be quite robust," Dunbar said.

Discovering the number was an accident; Dunbar was looking at the grooming habits of primates and trying to figure out why they spent so much time doing this activity. While he was trying to come up with an answer, he looked at their brain size and how it related to the size of their social group. That's when he realized that he could apply this theory to humans and determine the size of social groups that could be predicted for humans as well.

While he came up with the number 150, he said it's really a range; 100 for the less social and 200 for the social butterflies among us. For Dunbar, the number 150 is actually split up into a series of layers: 5 intimate friends and family, your closest group of people who support you; then 15 best friends and family (the people you'd turn to in a time of need or people you could confide in), 50 good friends (those you'd invite to an intimate party), and the rest who are just friends. The people in these groups can change at any time and may even leave them, but the numbers usually remain the same.

It turns out that the number 150 is common in human social circles.

It was the average size of English villages, church parishes, typical Amish communities, and basic military units.

Although we don't know how the brain handles all these friends, we do know that these numbers correlate with the overall size of certain areas of your brain. The area of interest is a loop of neurons in the prefrontal cortex above the eyes and some in the temple lobe, alongside the ear. It's an area of the brain known to be associated with mentalizing, or the ability to understand another person's perspective. Dunbar believes that this points to the fact that there's a particular type of cognition involved in dealing with mentalizing. Since women tend to be better at this skill than men, they often have larger social circles than men.

The other aspect of this number is that monkey and ape friendships operate on two separate processes: the cognitive thinking involved with a relationship, such as how many favors are owed the other person, and the endorphin system of the brain, which relates to the area that suppresses pain and makes them feel good. Monkeys and apes create social relationships by grooming each other, which triggers the release of endorphins and builds friendship and trust. Interestingly, the average time these primates spend grooming each other correlates with the size of their social group.

Dunbar has found that the same thing happens when someone is placed in a brain scanner and is stroked as if being groomed—the person's brain lights up with endorphins. While humans don't groom in the same way as animals, we've evolved other ways to create a similar endorphin surge, but on a larger scale, including laughter, making music together, and language—such as gossiping. The response that people have to this type of "stroking" correlates with their attachment style and the number of friends they have.

People who are warm and greet each other with a kiss on both cheeks have the capacity to absorb lots of physical contact. And, for example, the Brits, who are reserved and don't touch their friends as much, have a lower density of endorphin receptors. "The endorphin system is essential to this whole process. It's very rewarding; it's an opiate. It sets up the platform for which you can build meaningful relationships," he explained.

According to Dunbar, exchanges of information are important to developing close friendships. Two of the most important information exchanges explore what the other person likes and dislikes, and how they see the rest of the world. Knowing that the other person has similar views is what makes a good friendship. Good friends tend to be very similar to each other in terms of their sense of humor, hobbies, and interests as well.

Establishing a basis of trust is also important, and if a friend is similar to you, then you'll know how much you can rely on her. The more information you have about her, the more closely you can predict her behavior in the future. "You have to be able to model the mind state and worldviews of this person or you'll keep making mistakes. You need to be able to know they won't be offended by something you do, and that, in times of need, they'll support you," Dunbar explained.

The quality of the friendship depends on the amount of time and effort that you put into it. If friends don't see each other, then the quality of the relationship declines. If they don't see each other for long enough, say six months or so, that leaves them feeling less emotionally attached, and they may then get bounced out of the group of 150.

The exception is very close college friends. Those friendships can usually withstand this decline. Family relationships are also resilient to neglect and usually remain constant throughout our lives. They can slide off Dunbar's layers, but they probably won't drop out completely. On the other hand, our friendships generally can change considerably over time, with up to 20 percent shifting every few years.

Those friends who do leave your social group may be your fe-male friends because, as noted earlier, female friendships tend to be more intense and therefore more fragile than male friendships. When asked why, Dunbar pointed to the process of reproduction, from an evolutionary perspective, as the cause. "We're trapped by the fact that we produce premature babies that are only half developed when they're born," he explained. Because women produce babies that are born a year premature compared with other primates, there is a very long period immediately after birth in which the human baby is completely helpless and is a massive drain on the mother. If human babies had been born at about 21 months—that would be the same stage that monkeys give birth to their babies, when they are already mobile and able to feed themselves.

Women need close friends that they can rely on to help with child birth and child care. If a woman needs to get something im-portant done outside of the home, she needs someone that she can exchange child care with that she knows she can rely on—someone with whom she can safely leave her baby, and know that he or she will be well cared for. "You need a real commitment."

For Kim, knowing that she had close friends she could rely on was a godsend.

As of this writing, she was doing well and started driving again. She still had hemiplegia on her left side, which affected mainly her left leg (previously she couldn't move her entire left side), but with continued therapy she was hopeful she would be able to walk with-out a leg brace and cane.

"I am feeling so good that we are planning a six-week holiday to Europe over the summer and a potential Chengdu sister reunion is in the works!" she said. "All the love and support has been over-whelming. I know that if I'm having a bad day, I can chat with my friends here or online, and I will feel so much better."

Chapter 10

Friends Forever

Making new friends and keeping old ones

It is one of the blessings of old friends that you can afford to be stupid with them.

—Ralph Waldo Emerson

WHEN HEDVA LEWITTES, 71, divorced her husband thirty years ago and immediately moved across the country from California to New York, she worried about feeling isolated and lonely. Would she be able to make it on her own? Would she meet new people? Fortunately, she had her friends and found them to be an incredibly important source of support for her.

"I identified with my maternal grandmother, a widow whom I perceived as very lonely and isolated as she aged. I thought about how aging might be different for me, and I realized that friendship was not only critical to mental health but also to physical health. People are better off if they're not socially isolated," said Lewittes, who studies aging. "One of the things I found was that I had people who said, 'Just call my name and I'll come whenever you call.' It's wonderful if you have a friend who will do that for you."

As women grow older, they sometimes find themselves drifting apart from their friends, and many find it hard to make new ones.

It's something that can be awkward to talk about. But there is a body of scientific research that shows people with solid friendships live longer, healthier lives. Friendships among women decrease blood pressure and stress, reduce the risk of depression, and increase longevity, in large part because someone is watching out for us.

Less Time with Friends

A recent study found that once women have children, they drastically reduce the amount of time they spend with their friends to barely five hours each week, down from fourteen hours a week before having a child. Yet, these new moms still need their friends, perhaps even more so.

A 2016 study found that soon after your mid-twenties, your social circle shrinks, and this decline continues for the rest of your life, or at least until retirement, when it plateaus. Both men and women continued to make more friends until the age of 25, when they started to quickly lose them, women faster than men. At that age, "people become more focused on certain relationships and maintain those relationships. You have new family contacts developing, but your casual circle shrinks." So we decide which friends are most important and valuable, and concentrate on keeping those. The theory is that as people age, they begin to decide who is most essential and valuable in their lives, and make a greater effort to hold on to those friends.

Many people believe it's harder to make friends once you leave college. And after the age of 30? Fuggedaboutit.

A *New York Times* article on the subject that first ran in 2012 was so popular that it has been republished and shared many times. In the story, Alex Williams recounted how difficult he found it to make good, lasting friends after college:

> In your 30s and 40s, plenty of new people enter your life, through work, children's play dates and, of course, Facebook. But actual

close friends—the kind you make in college, the kind you call in a crisis—those are in shorter supply.

According to the experts, the reason it becomes difficult to make friends is that we have internal alarm clocks that tell us it's time to concentrate more on what matters, such as our kids, rather than going to a party or checking out the latest bar or restaurant. It's also harder to meet the conditions required to make close friends: proximity, frequent interactions, and the ability to confide in each other—situations that are ideal in college.

Beverly Fehr however, disagreed that making new friendships becomes much harder after college. "In our society there's a lot of mobility, people moving for jobs, and they seem to be able to establish social networks in new environments. College years *are* easier years to make friends, with so many potential friends available— but that doesn't mean you're not making good friends down the road."

Fehr suggested that each life transition brings an opportunity to make new friends: changing jobs, having children, connecting to other mothers. When we're older, friendship opportunities are there, too—they're there throughout our life span.

Friends at Middle Age

Still, as we approach middle age, there's often an urge to clean house when it comes to our friends; with kids older and less dependent on us, or with no kids, we have more freedom to spend time as we see fit, so we might have a desire to remove the friends that don't feel positive, honest, or accepting. In her book, *The Female Brain*, Dr. Louann Brizendine said that as women age, their desire to help and please others starts to fade, as the brain circuits that cause women to care for and fix those around them, including friends and family members, are no longer stimulated.

On the other hand, women may find that some of their friendships actually deepen during this time, as they perhaps become more tolerant and less judgmental about their friends' faults.

In the survey that I conducted for this book, the results on how many close female friends each woman had were interesting: most women had five close friends; those aged 18–24 had an average of nine close friends; and even more remarkable, women over the age of 65 reported an average of twelve close friends, which seems to dispute what many experts say about women losing friends as they age.

For some people, making new friends happens mainly at work. But these friendships don't always last. Lewittes has had her own experiences with work friends.

"There's a real tendency to only want to be with people like you. There's a whole rhythm of friendship; what I discovered from my own relationships is that most friends are situational or contextual, such as work friends. These can become very close, but if you change your job, that can end the friendship. There's a point where you can move beyond that context and reach out and make a friend of that person. I spent a lot of time being disappointed. It wasn't that easy to make new friends after college," she said.

But she said it's only partly true that you *won't* make new friends once you leave university: "Here I am at 71 with lots of friends— many long-standing friends, some I've had for 52 years, and I'm still making new friends."

Lewittes believes that going to college opens people up to friendship, because it teaches people how to appreciate others who are not like them.

While people from more traditional cultural groups tend to keep their relationships within their own kinship networks, once you're exposed to new friends you become more open to different kinds of people.

So is there a trick to making and keeping friends, especially as we age? According to Lewittes, older women sometimes find it difficult to keep and maintain friendships, especially since some of their friends might become divorced or widowed, or may have moved away.

A difference in your situation in life can change your friendships. Lewittes found that as she aged, some of her friends were retiring while she was still working as a professor. She had one friend whose retirement eventually ended their friendship. "She kept harassing me, saying that I should retire. She plays bridge all the time. It's a hard transition to retire, and an open question for women who have been working all their adult lives is, 'Will I have the same friendship network that I had when I was younger?' I'm facing that now. I've taught for almost forty years. It's a very intense community and I have some really close friends there. This has engaged me for most of my adult life. Thinking of retiring is difficult—it's hard to know what will replace it."

Lewittes has another friend who doesn't have grandchildren and Lewittes said that when she talks about her own granddaughter, she can tell that this friend doesn't want to hear about her. "Somehow it's painful for her," she said. Similarly, she has a friend who never married. When her own daughter was growing up, she felt like this woman was judgmental, and for years Lewittes didn't talk about her daughter in front of her. But they hung in there, and they're still friends.

Health Benefits for Older Women

Friendships for older women can take on two main functions: companionship—someone with which to share activities and social rituals—and support—providing emotional sustenance during major life transitions, such as retirement, the loss of a partner, or moving to a retirement community.

In a recent pilot study in the Netherlands, two researchers interviewed a group of older women on friendship and loneliness. The participants then entered a program designed to help them improve existing relationships or develop new ones. At the start of the study, all the women said they were very lonely. A year later, they were questioned again and all the women demonstrated significant reductions in loneliness. They had developed new friendships and those who already had friends had increased their friendship networks. This finding shows that older women can change their social circles when they have the right social skills.

In the study I conducted for this book, one woman talked about how her friends helped her later in life:

> "Loyalty, support, understanding and of course togetherness. My husband of 47 years passed away very suddenly four years ago and my female friendships have become even more important to me. They provide emotional support as well as a place for me to enjoy the company of good friends. Before his death, my husband was truly my best friend. After his death, I realized the importance of having close relationships to counter the loneliness and emptiness I felt... especially in the first year after his death. I have always been a strong independent woman and have been told that I handled my husband's death with courage and grace. Having said that however, he was the love of my life and I miss him terribly. My family, including my five children, have been extraordinarily supportive and loving since his passing, but it is the peer friendships, in addition to my family, that have given me the real support."

There are skills to making new friends, especially as we age. Joining a group is a good start. And according to Lewittes, you need to be brave and willing to take the next step when you meet someone you like.

Where to Make Friends

Research has shown that for many women, being connected to a religious institution, such as a church, mosque, or synagogue, can provide both a feeling of community and new friends. Lewittes said that as she neared retirement age, she started to become active in her local synagogue—even though she hadn't been a member of a temple for the past forty years. She thought it might be a good place for her to transition to when she decided to finally leave teaching, and she had a yearning to reconnect with Jewish women. She's now making friends through her synagogue, and she's amazed to find that people are reaching out, emailing and calling her.

For some older black women, the church has a provided an important framework for friendship. These relationships can be more practical in some ways, and many of them include older and younger women connecting together.

Betty, 81, found her community in her New Jersey church, which she's been attending for the past thirty years. She had a tight-knit group of friends there; they started out with around twenty women, but are now down to eight. "If one of us has a problem, we're there for each other. We take each other out for birthdays, and we're a great support group for each other. We'll talk about health issues, or something we might have gone through. When someone passes away in their family, we go to their houses and bring them food, and we are there for them," she said. "When one of the women had cancer and was in hospice, we were there with her every day. Her children were grown and she didn't have a husband, so we'd sit and read to her."

She said that membership in her church, where her husband was once a minister, has declined, but she's still an active member and sings in the choir. Betty is lucky that she also has a community of friends at her gym, where she goes every day to do yoga or cardio or to swim. She and her friends there have been going to the same classes for the past ten years.

She feels supported by her friends.

"If I had a problem, I know they'd be there for me. My mother, who is 101, lives with me. She's very active, but if something happened to her, I know they'd all help me," she said.

Lewittes conducted a study on women and friendship later in life, in which she found that for many older women, being of the same religious or ethnic background gave them a sense of their common past and helped them connect with new friends. I know that's the case for my own mother, who is an immigrant from Argentina, and who feels most connected to other women she's met who came from the same country and who speak the same language.

While Lewittes said she doesn't think of herself as the most secure person in the world, her work in the field of friendship has taught her the social skills necessary to meet new people, starting with making it apparent that she wants to make new friends. "You can feel that from people, that they're open to having friends. When people come along that I like, I make an effort. You need social skills to cross a barrier and make a personal connection, as well as tolerance and understanding. But I now have experience of going out in the world and meeting people. There are fascinating generational differences. This is why making friends at school and through work in early adulthood can be so important. For me friendship has been part of a process of both professional and identity development. Over the years, my long-term friends and I have worked to create mutual contexts and networks. I think this was true of some of the women I interviewed as well, although they often maintained their relationships by developing connections between their families."

Lewittes remembered when she joined the temple and met another woman with whom she hit it off with right away.

"She came up and said, 'Could I get your email address?' She was very warm and brave, even though she described herself as not very self-confident. Being brave means being aware that sometimes people won't respond to you," she said. "You can't force friendships, but you can be open to them. And you have to have realistic expectations about them. There are times I wanted friends and people weren't available. There were times I rejected friends—when I got married and had a child—and I was very picky. Sometimes it takes being patient until you connect with someone. There are a lot of people you don't click with or who don't want to be friends. If you take it personally every time, it will be hard. You need to be willing to get rejected—but to get over it, too."

Satisfaction with Age

Studies have also shown that, although their social networks may decrease as they get older, the interactions that older adults have with their friends are found to be more satisfying than those of younger adults.

In a study conducted by Gloria Luong, a professor of human development and family studies at Colorado State University, she found that life experiences were a factor. "Getting older confers greater wisdom. So even though the social networks might be smaller, they tend to be higher quality, giving them more meaning and satisfaction in their social interactions," she said. "As we get older we have a sense of time running out, and while this might be seen as a bad thing, it actually helps us prioritize our goals that are important to us. Older adults don't want to waste time on people who bring them conflict or stress. They want to use their time in a wise way that helps them focus on the things that matter."

When we are younger, we might be more willing to network with people who are irritating or unpleasant, like our boss, for instance, because he or she might help us to achieve our long-term goals. That changes as we age.

Luong's survey also showed that people are less likely to instigate conflict with older adults.

For example, we start to become aware that Grandma won't be around forever, so we decide to be nice to her and avoid conflict. She gave the example of the person at Thanksgiving dinner who makes racist or annoying remarks—if it's an older person, we might decide it's not worth bothering about it, or we might be more forgiving, so we'll leave them alone. Luong also cites negative stereotypes about aging, such as thinking older people are frail, not cognitively intact, or unable to change, as actually contributing to reasons people may treat older people more kindly.

Senior centers can be a great way for older women to make friends—although some complain that the social groups in them can be cliquey. And according to Lewittes, retirement communities can sometimes be comprised of widows who are from tight family kinship networks that can make others feel left out. One woman moved out of a "55 and over" development because she felt like all the women had already made their friends, and she couldn't break into any of the groups. But in one senior center that Lewittes studied, they had established a welcoming ritual, where someone would always come over and shake hands with a new person, making the transition much easier.

Sometimes people become better able to make friends when they age; creating new relationships and joining activities can help older adults relearn social skills. One of the subjects in Lewitte's study described the evolution of her involvement in her retirement community:

> Someone asked me to sit at a table; I think it was a crafts sale. "Sit at our table while we have a meeting." So I sat there for a while and I'm thinking, how could they go to a meeting and I can't go?

Why don't I go? (I was talking to myself.) Then finally I said next time they have something, I'm going to see what it's all about, and that's what I did. There was a friendly visiting committee here. I started and six months later I was asked to be chairperson. This is all new to me but it's not bad because I'm with other people.... I learned a lot; how to deal with people; how to listen—how to be outgoing. I felt (before) like I'm no good to anyone any more. What do I know? But it's easy. Just being friendly means a lot. Now I feel like I'm part of everything. I feel free.

Of course, some older women who are not very good at making friends may actually have a predisposition from earlier in life to be shy and withdrawn, and to have a smaller group of core friends.

Ronald Aday, a sociology professor at Middle Tennessee State University who specializes in aging, told me we develop our inclination early in life to the number of friends we'll have, and we continue on that pathway.

If we lose friends, we have a tendency to replace them. But some women don't have very large social groups with which they move through life; they might always have a small cohort of friends. And while many of us make friends and hold on to them over the years, when we lose some of the people in our group, we can have a hard time replacing them.

A Friend to Lean On

For many older women, having someone you can lean on and fall back on if something goes wrong is a godsend.

One of the biggest problems for older people is a lack of transportation. For those who have been living independently of family members, driving themselves often becomes a source of pride—and when they lose this ability, there can be extremely negative consequences; people may become isolated and lonely.

This is especially true for older people living in rural areas, where there are few social settings in which they can interact. Many people are strangers to their next-door neighbors. While we're connecting on our virtual social networks, online friends can be superficial; it's face-to-face social support that's important to many people. Aday believes women need to be more proactive about seeking out companionship and support—someone they can talk to or visit with. There are even companion websites on social media for helping seniors find friends, such as Stitch, and online chat groups such as silversurfers.

Experts also suggest checking out continuing education classes or auditing regular college classes for free, volunteering, going to the gym, getting a dog, attending church or synagogue, and joining groups at meetup.com; AARP also has an online community for older adults.

"Sometimes our choices are made for us in terms of our social group. If you have a friend who can't go places, you might have to replace them with someone else. And that leaves that person alone. It's a constant kind of challenge to maintain our convoy of friends and social support," said Aday.

Race Relations

Race can sometimes play a part in whether or not women will become friends. Sharon Lewis and Sara Jonsberg were faculty members at Montclair State University in New Jersey in the early 1990s, from different races and cultural backgrounds, when they struck up a friendship. They used their relationship to learn from and to teach each other—and their students—about race and racism in America.

"We gravitated toward each other as friends because of our similar intellectual and academic thinking. We had our differences, too, and not just race. Somehow throughout the friendship we kept coming back to those differences and problems—instead of rejecting them we decided to take them on. It wasn't easy by any stretch of the imagination. The success of our friendship was possible because we weren't afraid to undertake the difficulties and challenges involved," remembered Sharon.

As their friendship blossomed, Sara, who was 54 at the time, and Sharon, who was 38, began to learn from each other. They talked about and debated films and books they'd seen or read—including the 1992 movie, *Passion Fish,* in which a black woman is paid to be a nurse to a rich white woman in the South, who is wheelchair-bound after an accident. Sara loved the film; Sharon hated it. She saw it as the same old tale of a black woman supporting the growing awareness of a white woman, who wasn't conscious of the discomfort in their dynamics.

They found a poem by Adrienne Rich, called "Frame," about a white woman who watches—and does nothing—as a black woman is arrested for trespassing while trying to stay warm in a building lobby as she's waiting for a bus. "The way she looks at the problem of white and black women's relationships in that poem; that became a key piece of literature for us," said Sharon.

After many of their talks, they raised the question: Can black and white women be friends? They wondered about this, given the inherent imbalance of power in their own relationship.

"We were drawn together because we were both new and feeling a little uncertain about this new role and environment and place. Then we found we had similar interests; we were both interested in issues of oppression and inequality," remembered Sara, who grew up in Washington, DC, in the 1940s and 1950s when it was a profoundly segregated city. "I grew up knowing that and it didn't occur to me to question it. When I went back into teaching, I taught in an integrated situation and I started questioning the racism that I grew up with—and I kept at it. Meeting Sharon was an opportunity to work on that."

They discuss the issues that complicated and formed their relationship in an article titled, "Black and White Friendship," which appeared in the 2002 book, *The Quality and Quantity of Contact: African Americans and Whites on College Campuses.*

Sara said she learned through their relationship that a white woman isn't always aware of the power she has in a racist culture: "That's what Sharon helped me see more clearly. There are so many ways that just being white lends a kind of power in a racist culture. And she really helped me understand that in a way that I'd never known before. She helped me become more sensitive to the racial dynamic between us. It was always worth it to me to make that effort to try to be aware. It was unusual what we talked about. I suppose it was a measure of our friendship that we were talking about these things so early on. We felt comfortable enough to have those conversations."

Sharon was raised in a predominately white town on the New Jersey shore. She was fortunate that she didn't have to deal with racism there, but later, when she read about the history of segregation and racist policies in the United States, she began to understand why her father left the deep South, and she understood her parents' pain when they watched Civil Rights marches on TV.

When they met, Sharon was resentful at first that Sara didn't know the history of racism in the U.S. "There was that clash. But she's really come to understand now how privilege works in this country. And while she was learning about race, I was learning, too, about race and misogyny. Our friendship flourished as we researched, learned, and critically thought through and discussed the components that threatened a wholesome, nourishing cross-race friendship. Of course, with different races, each of us had different homework, but once the hard work was completed or launched, not only our courses/workshops, but our friendship flourished as well," said Sharon.

Sara welcomed their conversations. "I feel like being friends with someone is a constant learning experience. I'm always learning from her. Even the way she reads; she's a much more attentive and questioning reader than I am. I tend to go with the flow. She's more inclined to interrogate the text. She's taught me to become open to other ways of interpreting or seeing or thinking about things."

While they were both teaching, they had the opportunity to travel together to conferences, and that helped to further cement their friendship. They took a trip to Birmingham, Alabama, where they rented a car and drove through the South together. Sara said that during that trip they became aware of being together, as women of different races, in a way they hadn't before.

They traveled to Boston so that together they could view J. M. W. Turner's painting, "Slave Ship, Throwing Overboard the Dead and Dying, Typhoon Coming On," which is featured in the novel, *Free Enterprise*, by Michelle Cliff. Sara wanted to include the book on her course reading list, and the story sparked a conversation between them about race. The book is about the sources and uses of wealth in nineteenth-century slaveholding America, and in the novel, there is a conversation between two friends, a black woman and a white woman, about the painting. Ultimately, the conversation leads to the end of their friendship.

Sara and Sharon wanted to see the painting for themselves. Here is Sara's response, from their paper:

> Seeing the painting, we were dumbstruck. It is large, and something about it, some force, pulls the viewer right up to the scene and inside. Much of the painting's field is a dark, raging ocean, and in contrast a glaring white storm, is centered. For Sharon, the painting spoke of violence and destruction, but what's most

visible is the natural or environmental destruction—one can hardly see the endangered slave ship. I was struck by the glaring white typhoon at the center of the picture. I read the painting as Turner's notion of what Conrad once called, "the benign indifference of the universe."

At first, Sharon sat down and gazed at the piece from a distance. "I remember gazing at and exclaiming at the glaring white at the picture's center. Remembering how (the characters in the novel) are described as focusing on different components of the painting, I got up from the bench and walked up to the painting. I wanted to see details which from a distance are scarcely visible. I wanted to see what she had focused on, the foreground, the limbs and bodies thrown overboard. I remember seeing the iron chains around amputated limbs, bodies half submerged in the tossing sea which was surely about to claim them. No faces, I recall thinking—no faces. Then, I, too, began to speak an interpretation. For Turner, I thought, nature is far more destructive than self-interested, profit-fueled mankind. The brutality of the slave trade, for Turner, I read, is far less significant, less consequential, than nature."

How nearly the same but how different our four eyes saw. Sara saw Turner saying that nature ignores in the end all human effort, all human pain. He is not denying the horror of slavery. Indeed, he focuses eyes upon it, calling attention to its worst abuse, but he seems to be saying that in the end all will be wiped away, kind and cruel, evil and blessed alike. Sharon read Turner as conveying the notion that nature and the artist's act of depicting nature, is more significant than human cruelty; that humans and their "foibles" (such as greed, enslavement of one another) are trivial in light of the power of nature, that nature matters more as a subject than any vision of human behavior. The storm dominates, erases the bodies, erases the human atrocity, erases responsibility as well as torment.

They decided to include the novel in a literature course that they co-taught on black and white women writers. The class turned out to be life-changing—both for them and their students.

They invited the students to read selected fiction and nonfiction by black and white women writers and together they uncovered what the authors had to say about the future of the relationship between white and black American women. They sketched what they deemed the course's central questions:

> How are the writers defining "friend"? What are the markers or characteristics of "friendship"? What does "friendship" entail or require? Why is it that so much of the imaginative and theoretical writing by both black and white women cast doubt on the possibility of women's friendships across race? What is it about race or racial identity that thwarts or renders impossible meaningful relationships between white and black women? How are these writers defining "race," and what for them does "race" have to do with friendship? What is it about American history and/or culture that worries or forestalls women's cross-race relationships?

"We wanted students to share not only their personal experiences but also their impressions, questions, uncertainties, and analyses of the course reading material. We told students that we expected them to advance the critical and interpretive skills of all class members," said Sara.

They posed the question to their students: Can black and white women be friends?

Their answers confirmed the research the two women had done on the subject; the white students said "yes" and the black students said "no."

"We watched friendships develop across sexuality, gender, race, religion, ethnicity, and geographic region.... Students were exposed to new language...to speak their questions and concerns about race and oppression in America. We gave them permission to speak about race in mixed company, with sensitivity and grace," Sara and Sharon wrote in their paper.

Sharon remembered how she and Sara felt at the end of class. "We're both teachers and we got a high from seeing our students at the end of the semester come to some epiphany about who they are and knowing what happened in the world. When they came in, they couldn't even wrestle with an idea in an essay. They left the class with wonderful ideas. They'd ask, what am I going to do to make changes? That was exciting work for Sara and me."

Most of their students were planning to go on to become teachers themselves, and Sharon and Sara hoped they'd use what they learned in their class about race and racism in their own classrooms. Sharon says she still gets letters and phone calls from former students thanking her for enlightening them, and asking her to speak to their classes.

"It strengthened our friendship. It bonded us. It made us see that we weren't crazy, that this wasn't a whimsical academic question. This was something that really needed to be examined and thought about and taken to students," remembered Sharon.

She wishes that more teachers would have conversations like the ones they had in their classes.

Back when they were teaching, the pair attended workshops and conferences and tried encouraging women across all races to have the same kinds of talks that they had with their students. "We thought we had generated the kinds of questions that could be used for all people when there's a power differential. These questions could be used to have conversations, with some calls to action after that."

I asked Sharon the same question they asked their students: Can black and white women be friends?

"They can be friends, conditionally. They need to do a lot of work. It's not a TV Hallmark friendship," she said. "As a duet we were up against a lot. But Sara is a relentless optimist. She digs in her heels with hope we can get it together and be a better nation. And writing saved us. When we couldn't have the conversations, we'd have to write. We've got tons of letters. And that would help. Writing gets us to discoveries and more questions."

After all these years of friendship, Sara doesn't seem quite sure of their level of intimacy. "I think it's very difficult. You have to figure out how you define friendship—is it exchanging recipes, or is it something deeper that lays bare the soul? If that's the case. I would call us friends. She seems to feel we're friends and I think we are, too."

Sharon was more sure: "Sara? Well, I have five good friends, and she's one of them. She's one of my dear, best friends."

Both are now retired. They have been friends for thirty-five years.

The Shine Theory: Famous Friends and How They Influence Us

In the 1950s, Marilyn Monroe helped Ella Fitzgerald secure a gig in a nightclub that had refused to book her because she was black. Marilyn promised the manager of the club that she'd book a table in the front row every night that the jazz singer performed—and it worked. The audience turned out in droves, and this unlikely pair from two very different backgrounds eventually became lifelong friends.

Famous friends intrigue us, but they also teach us something: Women can help each other get ahead.

Tennis stars Martina Navratilova and Chris Evert, talk show hosts Oprah Winfrey and Gayle King, and activists Gloria Steinem and Marlo Thomas: All are famous women who had good friends to help them achieve what they set out to do in their lives. And they did. There's even a name for it: the Shine Theory.

Ann Friedman, a radio host and journalist who coined the phrase along with her podcast partner, Aminatou Sow, said the concept has been around a long time—they just put a name to it. According to Friedman, in her line of work she often meets exceptionally talented, successful women, and she wondered about feelings of competition that females sometimes have with one another. So she decided to find a way to get beyond that.

Friedman and Sow had talked casually about their own friendship, and how they supported each other's careers. They realized that if they had to make a difficult work decision, such as taking a new job, it helped to talk it over with a good female friend. "Me working on you is you working on me," explained Friedman. She thought about all that women could accomplish if they worked together. In 2013, Friedman wrote an article, "Shine Theory: Why Powerful Women Make the Greatest Friends," for The Cut, an online style section for *New York* magazine: "Here's my solution—when you meet a woman who is intimidatingly witty, stylish, beautiful, and professionally accomplished, *befriend her*. Surrounding yourself with the best people doesn't make you look worse by comparison. It makes you better."

After the piece ran, the idea took off.

Friedman and Sow heard from older women who told them how revolutionary the idea was, saying, "I wish someone had said that to me when I was starting out." For younger women who are just embarking on a career, it can seem like everyone is competing for the same thing, so the idea of the Shine Theory is radical.

"We hear from people who say that it's led to healthier working relationships with other women. It's changed how they view other professional women," said Friedman. "I thought it was important to write about this idea. It's a name for something that happens naturally in healthy relationships among peers. You can each have distinct career goals, and be excited for the other person to achieve that goal—as opposed to *not* wanting the other person to get ahead."

Friedman said the Shine Theory is not the same thing as friendship; it falls somewhere between friendship and mentorship. It's a long-term investment in someone else, and it's about building mutually supportive relationships with other women. It's not just about networking, and it can work for women in different careers.

The point of the theory is to shore up one's contacts and become mutually invested in another person's success, thus making your own network more powerful. Thinking that there are limited spaces for you in the career world can have a negative effect on how you conduct yourself with other people.

Friedman said she's interested in undoing the damage that a sexist society has done to women—pushing them to see other women as competition when they could be allies. Friedman believes that the concept of women *not* helping other women is mistakenly part of the scarcity mentality: the idea that there aren't enough good jobs to go around.

She cites comedians and actresses Tina Fey and Amy Poehler as examples of women who have practiced the Shine Theory and benefited from it: The pair, who have been friends for twenty-four years, met as struggling improv comedians in Chicago when they were in their twenties.

When Fey moved to New York to write for *Saturday Night Live,* she tried to convince Poehler to join her; Poehler came four years later, in 2001. When Fey wrote and co-starred in the teen comedy hit *Mean Girls,* Poehler had a show-stealing part as the "cool mom" in the film. A few years later, they became the first female co-anchors of "Weekend Update" on *Saturday Night Live.* By 2013, the best friends were cohosting the Golden Globe Awards ceremony. A *New York Times* interview with them after their film, *Sisters,* was released, described them as being like "Lean In," but funny. In the article, Fey talked about how their success didn't come at the expense of others—especially other women.

"When we choose projects, we do have our own internal Bechdel test," Fey said. About their film, *Sisters,* which they also produced, she said, "These are women who are in conflict, but they're not in competition. And it is about shaking off roles that they were given early in life that they now grew out of. Whether overtly in the story or not, we definitely are always looking at things that feel true to us."

Friedman explained that when women are competing with each other for jobs, as Fey and Poehler did, there can be a feeling of powerlessness, as though there's somehow less for you. But that concept of scarcity is a lie reinforced by capitalism, and it's detrimental for women to think that way.

Rather, it's more constructive to believe that if your friend gets a book deal, for instance, it will help you because you'll then have more knowledge of the publishing world that you can access through her. While it's unrealistic to say that you'll never be jealous or envious of a friend or colleague, it's your actions that are important. Pooling resources and contact information with others is a better way for individuals to get what they want, rather than tearing each other down.

"If you're truly in this mentality, then you'll be happy for your friends when they get what they're working for. I want to live in a world where my brilliant friends are rewarded for their labor, and to know that women make a better ally than an enemy," said Friedman. "The Shine Theory is that if I don't shine—you don't shine. If you're investing in people in your network, then in the same way, you're investing in yourself. The model is collaboration over competition; not keeping everything for yourself."

Linda Carli, a psychology professor at Wellesley College, studies women leaders and is an authority on gender discrimination and the challenges faced by professional women. She also wrote the book, *Through the Labyrinth: The Truth About How Women Become Leaders*. Carli has found that women and men communicate very differently, which can lead to disparities in their careers.

It starts early; when girls issue directives, boys ignore them, but when boys issue directives, other children listen and follow them.

While women are more collaborative in their language, they'll receive negative feedback if they're perceived as criticizing others at work—even female literary critics are condemned for this critical edge. Women also get in trouble for bragging, disagreeing, or negotiating, according to Carli; society believes women should negotiate to help others but not themselves.

"There are women who feel like if they align themselves with other women, it will hurt their reputation. They think it's too risky, so they distance themselves from women as a form of self-protection. That's a queen bee mentality," Carli said. "There are such powerful social pressures penalizing women for their behavior. It leads women to be much more agreeable, pleasant, collaborative, and more attentive to others. If you're in a position of having to moderate your behavior for being too assertive, then you'll be reluctant to act that way."

Perhaps women like Friedman and Sow, and the Shine Theory, are starting to change this need for self-protection. We can only hope.

Notes

Chapter 1: A History of Friendship

One of the earliest accounts we have of female friendship is the story of Ruth and Naomi: Wendy Amsellem, "The Book of Ruth: A Celebration of Female Friendship," Jewish Week Media Group, May 28, 2014, http://jewishweek.timesofisrael.com/the-book-of-ruth-a-celebration-of-female-friendship/.

Victorians accepted and even encouraged friendship between women: Sharon Marcus, *Between Women: Friendship, Desire and Marriage in Victorian England* (Princeton University Press, 2007).

Here is an excerpt from a letter that Mary Hallock Foote wrote: Erna Olafson Hellerstein, *Victorian Women: A Documentary Account of Women's Lives in Nineteenth Century England, France and the United States* (Stanford University Press, 1981).

In the 1800s, some young women in China: Lenore Lyons, *A State of Ambivalence: The Feminist Movement in Singapore* (Brill, 2004).

Chapter 2: The Science of Friendship

The aggression that is fundamental to being human: Heather Whipps, "The Evolution of Human Aggression," LiveScience, February 25, 2009, https://www.livescience.com/5333-evolution-human-aggression.html.

Jones divided the types of gossip into four categories: Deborah Jones, "Gossip: Notes on Women's Oral Culture," *Women's Studies International Quarterly* 3, nos. 2–3 (1980), 193–198.

Another reason why women behave so differently: Ovidiu Lungu, Steéphane Potvin, Andràs Tikàsz, and Adrianna Medrek, "Sex Differences in Effective Fronto-Limbic Connectivity During Negative Emotion Processing," *Psychoneuroendocrinology* 62 (2015), 180–188.

Güroğlu said that her findings could provide a neurological explanation: Berna Güroğlu, Gerbert J. T. Haselager, Cornelis F. M. van Lieshout, Atsuko Takashima, Mark Rijpkema, and Guillén Fernández, "Why Are Friends Special? Implementing a Social Interaction Simulation Task to Probe the Neural Correlates of Friendship," *NeuroImage* 39, no. 2 (2008), 903–910.

The results of their study suggested that facial recognition may be separate from general intelligence: "Face Recognition Ability Inherited Separately from IQ," Massachusetts Institute of Technology, January 20, 2010.

He conducted a study in 2007: Joshua M. Ackerman, Douglas T. Kenrick, and Mark Schaller, "Is Friendship Akin to Kinship? *Evolutionary Human Behavior* 28, no. 5 (2011), 365–374.

Chapter 3: The Evolution of Friendship

This was backed up in a 2016 study: Laura Almeling, Kurt Hammerschmidt, Holger Sennhenn-Reulen, Alexandra M. Freund, and Julia Fischer, "Motivational Shifts in Aging Monkeys and the Origins of Social Selectivity," *Current Biology* 26, no. 13 (2016), 1744–1749.

The study showed that low-ranking "new girl" chimpanzees: Anne Pusey, "Lowly 'New Girl' Chimps Form Stronger Female Bonds," *Animal Behavior* (July 2015).

Her research has found a relationship between animals who have social connections and their ability to survive: Lauren J. N. Brent, Steve W. C. Change, Jean-François Gariépy, and Michael L. Platt, "The Neuroethology of Friendship," *Annals of the New York Academy of Sciences* 1316, no. 1 (2014), 1–17.

This is especially true for humans: Jorg J. M. Massen, Elisabeth H. M. Sterck, and Hank de Vos, "Close Social Associations in Animals and Humans: Functions and Mechanisms of Friendship," *Behaviour* 147, no. 11 (2010), 1379–1412.

Chapter 4: Women Versus Men

This was borne out in research on how genders cooperate: Leonie Gerhards and Michael Kosfeld, "I (Don't) Like You! But Who Cares? Gender Differences in Same Sex and Mixed Sex Teams," CESifo Working Paper Series no. 6523, July 12, 2017.

Research comparing the strength of boys' friendships with girls': Amanda J. Rose and Steven R. Asher, "The Social Tasks of Friendship: Do Boys and Girls Excel in Different Tasks?" *Child Development Perspectives* 11, no. 1 (2016), 3–8.

Another study supported this: Stefan Robinson, Adam White, and Eric Anderson, "Privileging the Bromance: A Critical Appraisal of Romantic and Bromantic Relationships," *Men and Masculinities,* October 12, 2017.

In one study, participants said that while both men and women experienced: E. Ashby Plant, Janet Shibley Hyde, Dacher Keltner, and Patricia G. Devine, "The Gender Stereotyping of Emotions," *Psychology of Women Quarterly* 24, no. 1 (2000), 81–92.

The study also found that for women, friendship was a means to: Gindo Tampubolon, "Women Are Better Friends Than Men," 2007, http://ec.europa.eu/research/infocentre/article_en.cfm?id=/research/head lines/news/article_07_03_22_en.html&item=&artid=.

Chapter 6: Mon Ami

Different styles of friendship vary by culture: Roger Baumgarte, "Conceptualizing Cultural Variations in Close Friendships," Online Readings in Psychology and Culture, International Association for Cross-Cultural Psychology, September 1, 2016.

In one study, participants said that while both men and women experienced: E. Ashby Plant, Janet Shibley Hyde, Dacher Keltner, and Patricia G. Devine, "The Gender Stereotyping of Emotions," Psychology of Women Quarterly 24, no. 1 (2000), 81–92.

A team of researchers was curious to find out if emotional support was equally vital: Wendy Samter, Bryan B. Whaley, Steven T. Mortenson, and Brant R. Burleson, "Ethnicity and Emotional Support in Same-Sex Friendship: A comparison of Asian-Americans, African-Americans, and Euro-Americans," *Personal Relationships* 4 (1997), 413–430.

Chapter 7: The Breakup

According to Dunbar, who conducted a study on relationship maintenance and decay in 2010: Sam G. B. Roberts and Robin I. M. Dunbar, "The Costs of Family and Friends: An 18-Month Longitudinal Study of Relationship Maintenance and Decay," *Evolution and Human Behavior* 32, no. 3 (2011), 186–197.

While she was in graduate school, Jalma began to look into studying friendship dissolution: Katie S. Jalma, "Women's Friendship Dissolution: A Qualitative Study," dissertation submitted for PhD, University of Minnesota, December 2008.

One study found that most middle school friendships: Brett Laursen, "New Adolescent Friendship Study Confirms 'Birds of a Feather Flock Together—Stay Together,'" Florida Atlantic University, July 20, 2015.

Chapter 8: Friending and Unfriending

In one study, it was found, (not surprisingly) that people tended to put their best foot forward: Lin Qui, Han Lin, Angela K. Leung, and William Tov, "Putting Their Best Foot Forward: Emotional Disclosure on Facebook," *Cyberpsychology, Behavior, and Social Networking* 15, no. 10 (2012).

Still, the study found that "nearly half of survey respondents: Emily Drago, "The Effect of Technology on Face-to-Face Communication," *Elon Journal of Undergraduate Research in Communications* 6, no. 1 (2015), 13–19.

In a groundbreaking 2016 study conducted by Primack: Liu yi Lin, Jaime E. Sidani, Ariel Shensa, Ana Radovic, Elizabeth Miller, Jason B. Colditz, Beth L. Hoffman, Leila M. Giles, and Brian Primack, "Association Between Social Media Use and Depression among U.S. Young Adults," *Depression and Anxiety* 33, no. 4 (2016), 323–331.

A recent study found that overall, the use of Facebook was negatively associated: Holly B. Shakya and Nicholas A. Christakis, "Association of Facebook Use with Compromised Well-Being: A Longitudinal Study," *American Journal of Epidemiology* 185, no. 3 (2017), 203–211.

A 2017 study found that social media is stressing people out: Anna Vannucci, Kaitlin M. Flannery, and Christine McCauley Ohannessian, "Social Media Use and Anxiety in Emerging Adults," *Journal of Affective Disorders* 207 (2017), 163–166.

Another study found that quitting social media made people happier: Morten Tromholt, "The Facebook Experiment: Quitting Facebook Leads to Higher Levels of Well-Being," *Cyberpsychology, Behavior, and Social Networking* 19, no. 11 (2016), 661–666.

Chapter 9: A Friend Indeed

A 2016 study by Alexander Miething on close friendship and life satisfaction among men and women: Brian Joseph Gillespie, David A. Frederick, Lexi Harari, and Christian Grov, "Homophily, Close Friendship, and Life Satisfaction among Gay, Lesbian, Heterosexual, and Bisexual Men and Women," *PLOS One* (2015).

In the landmark Nurses' Health Study from Harvard Medical School: David Spiegel, Helena C. Kraemer, Joan R. Bloom, and Ellen Gottheil, "Effect of Psychosocial Treatment on Survival of Patients with Metastatic Breast Cancer," *The Lancet* 334, no. 8668 (1989), 888–891.

An offshoot study of the nearly three thousand nurses who had taken part in the Nurses' Health Study: Candyce H. Kroenke, L. D. Kubzansky, E. S. Schemhappmer, M. D. Holmes, and I. Kawachi, "Social Networks, Social Support, and Survival After Breast Cancer Diagnosis," *Journal of Clinical Oncology* 24, no. 7 (2006), 1105–1111.

A landmark 2000 UCLA study: Shelley E. Taylor, Laura Cousino Klein, Brian P. Lewis, Tara L. Gruenewald, Regan A. R. Gurung, and John A. Updegraff, "Biobehavioral Responses to Stress in Females: Tend-and-Befriend, Not Fight-or-Flight," *Psychological Review* 107, no. 3 (2000), 411–429.

Until the UCLA study was released: Jean-Philippe Gouin, C. Sue Carter, Hossein Pournajafi-Nazarloo, Ronald Glaser, William B. Malarkey, Timothy J. Loving, Jeffrey Stowell, and Janice K. Kiecolt-Glaser, "Marital Behavior, Oxytocin, Vasopressin, and Wound Healing," *Psychoneuroendocrinology* 35, no. 7 (2010), 1082–1090; and Janice K. Kiecolt-Glaser, Jean-Philippe Gouin, and Liisa Hantsoo, "Close Relationships, Inflammation, and Health," *Neuroscience and Biobehavioral Research* 35, no. 1 (2010), 33–38.

Chapter 10: Friends Forever

A 2016 study found that soon after your mid-twenties: Kunal Bhattacharya, Asim Ghosh, Daniel Monsivais, Robin I. M. Dunbar, and Kimmo Kaski, "Sex Differences in Social Focus Across the Life Cycle in Humans," *Royal Society Open Science,* 2016.

In a recent pilot study in the Netherlands: Nan Steven, Theo Van Tilburg, "Stimulating Friendship in Later Life: A Strategy for Reducing Loneliness in Older Women," *Educational Gerontology* 26, no. 1 (2010), 15–35.

In a study conducted by Gloria Luong: Gloria Luong, Susan T. Charles, and Karen L. Fingerman, "Better with Age: Social Relationships Across Adulthood," *Journal of Social and Personal Relationships* 28, no. 1 (2010), 9–23.

Bibliography

Baumgarte, Roger. *Friends Beyond Borders: Cultural Variations in Close Friendship.* CreateSpace Independent Publishing Platform, 2013.

Bekoff, Marc, *The Smile of a Dolphin: Remarkable Accounts of Animal Emotions,* Discovery Books, 2000.

Benenson, Joyce F. *Warriors and Worriers: The Survival of the Sexes.* Oxford University Press, 2014.

Brizendine, Louann. *The Female Brain.* Harmony Books, 2007.

Caine, Barbara. *Friendship: A History.* Routledge, 2014.

Dominczyk, Dagmara. *The Lullaby of Polish Girls: A Novel.* Spiegel & Grau, 2014.

Ferrante, Elena. *My Brilliant Friend; the Neapolitan Series.* Europa Editions, 2012.

Gershon, Ilana. *The Breakup 2.0: Disconnecting Over New Media.* Cornell University Press, 2012.

Hellerstein, Erna Olafson. *Victorian Women: A Documentary Account of Women's Lives in Nineteenth Century England, France and the United States.* Stanford University Press, 1981.Fine, Cordelia. *Testosterone Rex: Myths of Sex, Science and Society.* W.W. Norton & Company, 2017.

Holland, Jennifer S. *Unlikely Friendships* Series. Workman Publishing Company, 2011.

Hruschka, Daniel J. *Friendship: Development, Ecology and Evolution of a Relationship.* University of California Press, 2010.

Marcus, Sharon. *Between Women: Friendship, Desire and Marriage in Victorian England.* Princeton University Press, 2007.

Messud, Claire. *The Burning Girl.* W. W. Norton & Company, 2017.

Messud, Claire. *The Emperor's Children.* Vintage, 2007.

Midorikawa, Emily, and Sweeney, Emma Claire. *A Secret Sisterhood.* Houghton Mifflin Harcourt, 2017.

Raymond, Janice. *A Passion for Friends: Toward a Philosophy of Female Affection*. Beacon Pres, 1987.

Rinaldi, Ann. *An Unlikely Friendship: A Novel of Mary Todd Lincoln and Elizabeth Keckley*. Harcourt Children's Books, 2007.

Rosetti, Christina Georgina. *New Poems by Christina Rossetti: Hitherto Unpublished or Uncollected*. Macmillan, 2016.

Stanton, Theodore, and Harriet Stanton Blatch [eds.]. *Elizabeth Cady Stanton: As Revealed in Her Letters & Diary*. Forgotten Books, 2012.

Offill, Jenny, and Elissa Schappell [eds.]. *The Friend Who Got Away: Twenty Women's True Life Tales of Friendships That Blew Up, Burned Out or Faded Away*. Broadway Books, 2006.

Tannen, Deborah. *That's Not What I Meant! How Conversational Style Makes or Breaks Relationships*. William Morrow Paperbacks, 2011.

Terrell, John Edward. *A Talent for Friendship: Rediscovery of a Remarkable Trait*. Oxford University Press, 2014.

Turkle, Sherry. *Alone Together: Why We Expect More from Technology and Less from Each Other*. Basic Books, 2017.

Yalom, Marilyn, and Theresa Donovan Brown. *The Social Sex: A History of Female Friendship*. Harper Perennial, 2015.

Young, Rosamund. *The Secret Life of Cows*. Faber and Faber, 2017.

Acknowledgments

Without my dear, wonderful friends, this book would not exist.

I'd like to thank all the many, many people, including my friends, who let me share their stories, including Kim Dallas, Kuelli George, Sofia Bermack, Hayley Baldwin, Barbara Greer, Soo Najarian, Carol Apprendi, Heidi Lieb, Masela Obade, Megan Blumenreich, Jennifer Burke, Alison Javens, Debbie Harner, Julia Gaspar, Mike Searls, Steve Strunsky, Belinda Edmondson, Candy Cooper, Michelle Vago, Denise Diamond, Susan Steer, Betty Ford, Catherine Platt, Erika Leavitt, Sigrid Jahnsen, and Avalon Floyd.

Also, I want to offer my gratitude to the brilliant writer Claire Messud, who so kindly wrote the foreword for this book and was graciously interviewed about her novels.

I want to thank my amazing researcher, Brooke Schwartz, who helped me find the studies that I used, and who put together my invaluable research survey on friendship among women.

I also want to thank the following for their grace and generosity when I interviewed them: Dr. Amanda Herbert, Dr. Roger Baumgarte, Daniel Hruschka, Emily Midorikawa and Emma Claire Sweeney, Jennifer S. Holland, Joyce F. Benenson, Hedva Lewittes, Dr. Lauren Brent, Sara D. Jonsberg, Sharon A. Lewis, Katie Jalma, Laura Miller, Laura Eramian, Agustín Fuentes, Robin Dunbar, Ronald Aday, Marc Bekoff, Jacob Vigil, Ashby Plant, Josh Ackerman, Berna Güroğlu, Dagmara Dominczyk, Maria DiBattista, Linda

Carli, Clare McManus, Gloria Luong, Ann Friedman, John Edward Terrell, Ana Schwartz, Joan Silk, Anne Pusey, Marina Cords, Janice Raymond, Sharon Marcus, Dr. Brian Primack, Ilana Gershon, Jolynna Sinanan, Yan Ge, Ellen Baumel, Sigrid Jahnsen, Joel Block, Wendy Samter, Beverley Fehr, Gina Costa, Susan Shapiro Barash, and anyone I may have forgotten.

Also, sincere thanks to:

my amazing agent, Jane Dystel, who believed in me and in the importance of this subject and made it all happen.

my incredible editor and publisher, Laura Mazer, who made the whole process of writing a book a dream.

Deborah Davis, for her always wise advice, and for being so positive and encouraging throughout this process.

the Montclair Public Library, for help in tracking down research that I needed.

my children, Lucas, Will, and Owen, who always cheered me on and made me feel like I was doing something worthwhile and important.

my sister, Michelle, for being a great friend, as well as a sibling. She always rooted for me. And my mother, for her support.

my in-laws, Tony and Joy, for their advice and editing and for sending me books to read.

And finally, I want to thank my husband, Simon, for encouraging me to keep writing and for always supporting me.

About the Author

Jacqueline Mroz is a veteran science writer and journalist. Her articles have appeared in the Science section of the *New York Times*, and the *New York Post*, *The Bergen Record*, *Parents* magazine, and *New Jersey Monthly* magazine. Jacqueline has been interviewed on national radio shows and television, including *The Today Show*, about her work. She has taught journalism at Montclair State University and Rutgers University. Jacqueline lives in Montclair, New Jersey, with her husband and three children. She is grateful for her many, wonderful friends.